VACTOR

VACTOR

초판 1쇄 발행 2023년 8월 22일

지 은 이 Andrew. H. Kim
발 행 인 권선복
디 자 인 김소영
전 자 책 서보미
발 행 처 도서출판 행복에너지
출판등록 제315-2011-000035호
주   소 (07679) 서울특별시 강서구 화곡로 232
전   화 0505-666-5555
팩   스 0303-0799-1560
홈페이지 www.happybook.or.kr
이 메 일 ksbdata@daum.net

값 22,000원
ISBN 979-11-92486-91-8 (13320)

도서출판 행복에너지는 독자 여러분의 아이디어와 원고 투고를 기다립니다. 책으로 만들기를
원하는 콘텐츠가 있으신 분은 이메일이나 홈페이지를 통해 간단한 기획서와 기획의도, 연락
처 등을 보내주십시오. 행복에너지의 문은 언제나 활짝 열려 있습니다.

VACTOR

A Pioneer of Excellence and Prosperity

Andrew H. KIM

도서
출판 행복에너지

Human history is the history of value creation. From the moment humans existed on Earth, they had to create value for survival. Individuals, groups, and nations that succeeded in creating value have survived and prospered, while those who did not disappeared into the dark side of history.

In the era of the Fourth Industrial Revolution, also called the digital age, "knowledge and ideas" rather than land, labor, and capital become key resources more than ever before. And "creativity and cooperation" will become even more important virtues, and the ability to create value based on them will be the key to success and prosperity. The question is how to create value.

But surprisingly, we have never learned about "value creation" through regular school education starting from elementary school. There are no courses that deal with value creation, no teachers teach it, and no test of how much you know about it.

What's even more surprising is that while everyone is talking about job shortages, few people are talking about the importance of value creation. Many educators insist on prior education in English, mathematics, music, and art prior to elementary school. However, it is difficult to find an educator who emphasizes the necessity of education that creates value in one's life.

People are not Robinson Crusoe on an uninhabited island. We live in groups and societies. Humans have progressed toward meeting their needs through exchange and trade with others rather than self-sufficiency. Because it is not only efficient, but also enriches human life.

Schools and the state try to teach community members the virtues they need to live with others. The world extends this to global citizenship education. The SDGs (Sustainable Development Goals), an agenda that was resolved by 2030 in 2015, are 17 common goals for humankind to realize the ideology of sustainable development.

The Sustainable Development Goals (SDGs), also known as the "2030 Agenda for Sustainable Development", have the slogan of "Leave no one behind" and have five areas: Human, Earth, Prosperity, Peace, and Partnership. 17 goals and 169 detailed goals are presented as the direction for humanity to move forward.

Education is a key factor in realizing the SDGs (UNESCO, 2017). Education is not limited to SDG4, but is organically related to the other

16 goals. Therefore, the United Nations has declared that improving access to quality education is the most essential requirement for sustainable development, poverty eradication, gender equality, and youth participation in society.

UNESCO presented "Four Pillars of Education" in 1996. That is, Learning to know, Learning to do, Learning to live together, and Learning to be. And OECD (2000) advocated a "Learning Society." This is an educational philosophy that puts education as the core of national economic development and that education should go beyond formal learning and expand into an informal learning center to support the knowledge economy.

However, none of the above argues for education to create value. The UN, UNESCO and OECD do not educate individuals on how to independently improve their lives and how to create greater value in collaboration with others.

Transactions can create value (especially economic value). Transactions take place from person to person. And it takes place between an individual and the various groups surrounding that individual. Therefore, parents, teachers, and employers should educate their children, students, and employees about the actual transactions that take place there.

With this problem in mind, Korea's ABLE Academy created <ABLE

Education> as the result of four years of preparation since 2012. Traditional education is a process of learning knowledge and concepts hierarchically. On the other hand, Able educates learners to create value in the field of their lives.

ABLE stands for Arts, Business, Law and Economics. ABLE is an educational program created by extracting and converging mainly value creation theories and examples from among the contents of the four disciplines.

Arts(Humanities), the A of ABLE, was once neglected because it did not make money. However, the humanities are the foundation of creativity that only "humans" can do. Therefore, it is one of the important elements of ABLE.

Here, "A" includes not only the humanities such as literature, history, and philosophy, but also the arts such as music and fine arts, and social sciences such as psychology and sociology, etc.

ABLE's "BLE" is business administration, law, and economics, and these disciplines are relatively more practical than the Arts(humanities) and have abundant learning cases suitable for learning how to create value.

ABLE's goal is to make learning at school meaningful in society through ABLE education under the big theme of "value creation."

ABLE is a "self-help" education that helps people to create a better tomorrow through value creation by exerting creativity in the field of life, even though each person has different circumstances and resources. It is also an education that reminds one to cooperate with others as a member of the community in order to get what one wants.

Mark Twain said that no amount of evidence can convince a fool. Albert Einstein said that Insanity is doing the same thing over and over and expecting different results. Both emphasize the importance of education and enlightenment.

Educator John Dewey emphasized the importance of educational system innovation by saying, "If we teach today's students the way yesterday, we rob them of tomorrow." ABLE helps humans make better choices between stimuli and responses. We are not Pavlov's dog, Thorndike's cat, or Skinner's dog.

ABLE educates people to create better lives through better thinking and decisions. Most people are unaware of how information is processed in their brains. But most of them see no problem with what they think. That's why they always think the same, and in the end their lives don't improve.

In the United States, STEM education is implemented in K12. STEM stands for Science, Technology, Engineering and Mathematics. STEM does not educate the four listed separately, but approaches them as one discipline by integrating them.

Former President Obama emphasized the importance of revitalizing the economy through STEM, saying that STEM is the future of America. Meanwhile, Gates concedes that STEM is important, but argues that it tends to only benefit students with aptitudes for math and science. In fact, relatively few people have STEM aptitudes.

Science and technology are the key to unlocking the future. However, STEM education preferably focuses on people with STEM aptitudes. We can't all be Albert Einstein, and we don't have to. It is entrepreneurs who turn the ideas of geniuses into great business models. Also, anyone should learn how to create value in their lives and lead them to a better life.

That's why all students, whether they are science geniuses or stupid, must be educated in both STEM and ABLE. However, it is desirable for science geniuses to take SABLE, and for students who are not, to take ABLEs. Here, a "big S" in SABLE represents a large concentration on science, and a "small s" in ABLEs represents a little concentration in science. In other words, science geniuses should be educated with a focus on science. However, they also need to be supplementarily trained in ABLE.

On the other hand, general students should be educated focusing on ABLE. However, they also need to receive complementary science education in a relatively small proportion.

It should be noted that I wrote this book based on ABLE. Because we are all in the same position in that each of us has to create value in our own lives. It is also because we are all alike in our desire to achieve "prosperity" by demonstrating "excellence" in our lives. And because we are alike in that we are "humans (not animals)" who can create better lives through better thinking and decisions.

Throughout this book, I consistently try to show that better learning, better thinking, and better decisions can enhance "performance." And many parts of the book are quoted elsewhere. But running through all of this is my intellectual and moral realization. Everything in this book is based on my view of the world and man.

I look at "the world as a system" from the point of view of value creation. That is why I emphasize that individuals, groups, and businesses must succeed in value creation in order to survive and prosper.

I explain what and how humans in particular have to do to create value. Everyone should know how to understand the system and make better decisions. So I have presented various mental models in this book.

Finally, I hope that readers will discover in this book what mechanisms link individual performance to success, how individuals can excel as human beings, how to prosper economically and enjoy meaning in life. Excellence and prosperity are good and beautiful. Each of us has dignity as a human being and we are entitled to enjoy it.

Seok-Jin Kang

(Chairman of CEO Consulting Group, former Chairman of GE Korea)

Called "Jean Kang," I worked as a GE Man for 30 years, 22 of which as Chairman of GE Korea. I received my doctorate in the Netherlands on the subject of value creation, and the author of this book, Professor Kim, created an educational alternative for the future of mankind on the subject of value creation. That is ABLE education.

Professor Kim points out that although value creation is the key to the survival, prosperity and development of individuals, groups, companies and nations, our education system does not teach or learn about value creation in depth. This is a sharp insight that is very future-oriented.

Not only is there no content on value creation in the regular curriculum from elementary to high school, and even in universities, almost all university departments, except for business administration, do not teach value creation. Professor Kim asks why Vincent van Gogh could not escape poverty all his life. He questions why the lives of Thomas Edison and Nikola Tesla were so different.

Professor Kim emphasizes that there are prerequisites for the ideas of Vincent van Gogh or Nikola Tesla to go beyond ateliers and laboratories and lead to value creation in real life.

That is, they must understand human needs, businesses and customers, and have knowledge of the systems of the market and the state. I've been a global executive my whole life, and this is an often overlooked but very important and relevant point.

In the age of digital economy and artificial intelligence, the ideal talent that ABLE education is looking at is a Vactor. Vactors create useful value for themselves and the world in an open space. I was fascinated by Professor Kim's ABLE education, and I have been very honored and happy to participate in his global activities to nurture Vactors based on ABLE education.

Professor Kim, the author of this book, is a very unique person who has done three wonderful jobs that others cannot achieve in their lifetime. He was an elite administrator, a challenging entrepreneur, and now famous as a creative educator. He was born in Korea, studied in Japan, China, the United States and Russia, and is currently working as a 21st century renaissance man across national borders. Professor Kim is a proud Korean.

As a person who knows and cherishes Professor Kim's abilities and personality, I expect this book to be widely read all over the world for a long time. I believe and expect that the beautiful world the author dreams of will surely come true on this land.

Zeidula Yuzbekov

(Emeritus professor at Moscow State University, Honorary Economist of the Russian

Federation)

Andrew KIM is the creator of ABLE education, His writings and lectures are already famous in Russian universities including Moscow State University. Professor Kim's wonderful lecture has been a great inspiration to Russian entrepreneurs, scientists, and artists, from Altair (Sirius), a gifted student of science and art in the Russian Federation.

Since I first met Professor Kim in 2011 as a visiting professor at Moscow State University, I have maintained a valuable relationship for more than 10 years. He is a warm-hearted person and very wise. From my experience, students at Russian universities who have listened to his lectures respect Professor Kim and consider it a great honor to learn from him. Students are eagerly waiting for the day to listen to Professor

Kim's lecture.

I know very well that students respect Professor Kim as a human being. Because he really loves his students. He not only imparts knowledge to his students, but also gives them insight into the future. He guides students to the path of self-reliance based on creativity and cooperation without blaming the natural environment and resources.

I am a witness who witnessed that Professor Kim has been changing Russia through ABLE education. I am well aware that this book is not an ivory tower theory, but wisdom from Professor Kim's life. Through the theme of value creation, he is connecting Russia's education, jobs and innovation.

Also, Professor Kim is devotedly helping the development of my hometown, Dagestan. As a visiting doctoral scholar at Dagestan State University and Dagestan State Technical University, he is striving for regional development and innovation. He also serves as an advisor to Russia's sports hero Khabib Foundation for Education and Sports. I take this opportunity to thank him for his passion and dedication.

This book shows through various examples that a Plus Sum world where everyone can create and enjoy a better life is possible, rather than a Zero Sum Game of "your pain is my happiness." It is a truly treasured book full of Professor Kim's philosophy and wisdom.

I highly appreciate Professor Kim's excellent ideas. I hope that his sincere ideas become trees and forests, becoming a jungle of hope that covers this country and the world.

- Byung-seon Kwak
(Former President of Korean Educational Development Institute, President of Korean Educational Research Association)

People want wealth, fame and success. So they set goals and work hard. However, happiness in this process is uneasy and tiring. The author emphasizes that excellence is a process of growth and maturity rather than results and performance.

- Jong-in KIM
(President of Oikos University)

Professor Kim is a very genuine figure dedicated to the advancement of democracy and education in Korea. I hope that the ABLE education he created will spread beyond Russia and the United States to the world.

- Ki-su Lee
(Emeritus professor at Moscow State University, former president of Korea University)

Albert Einstein said that the highest value he pursues in nature is beauty and simplicity. His energy equation is exactly that. As the author says, the excellence of our lives also comes from simplicity.

- Sang-hee Lee

(Chairman of the Green Life Institute, former Minister of Science and Technology)

Humans must learn to look into the future and prepare for it. This book helps learners grow into capable subjects who can fly on their own. This book plays a valuable role that parents and teachers cannot properly do.

- Si-hyung Lee

(Doctor of Medicine, Director of Serotonin Cultural Institute)

The author of this book tells us the wisdom and strategies of the world, which we seem to know at first glance, but in fact do not know well. I hope this book will be widely read by young people.

- Kwon-taek Im

(film director, Awarded Cannes Best Director)

It is necessary to train young people to find their own values and create value for themselves. This book is asking young people the fundamental question of "how and what to live for."

- Tae-hee Lim

(Gyeonggi-do Superintendent of Education, Former Minister of Employment and Labor)

Under what conditions can humans be happy? As the title of this book suggests, it will be when someone celebrates excellence and prosperity. I expect that this book will contribute to creating a more humane society, a peaceful and beautiful world.

- Ki-pyo Jang
(Director of the New Civilization Policy Institute, former Representative of the Social Democratic Party of Korea)

Professor Kim is full of challenging spirit. I think he is a role model for young people as a renaissance figure in the 21st century. I congratulate his new book, which is thrilling just by its title.

- Kil-saeng Chung
(Former Chairman of the Korea Academy of Science and Technology)

Economists often fail to give an easy explanation of capitalism. However, the author very easily explains how each of us can create a better tomorrow by creating value in the capitalist system.

- Sung-hee Jwa
(Director of the Park Chung-hee Academy, former Director of the Korea Economic Research Institute)

The author says that anyone can excel. Moreover, he emphasizes that we can all prosper. The secret is simple. It's about using our brains well. From better thinking to better decisions and better execution, and consequently better performance.

- Soon-won Chung
(Chairman of ESG at LX Holdings, former CEO of Hyundai-Kia Motors)

In his book <Leonardo da Vinci's Perspective>, the author suggested looking at problems from various angles, showing that everything in the world is connected. And this book also tells us how to look at the system surrounding us.

- Sang-dae Han
(Chairman of Korea Thanks Committee, former Prosecutor General)

The lives of those who set their own goals and strive for them are all excellent. Nobel laureates, Olympic medalists, Fortune 500 entrepreneurs aren't the only ones who excel. If someone outgrows the past, he or she is already excellent.

- A. Abdurakhmanov
(Chairman of the Khabib Foundation for Education, Sports and Social Initiatives)

Economics studies optimization under constraints. However, the world of the author is rich, not scarce. He pursues plus-sum, not zero-sum. I always support his journey towards common prosperity of mankind.

- Aleksandr Nekipelov
(Dean of Economics, Moscow State University, Vice President of the Russian Academy of Sciences)

This book is already interesting just for its title. The author even cites "retrograde analysis" as one of the mental models. This is a powerful decision technique often used by chess masters.

- Andrey Selivanov
(Head of the Department of the CIS State Committee, deputy of the State Duma 1993-2003, 16-time world champion on chess composition)

We want an excellent and prosperous life. But very few succeed and most fail. Professor Kim connects a very difficult topic to the flourishing of individuals and communities from the point of view of value creation.

- Arthur Demchuk
(Professor, Faculty of Political Science, Moscow State University, President of the Society for Comparative Political Science)

Professor Kim has aspirations for a "better society." I am grateful to him for his dedication to fostering the gifted youngsters(Sirius) of the Russian Federation. I can't wait to read this wonderful book in Russian.

- Nazim Balamirzoyev
(Rector, Dagestan State Technical University of Russian Federation)

Students at Moscow State University love Professor Kim's lectures. His lectures are always exciting, informative and even insightful. I really appreciate him giving me the why and how that everyone must create value in order to excel and prosper.

- Maria Alexeeva
(Graduate student at the Faculty of Economics, Moscow State University)

Preface ·· 004

Acclaim for Andrew KIM and ABLE education ················· 012

Praise for <Vactor: A Pioneer of Excellence and Prosperity> ·········· 016

Prologue ··· 026

Part I.

Space between Stimulus and Response: Decision and Choice

Chapter 01. Map to understand the world: Mental Models

1. Perspectives on Human beings ································· 041

  1) Psychoanalysis and Behaviorism ························· 041

  2) Cognitive Development Theory and "Cognitive Revolution" ········ 045

2. How does the human brain process "information"? ············· 046

3. Mental Models (MM) ··· 052

4. Functions of Mental Models ································· 060

5. Mental Models as Lenses, Biases and Tools ················· 065

  1) Lenses ·· 066

  2) Biases ·· 068

  3) Tools ·· 070

6. Hard mental models and Soft mental models ················· 075

Chapter 02. Understanding how the System works

1. Systems and Mental Models ································· 086

  1) What is a System? ··· 086

  2) System and IPO model ····································· 091

  3) Little's Law ·· 093

2. Mechanism of some Systems ································· 100

  1) A system called a fan ····································· 100

  2) "Organizations" and "Corporations" ························· 106

  3) Business system ··· 110

  4) System called "Capitalism" ································· 112

  5) The system of "Money": Compounding and Leverage ········· 122

Chapter03. Improvement and Utilization of the System

Before started ·· 130

1. How to improve the system ··· 131

   1) One Level Higher ··· 131

   2) Theory of Constraints ··· 134

   3) First principle ·· 141

2. Use of feedback loop ·· 145

   1) Understanding feedback loops: some examples ······························· 147

   2) Use of feedback loop ·· 149

   3) What well-designed feedback loops have in common ···················· 152

3. A system called "Luck" ··· 155

   1) Magic potion ·· 156

   2) 4 stages of luck and "luck surface area" ······································· 156

   3) Improving the luck system: 5 ways to increase your "luck surface area" ············ 158

Chapter 04. Decision-making methods for value creation

Before started ·· 161

1. Making a decision ··· 163

   1) Long-term: Regret Minimization ·· 163

   2) Medium-term: Pareto Principle ·· 166

   3) Short-term: ICE ·· 167

   4) Immediate: Eisenhower Matrix ·· 170

2. Systems thinking ··· 171

3. Game theory ··· 180

4. Second-order thinking ··· 187

5. Marginal thinking and sub goals ··· 191

   1) Marginal thinking and holistic thinking ··· 191

   2) Sub goal ··· 197

6. Numeracy and Analytical Thinking ··· 200

7. Optimization: Linear Programming ··· 207

8. Probabilistic Decision Making ··· 211

   1) Bad Decisions but Luck vs. Good decisions but bad luck ·············· 214

   2) Think Like a Poker Player ·· 215

   3) How to think of betting in three steps ·· 215

9. Backwards reasoning ··· 217

10. The 3 stages of decision making and simplification ································· 221

Part II.

Competence and Performance

Chapter 05. Meta-cognition and Circle of Competence

1. Value creation and Competence ································· 230

2. Competence and Meta-cognition ························· 236

3. Competence and Circle of Competence ··············· 247

  1) What is the circle of competence? ····················· 247

  2) If so, how can you find your circle of competence? ··············· 251

4. Negative capability ··· 254

Chapter 06. Pareto's Principle

Episode: Reverend John Maxwell ·························· 263

1. Non-linear: efforts and results ························· 265

2. Pareto Principle and Performance ····················· 268

3. Focus on High-value areas! ···························· 276

4. Practice the Pareto Principle! ·························· 284

Chapter 07. A Critical Review of the 10,000-hour rule

1. 10,000-Hour rule ··· 287

2. Original source of the 10,000 hour rule ··············· 288

3. In-depth review of the 10,000 hour rule: ·············· 292

  1) When effort and performance are not related. (Luck) ············· 292

  2) If the aptitude is not right for you ···················· 294

  3) When the amount of effort is not enough ·············· 297

  4) When quality is more important than quantity of effort ·············· 298

4. A more realistic alternative for us ····················· 299

Part III.

Mindsets

Chapter 08. Expansion and Strengthening of Competence

Before Started ·· 304

1. What's wrong with staying in your comfort zone? ······· 305

  1) If you settle in your comfort zone, there is no growth, but rather stagnation. ········ 305

  2) Comfort zone and safety zone are not the same. And the safety zone changes. ····· 308

2. Get out of your comfort zone? ································· 311

   1) Model 1: comfort zone → fear zone → learning zone → growth zone ··········· 312

   2) Model 2: comfort zone → "Stretch zone" → panic zone ············· 314

   3) Synthesis of the two models ································· 315

3. Mindset that drives people ································· 321

   1) Fixed mindset and Growth mindset ···················· 321

   2) From limits of Growth mindset to Vactor mindset ············· 323

4. What are the beliefs that give us strength? ················· 328

   1) Message from Steve Jobs ································· 329

   2) The Grounds and Amazing Power of Beliefs:

      The Hidden Link to the Growth Mindset (or Vactor Mindset) ········· 332

   Further reading: An episode of Dr. Youngwoo Kang ·········· 338

Chapter 09. Value creation based on the Plus-sum mindset

1. Competition and Zero-sum ································· 344

2. Plus-sum and Plus-sum mindset ···························· 348

3. How to create value? ································· 357

4. How to create value? : Case Study ························ 364

   Further reading: <One red paperclip>-from Plus-sum ········· 369

Part IV.

Social Networks

Chapter 10. The Impact of Social Networks on Success and Prosperity

1. How did Einstein become a celebrity? ····················· 384

2. Mixed fortunes of SAMO partners. ························ 394

3. Lessons from Einstein and Basquiat ······················ 401

4. Social Networks ································· 410

   1) Weak ties ································· 410

   2) Success formula : "3 Elements of Success, PIE" ············· 415

   3) Value network ································· 417

Epilogue ································· 424

People are working hard under the hot sun. This work is <The Red Vineyards at Arles>, painted in 1888 by Vincent van Gogh.

Vincent van Gogh was born in 1853 in the small town of Zundert in the Netherlands. He lived in Paris from 1886 and moved to Arles in the south of France in 1888. He painted this picture at this time.

Vincent left about 900 works and 1100 sketches. However, among his 900 works, this painting was the only one sold during Vincent van Gogh's lifetime. The person who bought this work is Anna Bosch, a painter, and she is the sister of a friend of Van Gogh. Anna Bosch bought this painting in 1890 for 400 francs. And this painting was purchased by a Russian rich man named Ivan Morozov, and is currently on display at the Pushkin Museum.

Vincent worked as an employee at the gallery for 7 years. But he hadn't worked to earn money since 1880. He only painted for 10 years. So he always had financial support from his brother Theo, who worked as an art dealer. When he writes to Theo, he almost always asks for money to be sent.

Vincent says he will pay Theo back when he makes money someday. However, none of his paintings were sold, except for <The Red Vineyard>. Why didn't his paintings sell?

It is difficult to conclude with only one reason, but there are several clues to understand the reason.

In a letter to his brother Theo, Vincent says that an artist should not paint while considering whether his own works are worth selling. He says that an artist should put something good in his works. According to letters and documents he exchanged with his brother Theo and his family and friends, he pursued "light and freedom" and vowed not to be preoccupied with "worldly things."

There are several backgrounds for Vincent's aversion to "secular things." First, let's move on to a time before he started painting as a painter.

Vincent dropped out of school and worked as an employee at the Gupil Gallery in Hague (1869) and London (1873). He got a job there because his relative was a famous art dealer.

Although Vincent himself was an employee of the gallery, he often quarreled with his customers, thinking that "trading in art was the same as stealing", and of course he was kicked out of his job.

Meanwhile, a contemporary of Vincent was an Englishman named Joseph Duveen. Like Vincent, his relative was an art dealer, and young Joseph worked there as an employee. However, Vincent and Joseph's attitudes towards "art" were completely opposite.

Duveen noticed that Europe had a lot of art but no one could afford it, whereas America had a lot of money but no art. And he said he would connect the two and put it into practice.

As a result, Duveen left his name as the most unique as an art dealer and received the title of "Sir" from the British royal family. He donated many of his collections to the British Museum and a separate gallery space named after him was established.

A little before Vincent was Henry David Thoreau, an American philosopher, poet, and essayist. His ideas of civil disobedience are known to have influenced many people, including Lev Tolstoy, Mahatma Gandhi, Martin Luther King, and Nelson Mandela.

By the way, his work <Walden(1854)> contains a very interesting anecdote about an Indian basket weaver. The Indian who appears in this book shouts at the white lawyer who refuses to buy the baskets he has woven, "So you're saying that we should all starve to death?"

Thoreau says in this story that it would be foolish for an Indian to yell at a lawyer for a basket. He says:

He had not discovered that it was necessary for him to make it worth the other's while to buy them, or at least make him think that it was so, or to make something else which it would be worth his while to buy.

The "value(=worthwhile)" that Thoreau is talking about here means economic value. Economic value refers to the value of money. Replace the Indian in this story with Vincent van Gogh.

Vincent made an earnest request in a letter to his brother Theo. "Why don't people buy my paintings? Why are my paintings not selling? Please let me know how I can sell my paintings."

However, he did not think of painting a picture that would be attractive enough for someone to pay money for. His request ended in an empty cry like an Indian selling baskets.

Pablo Picasso and Vincent van Gogh were painters of similar talent. However, the lives of the two unfolded in extreme opposite ways. While Picasso lived a life of success, Gogh lived a life of failure.

As we commonly know, Vincent van Gogh was clumsy both academically and professionally. He was a drunkard and frequented brothels. And he cut off his own ear.

Pablo Picasso was already a millionaire in his early thirties. His success accelerated as he got older. Gogh was poor in his twenties, poor in his thirties, and poor at the time of his death.

His reputation as a painter was also gloomy. His paintings did not attract people's attention. He lived without making his name known as a painter and died like that.

In some ways, Gogh was a painter of greater talent than Picasso. He left over 2,000 works in just 10 years from 1880 to 1890. Even people who don't know him know <Sunflowers> and <Starry Night>. He worked harder than anyone else.

Nevertheless, we love Vincent van Gogh's work. We feel intense sympathy for his life when he passed away tragically at the age of 37. Why?

Perhaps it is because our lives, like Vincent van Gogh's, are dotted with many mistakes and failures. However, there is a little-known fact about Gogh. Looking at the letters that Vincent sent to Theo, he is not the alcoholic, schizophrenic and cranky Gogh. He constantly introspected, pondered deeply, and was cautious about his life to the point of being desperate.

Perhaps, for Gogh, "Absinthe", an alcoholic drink with 70% alcohol, was a painkiller for him to continue painting even in the frustration and pain of life. Absinthe may not have been a delirium-causing curse for Gogh, but a source of inspiration.

Vincent van Gogh told his brother Theo:

"Later, people will definitely recognize my paintings, and when I die, they will definitely write about me."

His words came true like a prophecy. Numerous books have been published about him. His life, like a drama, was also made into a movie. And while we are enthusiastic about his painting, the result of his pursuit of light and freedom, we sympathize with his short life as an artist.

A man named Vincent van Gogh.

From a secular point of view, he seems to have failed his parents' expectations and made his brother hard, and he failed every time he did. Is he a Loser who does not know the world? He also called himself valueless. Did he live a worthless life? What about you if he is your child or friend?

The subject called "human life" is difficult indeed. We don't know what's right or wrong, where to go or how to go. However, if possible, we want to live a life that is economically prosperous, respected by others, and contributing to society. At least we don't want to live a life pointed at by others. This would be human nature.

If so, we should ask the following questions:

How can we live a life of excellence and prosperity?

gdp-world

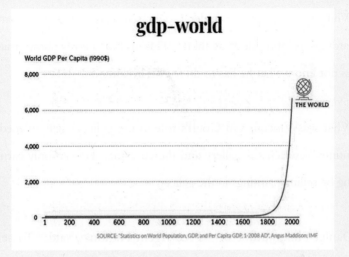

World GDP Per Capita (1990$)

SOURCE: "Statistics on World Population, GDP, and Per Capita GDP, 1-2008 AD", Angus Maddison; IMF

This graph shows the growth of human GDP over the last 2000 years. It has grown dramatically since the 1800s. Depending on the era, the protagonists such as hunters, farmers, merchants, and entrepreneurs were different. However, all of them have one thing in common: they are the protagonists of value creation in each era.

Value creation is any process that produces more valuable outputs than inputs. The people and groups that succeeded in value creation were the protagonists of history.

Human history is the history of value creation. From the moment humans existed on Earth, they had to create value for survival. Farmers grow crops, doctors treat patients, and car salesmen sell cars. All professionals have their own roles.

While working as an art dealer, Gogh used to quarrel with customers, regarding "painting deals as theft." This attitude clearly shows that he does not know what he has to do for his livelihood.

What was Vincent van Gogh's role in the gallery? It is to mediate paintings between the gallery and the customer. He can only earn his living by selling paintings in the gallery.

Daniel Pink, author of <Free Agent Nation>, said, "To sell is human." A gallery can survive and prosper only when its paintings are sold to customers. Vincent is only eligible for his salary if he creates "economic value" for the gallery. However, Vincent was ignorant of this obvious logic and had a bad attitude as an employee.

If Samsung Electronics sells a smartphone at a price of $1,000, Samsung Electronics must provide customers with a value of more than $1,000. If you paid more than the value you get from your smartphone, this could mean you've been ripped off or you're a philanthropist. And Samsung Electronics can survive only when its various costs, such as wages for its employees and costs to suppliers, are less than $1,000.

$$Cost < Price < Value$$

This seems obvious at first glance. However, it contains a very important logic. This is because this is the basis for a company's survival.

This is called "Survival Inequality."

You must provide value to your customers. That way you can get a reward. If you are an employee, you must provide value for the company you work for. Most employees are unaware of this fact.

And you must provide the company with greater value than the salary you receive. Only then can both the company and you survive. Going to work is only a necessary condition for receiving a salary. That's not enough.

We explored the meaning of "value creation" through the Vincent van Gogh's episode. Our survival and prosperity depend on value creation.

In the mid-2000s, I had an opportunity to deeply reflect and realize the meaning of my work and life. And I have been boiling that realization as the motto of my life until now. It is the following one sentence.

"To justify your existence,
you must leave useful value in the world."

And since 2012, I started interdisciplinary research on the topic of "value creation." And I educated students, entrepreneurs, scientists and artists on this topic. Finally, in 2016, I created <ABLE education> focused on value creation and first conceived the concept of "Vactor", a pioneer of excellence and prosperity.

A Vactor here is a person who creates value. Vactor is an abbreviation for "value creator." Vactors are people with practical wisdom to solve life's problems. In mathematics, a scalar has only magnitude, whereas a vector has both magnitude and direction. By analogy, a Vactor can be said to be the shape of such a vector.

$$\text{scalar} : \text{vector} = \text{Scholar} : \text{Vactor}$$

Scholars usually boast of their academic degrees and theoretical knowledge. On the other hand, Vactors are those who creates "useful value" in the field of lives not in an ivory tower.

These are people with practical wisdom to solve life's problems. Wherever they are, they always live an intellectual life. Intellectual life enables us to create value more effectively. It leads us to a life of excellence and abundance.

And here, "intellectual life" is the life of the intellect, that is, the life of thoughts, knowledge and ideas. So, it does not mean the life of a scholar, intellectual, expert, or knowledge worker. This is not the same as the "professional life" associated with your job.

If someone is actively using their brain to think better and make better decisions in their life, then they are living an "intellectual life." So it doesn't matter who you are. It does not discriminate between men and women, the rich and the poor.

A person who lives an intellectual life has a balanced lens through which he views the world. He has both a telescope and a microscope. He also has "mental tools" to solve problems and create value in life and work.

To him, the world is rich. And he reaches out and holds the hands of others, creating plus-sum value for himself and the world. The "intellectual life" leads him to a life of excellence and abundance.

Through intellectual life, we can enjoy liberation from ignorance and escape from lack and fear. And we can demonstrate our excellence as human beings to the world and enjoy a prosperous life spiritually, socially and economically.

In order for individuals to improve their standard of living, continuous efforts are needed, not temporary. This is the principle that produces both public and private wealth. Unfortunately, there are always repeated budget wastes or big mistakes in government. Meanwhile, there are also market failures.

Even so, if we individuals can keep progress and reflection toward improvement, we can improve our living conditions. To him, the world is a school and a library. He is always in learning. He learns through reflection on his experience. Reflection leads him to live a moral life.

In the next part, I will explain how we can expand our capabilities and create value in our studies, work, business and life while living intellectually and morally. Let's all go on a wonderful journey!

Part I.

Space between
Stimulus and Response:
Decision and Choice

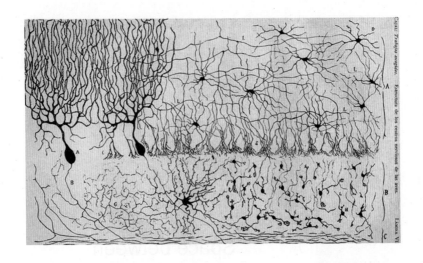

A fragment of the brain successfully stained

by S. R. Cajal (source: frontiersin.org)

We can get richer in life by avoiding stupidity than by having greater intelligence. The intellectual life helps us avoid folly in life and leads us to practical wisdom. After all, intellectual life brings us an excellent and abundant life.

Chapter I

Map to understand the world: Mental Models

1. Perspectives on Human beings

1) Psychoanalysis and Behaviorism

Psychology has a different view of human beings. Among these, there are several views on whether humans are born (Nature) or nurtured (Nurture). Here, "nature" means an innate quality, and "nurture" means a cultivated quality.

Nature and nurture can also be explained by heredity and environment. In general, human beings are shaped by these two forces.

Of these, let's look at psychoanalysis, behaviorism, and cognitive theory.

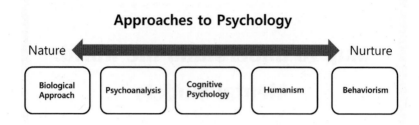

Approaches to Psychology

Nature ← → Nurture

| Biological Approach | Psychoanalysis | Cognitive Psychology | Humanism | Behaviorism |

Sigmund Freud's psychoanalytic theory compares the human mind to an iceberg, and divides the part floating on the water into consciousness and the much larger part underwater into unconsciousness.

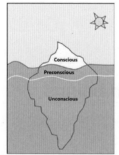

Psychoanalytic theory saw that unconscious desires and primal instincts, which occupy most of the human "mental world", dominate human behavior.

In response, Behaviorism argued that only observable behavior is worth studying. Behaviorism saw that the psychology of humans and animals could be objectively studied through observable and predictable behavior.

Soviet physiologist Ivan Pavlov observed conditioned reflexes in 1906 experiments on salivation in dogs. Following this, Thorndike of the United States led to the development of operant conditioning theory, proving that learning is due to the process and result of "trial and error" through a cat experiment in 1911.

Behaviorism believed that human personality is not determined by biological inheritance based on the results of animal experiments. They saw that human personality is formed through acquired experiences. They argued that human beings are not born with any particular inclination, but are born with a "blank slate" (Tabula Rasa), as if nothing was written on a piece of paper.

American psychologist John Watson argued in <Psychology as the Behaviorist Views it(1913)> that psychology should be the science of behavior, not the study of consciousness. In his book <Behaviorism(1924)>, he argued that all behavior can be controlled by the environment. He said:

"Give me 12 healthy children. Then I will raise them in my special, well-crafted world. I promise to train them to become one of my chosen professionals (doctor, lawyer, artist, merchant, president, or even beggar or thief) regardless of their talents, tastes, inclinations, abilities, aptitudes, or race."

Subsequently, Skinner conducted various animal experiments using the Skinner Box he devised. And based on the research results, he argued for operant conditioning. Here, "operant conditioning" refers to a method of increasing or decreasing the probability that a response will occur by selectively rewarding a response. Selective reward here means reinforcement and punishment.

According to Skinner, human behavior is motivated by environmental stimuli (Antecedents) and entirely determined by Consequences (i.e., selective rewards). Skinner called this assumption the ABC paradigm.

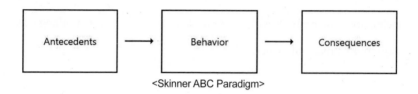
<Skinner ABC Paradigm>

Skinner saw that human behavior is sustained by rewards and punishments. According to this view, all human behavior is predictable and therefore controllable. He believed that human and social problems should be solved by properly manipulating the forces of the environment.

As seen above, behaviorists focus on stimuli in the environment and the organism's response to those stimuli, describing the relationship between "stimulus (S)" and "response (R)". For this reason, behaviorist psychology is sometimes referred to as "S-R psychology".

Behaviorists use the term "conditioning" instead of "learning." This implies that an organism is conditioned by environmental events. This is because behaviorists believe that internal human processes such as thinking, motivation, and emotion cannot be directly observed or measured and must be excluded from explaining the learning process.

2) Cognitive Development Theory and "Cognitive Revolution"

The Theory of cognitive development, proposed by the Swiss philosopher and developmental psychologist Jean Piaget, introduces the idea of internal mental processes or states (such as beliefs, needs, and motivations) between stimuli and responses. A comparison of this theory with behaviorism is as follows.

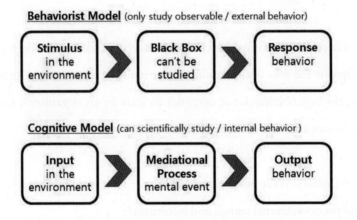

Behavioral approaches study only externally observable (stimulus and response) behaviors that can be objectively measured. They believe that they cannot study the internal behavior of a person because they cannot see what is going on in the human mind.

However, cognitive psychologists postulate that a mediational process occurs between a stimulus (or input) and a response (output). They are mediation processes because they mediate between the stimulus and the response. They come after the stimulus and before the response. The mediating (i.e., mental) events here may be memory, perception, attention, or problem solving.

For example, cognitive approaches suggest that gambling problems are the result of maladaptive thinking and faulty cognition. Gamblers are more likely to misjudge the amount of skill involved in a game of "probability" and enter with the mindset that the odds are in their favor and therefore they have a good chance of winning.

Therefore, cognitive psychologists say that understanding human behavior requires understanding these mediation processes. Cognitive psychologists consider it essential to look at an organism's mental processes and how they affect behavior.

So, what is really going on in our brains? How does our brain receive and process external stimuli and information?

2. How does the human brain process "information"?

See the picture below. This is <Representation>, a 1962 work by surrealist artist René Magritte. The image of people playing soccer is also included in a small frame on the left. Just like this, we have our own internal version of the external world.

Cognitive theory argues that our external environment is internalized as mental representations. "Representation" here refers to the way in which an individual mentally possesses an external object. However, these are not "replication" of the outside world, but "representation."

Various facts, concepts, and images that we know are classified and stored in our brains according to certain criteria, like a file box. It is difficult to find memorized information again if it is jumbled like trash in a trash can. But it is easy to find information if it is stored like a file in a file box. We work in the office by organizing paperwork like that.

In the picture on the left, external information is arranged in a certain category or structure, like files in a file box. Piaget called this "schema."

SCHEMA

Everything You Know

Because the concept of "schema" is abstract, it is difficult to understand easily and intuitively. I hope you first understand that schemas are formed in our heads.

Now, let's learn a little more about schemas.

Animals and humans survive by adapting to their environment. We perceive various external objects in the environment as "patterns". For example, we perceive a "bird" as an "animal" with wings, feathers, and a beak.

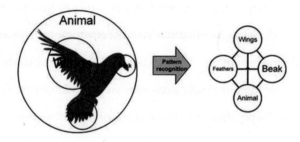

And we store the actual appearance of the bird in our brain as the schema on the left. That is, we remember a "real bird" as a "conceptual schema" with wings, feathers, talons and beak. We have a schema for birds. That's why we can distinguish numerous birds from other animals by calling them all "birds" despite their different appearances.

For example, whenever a child sees a sparrow, a swallow, a dove, a magpie, or an eagle in flight, he starts calling them "birds." And the parents who see it are delighted. The child has a schema called bird and generalizes the new experience to fit the existing schema. This is called "Assimilation."

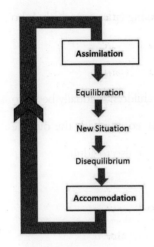

If the new experience fits the existing schema, the organism is in a state of cognitive equilibrium. However, a child who has learned that all flying objects are birds calls them birds even when he sees a flying airplane.

At this time, parents or teachers teach that both airplanes and birds fly in the sky, but airplanes are not birds. The child becomes momentarily imbalanced. But, as the child acquires new information that airplanes are not like the birds he knew (they have fur and flap their wings), he modifies the existing schema to fit the new information. This process is what we call "Accommodation."

In this way, human beings change their schema cognitively through interaction with the environment. This is human adaptation to the environment. In a word, it is a process of schema change. Adaptation is achieved through cognitive equilibration through assimilation and accommodation. Humans adapt to the environment by changing existing schemas or creating new schemas.

For example, John, who lives in the countryside, is going to transfer to a school in New York in a few days. John thinks all students in metropolitan cities are selfish. This is John's schema. John became friendly with Paul at the new school. Looking at Paul, who is kind and caring, John changed his mind that children in big cities are selfish. John now has a new schema for "city children."

Through this process of accommodation, children gradually begin to construct efficient and sophisticated ways of coping with the outside world. And this applies not only to children, but also to adults.

Now let's look at the types of schemas here.

① Object(or Entity) Schema: This helps to understand and interpret inanimate entities, including what different entities are and how they work. For example, there is a schema for what doors are and how to use them. A door schema can also include subcategories such as sliding doors, screen doors, and revolving doors.

② Person schema: This is a schema created to help us understand a specific person. For example, schemas about other people include the individual's appearance, behavior, likes and dislikes, personality traits, and so on.

③ Role schema: This is a schema that includes expectations about how a person who assumes a specific social role will behave. We hope the waiters are friendly. Not all waiters behave like that. However, our role schema for the waiter expects the waiter to be friendly. We have role expectations for firefighters, soldiers, doctors, lawyers, bosses and employees.

④ Event Schema: This is a schema containing the expected sequence of tasks and actions during a social activity or event. For example, when individuals go to the movies, they expect to go to the theater, buy a ticket, select a seat, set their cell phone to silent, and leave the theater after watching the movie. We have schemas for almost every social activity, including classes, work, worship and negotiations.

⑤ Self-schema: Humans have certain images about others. In this way, humans also have an image of themselves. That is, the concept of self. In particular, humans form beliefs about themselves. These self-schemas influence individual judgments about one's ability to organize and implement the course of action necessary to achieve a particular goal (i.e., self-efficiency).

According to research results, people with high self-efficacy have a strong belief that they can successfully perform certain behaviors and produce positive results. They imagine a success scenario that connects the present and the future and are not afraid of problems.

3. Mental Models (MM)

People interpret information and make value judgments based on their schemas. In other words, schemata influence our perceptions and interpretations of the world.

A person's perception or value judgment on new information is interpreted as a result of interworking with the existing schema. If the new information does not match the existing schema, the existing schema is changed to interpret the new information.

Meanwhile, there is a concept called "mental models" that is rapidly gaining popularity. In 1943, Scottish psychologist Kenneth Craik is believed to be the first to comment on the concept of mental models. He defined "mental models" as "an internal interpretation of the external world."

He said:

If the organism carries a "small-scale model" of external reality and of its own possible actions within its head, it is able to try out various alternatives, conclude which is the best of them, react to future situations before they arise, utilize the knowledge of past events in dealing with the present and the future, and in every way to react in a much fuller, safer, and more competent manner to the emergencies which face it.

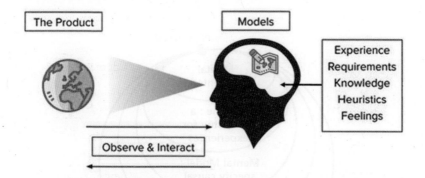

Like schemas, mental models are how we make sense of the world. Because we can't keep all the details of the world in our heads, we use models to simplify complex things into comprehensible, configurable chunks. Through the "mental model," the complex external world is reduced to a simple, easy-to-understand world.

Children assemble different types of plastic model toys. With this, children can picture real cars and airplanes in their heads. We understand reality with these models. Likewise, the theories, laws, principles, and rules in our heads are all models. It's called the mental model because it's in our heads.

There is an external stimulus and a response. Behaviorism thought there was a kind of black box between the stimulus and the response. And since that area could not be observed and measured, it was considered not to be studied. Cognitive psychology, on the other hand, has pioneered this field and brought about a cognitive revolution.

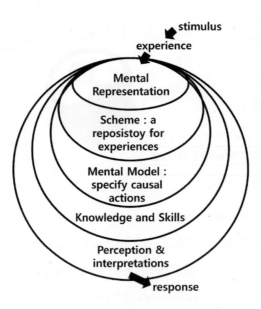

Humans construct mental representations from the experiences of external stimuli. And this is categorized as "schema." A "mental model" is a higher level concept than a schema and usually includes causal relationships. Further explanation will follow on this.

And all the facts, concepts, schemas, and mental models that humans have constitute human knowledge and skills. Humans use these tools to recognize, interpret, and respond to external stimuli. Behaviorism treats all these processes as a black box and simply sees the relationship between stimulus and response.

The most important thing in life is what happens inside your head. Because "quality of thought" is paramount to achieving an excellent and prosperous life, good relationships, good work, and good investments.

The idea that the thought process is the key to success competes with other human attributes such as enthusiasm, hard work, fighting spirit, and luck. Most of these things actually affect your success. However, your thoughts (especially decision-making) determine the direction that leads you towards or away from success. This is a very simple but very powerful fact.

See the picture below. Mental models consist of relationships between schemas. In this respect, mental models are higher order than schemas. "Mental models" help us understand the structure and mechanisms of systems.

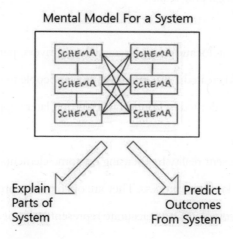

Mental Model For a System

Mental models allow us to analyze "causation", understand the components of a system and how it works, predict the future, and improve the system. We will learn about this in Chapters 2 and 3.

A map is not a territory. But we understand territory through maps.

On January 10, 1863, the London Underground opened, connecting 6 km between Paddington and Ferringdon. And in the early 1900s, as the London underground transport system was booming, commuters still struggled to understand how to get from A to B.

The original underground map was "realistic", though obviously a representation of reality, it still tended to leave people confused. Then, in 1931, a draftsperson named Harry Beck came up with an alternative that embraced a "conceptual representation" rather than even trying to represent "geographic reality."

He let go of locational accuracy-deleting rivers, parks and shifting locations--and created a diagram to empower people to quickly get from A to B. It was adopted in London in 1933 and later adopted worldwide.

Maps represent reality by focusing on some elements and not others, leaving out a lot in the process. They are open to interpretation. They are ultimately incomplete and inaccurate representations of reality.

Map vs Territory = Mental model vs Reality

Likewise, mental models are simplified representations of what they are trying to express. Mental models are often useful and necessary for us to take action in a complex world, but they are not accurate representations of reality.

The figure below illustrates the relationship between the real world, mental models, and decision making. Professionals have several mental models unique to their fields.

Mental models help us make sense of the world. For example, "theory of demand and supply" are mental models that help us understand how the economy works. And "Game theory" helps us understand how relationships and trust work. "Entropy" helps us understand how disorder and decay work

Professionals have several "mental models" unique to their fields. Each expert sees things differently.

When a botanist looks at a forest, he or she looks at the ecosystem, an environmentalist looks at the effects of climate change, a forestry engineer looks at the state of tree growth, and a businessman looks at the value of the land.

Nothing is wrong, but nothing can account for the full extent of the forest. Moreover, if you are only looking at a problem in one direction, you have a blind spot. And blind spots in the wild can kill you.

Charlie Munger, associate of Warren Buffett and vice chairman of Berkshire Hathaway emphasized the use of practical wisdom through understanding "mental models." He said:

If you memorize fragmentary facts and try to bring them back up, you really don't know anything. Facts cannot be in usable form unless they are hung together over the "latticework of mental models."

Here's a way to think differently. Learning knowledge from other disciplines can lead to better initial decisions about forest management. So the secret to good thinking is to learn and use different mental models.

That's why we have to build a "latticework of mental models" in our heads. It is a lattice in which each model operates in parallel with the others, or sometimes against each other. We must have models in our heads. And we need to place vicarious and direct experiences in the grid work of this model.

Charlie Munger says.

You may have seen students who just remember and try to bring back what was remembered. They fail in school and in life. You have to stake your experience on the latticework of mental models in your head.

We form "mental models" through learning and experience. Just as surgeons, firefighters and accountants have different majors in college, each profession has a different mental model required for someone to be successful.

If you want to be a mathematician or scientist, your brain needs to form mental models related to math and science. And the more experience you gain as a scientist, the better equipped you are with the mental model of science.

However, the excellence and prosperity of human life comes from "value creation." Therefore, everyone should have useful mental models for value creation.

The quality of our thoughts is proportional to the models we have in our heads and their usefulness in the situation at hand. The more models you have (the bigger your toolbox) the more likely you are to have the right model to see reality.

Even a brilliant scientist or artist can struggle if he doesn't know how to create value in his life. Such was the life of Vincent van Gogh. We will look at it in detail in Chapter 9.

4. Functions of Mental Models

Mental models do two things. And this is the basis for everything you do.

① Mental models help you evaluate how a system works. Here, "system" is a unified whole in which each element interacts each other and is intricately entangled. This includes both natural and artificial. Of course, people are also a system. We will look at this in detail in Chapters 2 and 3.

② Mental models help you make "better decisions" through "better thinking." We will look at this in detail in Chapter 4.

The world is made up of multi-layered systems. And that world belongs to those who understand that system. You can understand systems and make better decisions with the help of mental models. You create value through the system.

I will ask you two questions that will help you understand the above concept easily. First question. How do rocket engines work? Second question. What Type of Rocket Fuel Should You Use?

A rocket engine is a system that we can reverse engineer and understand. In simple terms, reverse engineering is a process of discovering the technical principles of a device, process, or system through structural analysis.

Reverse engineering often involves taking an object (mechanical device, electronic component, software program, etc.) to pieces and analyzing it. Therefore, reverse engineering is the most suitable learning method in the current era where you have to update your own knowledge and information before someone teaches you.

A rocket engine has many interdependent parts and you can understand how a rocket engine works through a mental model called reverse engineering. And you have to decide what type of fuel to use. Mental models guide you to the best answers to both questions.

Mental models are typically used to describe a person's mental representation of some physical system (such as how an engine or computer works), but can also relate to other types of systems (such as how a university or business works).

Mental models embody stored long-term knowledge about these systems that can be invoked when needed to direct problem solving and interaction with related systems.

Mental models can grow and evolve with experience, but represent largely static knowledge about the system. For example, the main function of the system, how it works, how different components affect other components, and how components behave when faced with different factors and influences.

An important concept related to this is "situation models." Unlike "mental models", which describe general knowledge about a system, "situation models" represent human knowledge and understanding of the current state of the system. While mental models are static knowledge, situational models are very dynamic.

This model can incorporate the values of various system parameters (such as fuel gauge level and motor speed), as well as the model's changes in situation over time. A higher level of understanding (Gestalt-type understanding of the state of the system in relation to human goals) and prediction of future states are also part of the corresponding situation model.

Here, Gestalt is German and corresponds to form or shape in English. Gestalt refers to the form and state of an integrated whole with complete structure and wholeness, not a whole made up of parts in psychology and philosophy. Gestalt psychology understands that humans are beings who perceive an object as a whole rather than as a combination of individual parts.

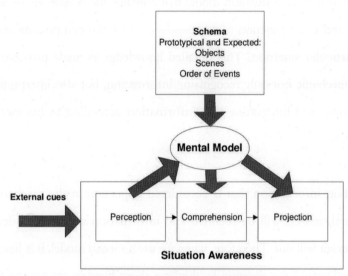

<The relationship between mental models
and situational models (situational awareness)>

Situation models provide a useful window into mental models. As you can see, situation models are not developed just by observing the world, but are heavily influenced by the underlying mental models someone has. Therefore, the situation model is also called situation awareness. Broadly defined, situation awareness is, after all, "a person's mental model of the world around them" in a particular situation.

For example, a mechanic might have a mental model of how a typical engine works. However, the mechanic can look at how a particular engine in a customer's vehicle is currently performing (for example, a carburetor problem).

He may have a situation model that contains the condition (new, worn, dirty) and exact function (model, horsepower, etc.) of the component under a particular situation. This detailed knowledge is made possible by the mechanic not only recognizing information, but also interpreting, filtering, and integrating that information according to his mental models.

Thus, information that is considered important in the mechanic's mental models will be retained and information that is considered irrelevant will not. Therefore, when we use a mental model, it is helpful to understand the situation by thinking about how we are interpreting the model according to the specific situation.

If you misperceive a situation, you risk applying an inappropriate mental model. Also, even if you applied an appropriate mental model, you may not have properly understood the mental model in the first place. Also, when you are trying to understand someone's thoughts (your child, boss or subordinate, partner, etc.), you can think of the mental model they use, given their general intellectual level.

This allows you to be more predictive of what he will be thinking in any given situation. Because situation models are the key to understanding mental models. Perhaps you can understand what I mean more easily if you think of yourself as negotiating or playing a game with someone.

5. Mental Models as Lenses, Biases and Tools

There are various mental models in the world. There are mental models devised or discovered by scientists and philosophers, and there are mental models that each person has through their own experiences. People see the world through these mental models (lenses) and solve problems in the world (tools). And they are caught up in biases.

So I categorize the various mental models into three categories: ① Lenses ② Biases ③ Tools

The mental model is, after all, the "lenses" through which you view the world (=system). We can see things far away and very small things through telescopes and microscopes. Telescopes and microscopes have lenses. We understand the mechanisms of the world through the lenses.

However, as the saying goes, "a map is not a territory," what we see through telescopes and microscopes is not what it really is. It is just an image that catches your eye. Several "biases" are at work here. At the same time, mental models are "tools" that help you make better decisions.

1) Lenses

Using a Lens whenever you analyze a problem means that you think about it in the context of this particular Lens. Plato and Aristotle, Van Gogh and Joseph Duveen all look at the world with their own mental models.

According to Heraclitus, all things change. He conceived things in constant movement and change. In contrast, to Parmenides, all things were unchanging and fixed. He emphasized the identity of existence. There was no change in his "lens".

In Ptolemy's geocentric "theory(=mental models)", the earth is at the center of the universe, and all celestial bodies including the sun revolve around the earth in about a day.

On the other hand, in Copernicus' heliocentric theory, the sun is at the center of the universe, and the earth, moon, and other planets revolve around the sun.

Adam Smith and Thomas Malthus saw the same thing differently. Smith saw population growth as a blessing, while Malthus saw it as a disaster.

For Smith, population growth meant an increase in the number of divisions of labor and the possibility of further subdivision of existing divisions. This promotes specialization. This is an increase in productivity and means economic growth. Economic growth means an increase in income and an increase in demand.

On the other hand, Malthus predicted that although the population increases exponentially, the food necessary for human survival increases arithmetically, so society will be extremely chaotic due to lack of food in the future. To him, population growth was a source of evil and a disaster.

Both Karl Marx and Joseph Schumpeter paid attention to the dynamism of capitalism and saw the subject of such dynamic destruction as capitalists and entrepreneurs. However, Marx saw the capitalist as an object to be overthrown, and Schumpeter highly valued the entrepreneur as the subject of innovation.

Depending on what "mental models" we have, even if we look at the same world (=system), it looks different.

Examples include mental models such as the laws of thermodynamics, the Pareto principle, Maslow's hierarchy of needs, and Theory of Constraints (TOC). You can choose one of them and use it to look at the problem and understand if there are similarities and relevant insights that can be borrowed from these models.

2) Biases

Biases are mental shortcuts that our brains use to make sense of the world around us. They shape the way we perceive the world, make decisions and interact with others.

Our biases are based on our past experiences and cultural and social norms. While biases can be useful in some situations—for example, helping us quickly identify danger—they can also lead us to make poor decisions.

There are a lot of biases that we humans fall victim to, but here are a few of the big ones that can really wreck your decision-making:

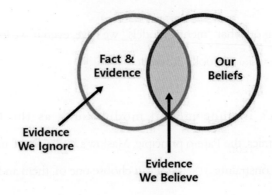

Confirmation Bias

One example I like to cite is "confirmation bias." This is the tendency to seek only the facts that confirm one's claims and beliefs. The dichotomy of thinking that all things or situations are black or white or that this is right and that is wrong is in line with the confirmation bias of believing what one wants to believe.

For example, if you believe that all politicians are corrupt, you may only seek out news stories that support that belief, while ignoring evidence to the contrary. This can lead you to make decisions based on incomplete or inaccurate information.

"Sunk cost fallacy" is the tendency to continue investing time, money, or other resources into something, even if it's not working out, simply because we've already invested so much. For example, if you've spent a lot of money on a car that keeps breaking down, you may keep sinking money into repairs rather than cutting your losses and buying a new car. This can lead to wasted resources and missed opportunities.

A much sadder and all-too-common example of the sunk cost fallacy is in relationships. A lot of people stay in bad relationships because they've been in them for so long and they feel like leaving would mean they've "wasted" all those years.

"Bias of overconfidence" is the tendency to overestimate our own abilities and underestimate the complexity of a situation. For example, if you're confident that you can fix a leaky pipe in your house, you may not realize that the problem is more complicated than you initially thought. This can lead to mistakes, wasted time and money, and potentially dangerous situations.

The key to avoiding the negative effects of biases on decision-making is self-awareness. By acknowledging that we all have biases, and being mindful of how they might be influencing our perceptions and decisions, we can make more informed and thoughtful choices.

Seek out diverse perspectives, challenge your own beliefs, and don't be afraid to admit when you're wrong. By doing so, you'll be better equipped to make decisions that align with your values and help you achieve your goals.

3) Tools

The last category is "tools", mental models that help us make decisions. These tools are mainly of the computational kind, such as game theory, linear programming, stochastic (or statistical) approaches, etc.

For example, you can make good decisions using "Thinking by Inversion", "Second-order thinking", "SWOT analysis", and "two-track analysis." So whenever you are ready, you can apply the tools to help you make the right decision.

So how do they work together?

When I have to make an important decision and have time to think (critically), I use the following approach.

① I look at a situation through various lenses. I apply the lens that I believe is best for the problem and see what I can learn from it.

② Then I look at potential errors in judgment that I may have made (or that others in this context may have made) and try to remove them from my judgment.

People generally think of themselves as self-centered. So while they can be good at detecting other people's biases, they're pretty bad at detecting their own. So, this is the hardest part.

③ Once the situation is clarified and the biases removed, it is time to see what tools can be applied to solve the problem. As you can see in the picture, "tools" support "work" and augment "thinking." And "work" requires "thinking." Tools that help us think are "mental tools."

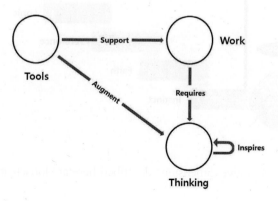

One of the biggest problems is that there are over 100 mental models of all three types, even on a limited list, and it is time consuming and difficult to go through even the most applicable ones. As such, this method is only suitable when, firstly, you have the time to decide, and secondly, you need to make decisions that maximize results.

But you don't have to worry. Based on my research, people usually already have some mental models they have learned from their experiences. And they tend to use those models intensively.

If you look through the list of 100 or so mental models, you will find some mental models that you are already familiar with and use in real life. You can gradually add new models to it one by one.

So how do mental models fit the cognitive dimension of human thought and behavior? Please refer to the following picture.

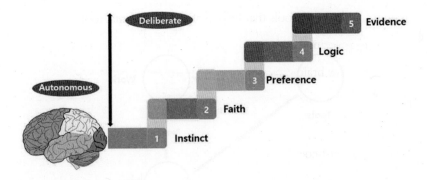

The five cognitive dimensions described here are loosely inspired by the first six levels of Leary's and Wilson's pseudo-scientific, but highly intuitive, eight-circuit model of consciousness, best described in Wilson's book <Prometheus Rising>.

Due to our most common cognitive biases the five cognitive dimensions of Mental Models typically work like below. Unlike animals, humans do not only have instincts, but also have reason. So, these aspects influence the human mental model. It can be classified into 5 categories.

First of all, it is instinct. Next is faith, preference, logic and evidence. When humans think, they are influenced by these factors. Even with a well-equipped logical thinking model, sincere religious beliefs hinder the movement to logic.

The Five Cognitive Dimensions of Mental Models are:

① Instinct

Our most primal Mental Models, like "Fight or Flight", are hard-coded into our brains and DNA. They are not even based on our own experiences but on our ancestors' experiences, natural selection and other evolutionary forces. Unfortunately, we can't easily get rid of the crap that is hard-coded into this dimension, we can only manage it.

② Faith

Since humans are driven not only by logic but also by "faith" (even false belief), it is good to have a grid of desirable mental models. If you have a strong belief in God, you are very unlikely to consider a different Mental Model in a higher dimension explaining the origins of mankind with logic or evidence.

③ Preference

Preference-based Mental Models is also the cognitive dimension of most idealists, who interact with the world as they would prefer it to be rather than how it is. The Semmelweis reflex explains how Mental Models from any of the other cognitive dimensions can end up in the preference bucket due to ego, social norms, moral constructs, etc.

④ Logic

Many, if not most, popular Mental Models of our time fall into this category simply because we use them as inductive arguments. Well-crafted theory can be very powerful as the foundation of Mental Models.

⑤ Evidence

Evidence-based Mental Models, the superior cognitive dimension for understanding the world, generally comes from logic-based models that are tested in the real world and found to accurately predict reality.

However, moving evidence-based Mental Models away from the evidence and into the inductive logic dimension can quickly turn into a slippery slope ride down to the lower levels of predictive capabilities.

As we have seen above, there are several factors that motivate people. What we must remember is that human beings are driven not only by "logic" and "evidence" but also by "instinct" and "faith" (even false beliefs). That's why equipping ourselves with desirable "mental models" is a good thing to improve our lives.

So, if someone adopts a worldview that says "painting trade is stealing" or "capitalism and entrepreneurs only create inequality," that person's life is going against the direction of value creation.

6. Hard mental models and Soft mental models

We learn new mental models and organize these models into a latticework of mental models. We might call this an additive approach. That is, new models are continuously added to the grid of existing models. The more nodes and connections, the stronger the model and capabilities. All in all, this approach leads us to make smarter decisions.

But on the other hand, what has not received much attention is that the majority of our mental models are implicit and are below our level of awareness. It is often more valuable to identify and discard existing hidden models than we are to attempt to learn new mental models. We can call this a subtractive method.

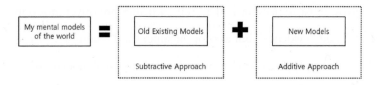

There is a fundamental reason why almost all popular treatment of mental models focuses on adding new models rather than discarding existing ones – they are targeting two very different kinds of models. One is easy to identify and "sell" but not as useful, while the other is harder to identify and package, but can be more transformative.

Two kinds of mental models

Different kinds of mental models can be found in a range of disciplines including cybernetics, architecture, cognitive psychology, systems dynamics and neuroscience amongst others. To keep our discussion simple, consider two generic types of mental models — hard and soft.

• Hard mental models are the ones common in popular discourse. These are models identified from various disciplines, packaged as a "rule" and put into language that we then learn and try to use in practice. By definition, they tend to be explicit and thus visible.

• In contrast, soft mental models are ones we're already using but unaware of. These are often not "languaged", personal to us and because of their proximity and common use, transparent to us. Nevertheless we use them and are influenced by them.

You can visualize the two types on a continuum:

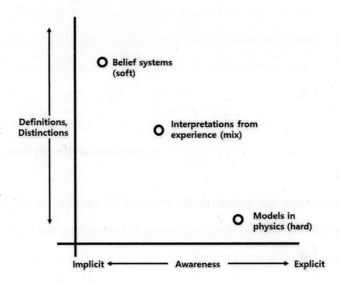

The X-axis of this figure represents our "Awareness". The farther from the origin, the more explicit, and the closer, the more implicit. The Y axis represents "Definitions or Distinctions". The further from the origin, the more fuzzy casuality, imprecise language, and subjective and personal, and the closer it is, the clear casuality, precise language, and objective and impersonal.

That is to say, your concepts and beliefs about your capabilities and competences are examples of soft mental models, whereas models derived from physics, such as the laws of thermodynamics, are hard.

Consider the following as a definition of soft mental models:

...the images, assumptions and stories which we carry in our minds of ourselves, other people, institutions and every aspect of the world. Like a pane of glass framing and subtly distorting our vision, mental models determine what we see. Human beings cannot navigate through the complex environments of our world without these 'mental maps'; and all of these mental maps, by definition, are flawed in some way.

— Peter Senge in <The Fifth Discipline>

Why are these soft mental models invisible? It's because they are what can be called "givens"— things we assume to be true, thus not treated as assumptions and go unexamined.

...We call them "big assumptions" because they are not currently viewed as "assumptions" at all. Rather, they are uncritically taken as true. They may be true, and they may not be, but as long as we simply assume they are true, we are blind even to the question itself.

— Robert Kegan in <Immunity to Change>

For example, the assumption about "rational humans" in economics has long persisted even though it is not true, leading people (even economists) to unwittingly assume that humans are rational. In response, Herbert Simon spoke of bounded rationality, and some economists have come to realize that there are no people in the neoclassical model.

A simple but powerful example of soft, hidden mental models is the "Kanizsa triangle." In 1955, Italian psychologist Gaetano Kanizsa developed this concept. This is a picture reminiscent of a white triangle through the arrangement of three pacmans shaped like claws.

If you look at the three pacmans that look like claws, a triangle emerges between them. You can see the outlines that don't exist, and the triangles that reveal the reality with those outlines are whiter than the white background. The white triangle, which does not physically exist, exists entirely in the viewer's mind. A virtual space that does not exist is revealed in the real space.

John Sterman of MIT puts it this way:

Most of us do not appreciate the ubiquity and invisibility of mental models, instead believing naively that our senses reveal the world as it is.

On the contrary, our world is actively constructed (modeled) by our senses and brain.

Research shows that the neural structures responsible for the ability to see illusory contours such as the white triangle exist between the optic nerve and the areas of the brain responsible for processing visual information. Active modeling occurs well before sensory information reaches the areas of the brain responsible for conscious thought.

Powerful evolutionary pressures are responsible. Our survival depends so completely on the ability to rapidly interpret our environment that we (and other species) long ago evolved structures to build these models automatically.

Usually we are completely unaware these mental models even exist. It is only when a construction such as the Kanizsa triangle reveals the illusion that we become aware of our mental models.

The Kanizsa triangle illustrates the necessity of active and unconscious mental modeling or construction of "reality" at the level of visual perception. Modeling of higher-level knowledge is likewise unavoidable and often equally unconscious.

This tells us something very important. Our world is actively constructed (modeled) by our senses and brain. Briefly, there sis difference between perception, interpretation and generation—we are generating reality as much as we are interpreting it.

We don't always see outside reality and then interpret it based on our models. This is what the additive approach is based on, and is only partially true. Rather we are creating reality itself using these models—which makes it even more critical to understand the ones we're already using, but not aware of.

Rather than a mirror or a camera that captures reality, we are more like a projector creating its own reality based on models running in our head. And most of these remain invisible and unexamined.

Our minds are not necessarily mirrors of reality, rather our reality is a mirror of our minds. Reality is up to our interpretation and we create it. This is a very important recognition because it shows that we can improve our lives based on our ideas. We will look at various examples of this in Chapter 9.

What you see is not really there; it is what your brain believes is there...Seeing is an active construction process. Your brain makes the best interpretation it can according to its previous experience and the limited and ambiguous information provided by your eye.

— Francis Crick in <The Astonishing Hypothesis>

In the metaphorical no less than in the literal use of "seeing", interpretation begins where perception ends. The two processes are not the same, and what perception leaves for interpretation to complete depends drastically on the nature and amount of prior experience and training.

— Thomas Kuhn in <The Structure of Scientific Revolutions>

But as we saw in the Kanizsa triangle, it goes one step beyond interpretation as well. We are actively generating reality as well, just like we generated the triangle that's non-existent. We cannot "unsee" the triangle, even when we are actively aware of its non-existence.

In the additive approach, the idea is that the new mental models will help us interpret better and thus respond better. But what gets left out is that mental models also "generate" or rather create my world. This is where the implicit, soft models play a large role and why leaving them out is a missed opportunity.

Examples of soft mental models

As a human being, mental models are a part and parcel of how we operate. The fact that we use them and even that many of them are wrong is not the problem. The real challenge is that we are primarily unaware of their influence, especially unhelpful ones that impede growth and development. Some examples of hidden mental models would include:

- "Leadership requires being an extrovert."

- "Meetings are a waste of time."

- "All leaders are power hungry."

- "You cannot learn anything past a certain age."

- "People don't change."

- "Even a normal person becomes inferior when he enters the National Assembly."

- "Russians are drunkards."

- "Japanese people are different from the outside."

- "The rich are materialistic and greedy."

- "The state is an instrument of the ruling class."

- "Talents and abilities are fixed."

Each of these models informs and influences my actions and how I go about it. Robert Hargrove, an authority on executive coaching, calls this an "unhelpful frame of reference."

Then why is the additive approach more popular?

Our efforts for improvement default towards additive rather than subtractive approaches. We want to go learn additional new ones without trying to figure out what's actually restricting us already. Why so?

The additive approach feels easy.

- Learning about new models feels and sounds easy. Identifying, updating or removing existing models on the other hand is much harder and takes time, effort, and attention. The additive model is seductive but equally ineffective for the most part, especially how we usually go about it—reading about them and thinking we "got it."

We think we "got it" about something, but it takes a lot of time and experience again before we really know about it. Just because you read a book or take lessons doesn't make that knowledge completely yours.

You are close to being able to say "got it" when you have vividly realized something through experience rather than simply knowing something. And you don't repeat trial and error again, and on the one hand, apply it to a new environment and create practical and economic value.

Creation sits at the top of Bloom's revised Taxonomy. And this is also an area where human intelligence can make a big difference compared to artificial intelligence from a low level of memorization and calculation.

• The subtractive model looks "soft" whereas the additive models looks analytical and "science backed". It's easier to package and sell the additive model.

The subtractive approach takes work.
• We've spent entire lifetimes relying on these hidden models, so of

course we can't get rid of them overnight.

• We see through them—their invisibility makes them harder to identify and tackle.

• We have defensive routines that actively work to prevent us from seeing the gaps and flaws in our reasoning.

• Perhaps what makes unlearning mental models so difficult is that it requires temporarily suspending judgement and preconceived notions. This makes causes discomfort and requires us to embrace what Keats called "negative capability."

Mental models play a key role in performance. We can either pretend to be getting better by reading about new ones, or do the hard work of identifying, examining and refining existing unhelpful ones.

Chapter 2

Understanding how the System works

1. Systems and Mental Models

1) What is a System?

By 1903, automobiles were made by hand, and automobiles were expensive luxuries that ordinary people could not own. Henry Ford, the founder of the Ford Motor Company, determined that mass production was essential to making automobiles widely available.

Henry got the inspiration for a conveyor belt one day at a slaughterhouse in Chicago and simplified the assembly sequence to a few steps to create a cheap car that ordinary people could own.

As a result, Ford conceived of a conveyor belt in automobile production in which the work is moved to a worker in a fixed position, rather than a worker going to a work table and working.

In 1913, Henry Ford began work on building a serial assembly line of Model T cars. The new system at the Ford plant in Highland Park, Michigan, USA, was the beginning of the world's mass production. It was a conveyor system.

Production using the assembly line brought about a major change in the industrial production method. Ford's production rose sharply from 19,000 in 1910 to 248,000 in 1913. After that, the number of cars made by Ford was equal to the number of cars made by all other companies.

In order for conveyor belts to be utilized, complex processes had to be standardized and simplified along with "division of labor" in which tasks were divided for each worker.

At that time, scientific management techniques were being researched to devise the most efficient method by observing the work process "scientifically".Taylorism, which is called "time and motion study" attempted by Frederick Taylor, standardizes repetitive tasks by measuring the work movements of "picking up, lifting, bending, and matching" with a stopwatch, and based on this, improves work ability.

The principles of Taylor's division of labor and scientific management come to light when combined with Ford's mechanical production system, the Conveyor Belt. Let's take a look at the evolution of this concept of a "system."

The 19th century French physicist Nicolas Carnot pioneered the development of the concept of a "system" in the natural sciences (thermodynamics). In 1824, he studied a system he called the "working substance" of a steam engine (here the water vapor in a steam engine) in reference to the system's ability to do work when heat was applied. The working substance can come into contact with the boiler, the cooling reservoir (flow of cold water) or the piston (actuated by pushing the working substance).

In 1850, German physicist Rudolf Clausius generalized the picture of "system" to include the concept of the surrounding environment, as shown in the figure below left, and began to use the term "working body" to refer to systems.

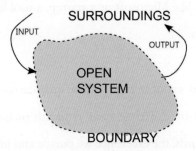

As we can see in the conveyor example, a system is a group of interacting or interrelated elements (e.g. belts, rollers, etc.) that operate according to a set of rules to form an integrated whole.

Systems have several common properties and characteristics, including structure, functions, behavior and interconnectivity.

Biologist and physicist Ludwig von Bertalanffy became one of the pioneers of general systems theory. In 1945, he introduced models, principles and laws that apply to generalized systems or subclasses, regardless of the particular kind, properties of their components, relationships or "forces" between them.

The world makes more sense when viewed as a patchwork of systems. Patchwork or "piecework" is a form of needlework in which pieces of fabric are sewn together into a larger design. Larger designs are usually based on repeating patterns composed of different fabric shapes.

A "system" is anything that has multiple parts that depend on each other. All machines and processes are systems at some level. For example, a business like Microsoft or a startup, a tool like a rocket or a keyboard is a system.

Processes such as economic growth or maintenance of romantic relationships, states of existence such as health or happiness, are all systems. In other words, the excellence we pursue and human prosperity itself are also part of the system.

Mental models help us understand how things (systems) work. What do you mean by mechanism? If you look at the dictionary meaning of mechanism, it says that it is the working principle of things. The principle that a machine runs is also a mechanism, and the principle that a certain situation runs is called a mechanism.

Mental models identify the key components of a system and how they interact. Each system can be reverse engineered into a mental model. This clarity is necessary for us to dramatically improve the system.

If someone improves the business system, that person can make more money. When someone improves the relationship system, that person gets deeper friendships.

2) System and IPO model

Systems in this world are very diverse and complex. Therefore, it is difficult for us to easily understand the system. If we focus on the characteristics and differences of each system, it becomes like a blind man touching an elephant.

Thus, by understanding what the common elements (rather than the differences) of the systems are, we can better understand the working mechanisms of the systems.

The system has the following common properties.

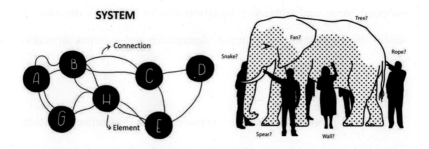

① A system has elements that make up the entire system.

② There are connections and interactions between the elements.

③ The system has a structure and function.

④ Generally, the system shows the process of input, conversion and output.

⑤ Many systems have feedback loops.

We can easily understand that systems are made up of wholes and parts. For example, there are small systems in the universe, such as galaxies, solar systems, and Earth, which interact as a whole and as parts. Therefore, I will omit further explanation on this.

In the figure below, the process can be seen as a kind of black box. The concept of input and output here is very broad. It includes stimulus and response, cause and effect, and effort and performance.

<IPO Model>

For example, calculators (including computers) calculate (convert) human-supplied input and provide calculation results (output). A thermostat senses the temperature as an input, determines and executes an action (heat on/off) as an output.

The IPO model is a general, abstract model that represents this. The IPO model is a very important and useful mental model for understanding the system. In addition to engineering, various IPO models have been developed for different fields.

For example, the political system theory devised by David Easton, an American political scientist, is a model that takes public demand and support as input and produces policies, laws, or budgets through a conversion process.

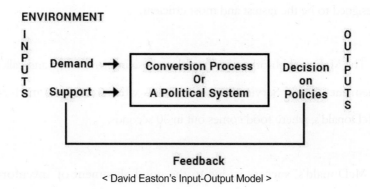

Feedback
< David Easton's Input-Output Model >

On the other hand, for reference, there is a useful mental model called "Input Goals." Most of the goals people set are "output goals" based on outcomes (becoming a millionaire or getting a six-pack). But the outcome is never in your control.

So this model suggests we focus on the input target. For example: Training twice a week for 1 hour every day (input) → slim body (output), or writing 2 hours a day (input) → being a good writer (output)

3) Little's Law

McDonald's is synonymous with fast food, famous for its "Big Mac" hamburger. Even when the McDonald brothers, who founded McDonald's, started their business, the most important thing was speed.

The McDonald brothers reduced the number of food choices and standardized the types of food. The movement of the kitchen was designed to be the fastest and most efficient.

The McDonald brothers put together these improvements and called them the "Speed Service System". This is what created the myth of McDonald's, where food comes out in 30 seconds.

McDonald's' success is due to the good alignment of inventory, output rate, flow and time in a stable process. Professor John Little of MIT's Sloan School of Business studied this scientifically.

The law discovered by Professor Little is called "Little's Law". The formula is:

$$L = \lambda \times W$$

In Little's Law, L is the average number of items within a system. Lambda(λ) is the average rate of items into and out of the system. W is the average time an item spends in the system.

The term may seem unfamiliar, but in a nutshell, it is a formula that states that the average number of customers staying at a restaurant or store$(=L)$ is the number of customers per hour who come to the restaurant$(=\lambda)$ multiplied by the average number of hours they stay$(=W)$.

It's a simple formula, but it's very useful because it generally holds regardless of the type of probability distribution.

If no one is in line, the waiting time is zero. Consider the meaning of waiting time. Waiting time means the time it takes for the last person in line to come to the front.

How many additional people can come in during this time? It is equal to the number of waiting time multiplied by the average arrival speed(=λ).

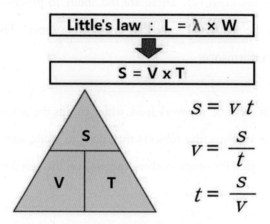

You will see that the formula $L = λ \times W$ is the same as the formula $S = V \times T$ in the end. Difficultly expressed as the average arrival rate, λ is a variable similar to speed (V).

Just as there is a difference in speed between individuals when climbing a mountain, the number of pending tasks in front of you and your ability to handle them are V and λ.

W, the average wait time in the system for an item, is the same concept as time (T). L, which is the average number of items in a queue, is the same concept as distance (S).

When students were in middle school, they found it difficult to intuitively understand the concept of speed (V). Likewise, the concept of average arrival speed (λ) is not easy to understand.

But it's easier to understand if you think of it as the ability of some system (restaurant, factory, etc.). These are the ability to process, solve, and digest. It is the ability to handle long lines of customers. These abilities represent performance.

Here, L is the L of the work load, which means the amount of work or load. For students, the subjects they need to study, such as English and mathematics, for office workers, the projects they need to handle are workload in front of them.

If you need to get from Moscow to St. Petersburg, there are several alternatives. Examples are airplanes, trains (high-speed trains and regular trains) and automobiles. The distance we have to travel (S) equals the workload we have to deal with (L).

The picture on the left shows a kind of overload due to overwork. How to solve these problems?

According to Little's Law, lambda is performance. So if you increase the lambda, you can handle more L. For example, you can improve work capacity by installing an additional assembly line when car orders soar, or by installing an auto pass at a toll gate that is blocked.

Let's look at Little's Law through the following situation. There is a restaurant that served 300 customers for 4 hours. Average meal time is 10 minutes. What is the average number of customers in the restaurant in this case?

The number of visitors per hour = the total number of visitors / visit time = 300 people / 4 hours = 75 people / hour. And since the average waiting time is 10 minutes = 1/6 hour, the number of customers in the store per hour is $75 \times 1/6 = 12.5$ people.

Therefore, you can refer to these numbers to prepare your operating facilities. If you add a 4-person table, you should prepare more than 4 tables and the number of employees should be prepared according to this capacity.

Little's law is also used to determine how much inventory a company should keep. It also tells how much cash a business needs to keep on average. This shows that the manager only needs to control two of three things: flow rate, flow time, and inventory.

This is because if any two properties are controlled and determined by L=λW, the other property is controlled. For example, when λ and W are determined, the value of L is determined automatically. This is a very important theoretical tool that process managers can consider when selecting or improving a process.

Let's solve the next problem.

There is a hotel that has an average of 135 guests per day. The hotel divides its guests into two types, one type is business customers and the other is simple tourist customers.

On average, business guests visit hotels twice as often as leisure guests and stay on average 1.8 nights. Simple tourists stay 3.6 nights on average. Business customers pay an average of $250 per night, and leisure customers average $210 per night.

① How many guests are staying for each type of guest?

Business guests : $135 \times 2/3 \times 1.8$ [$\lambda=135 \times 2/3$, W=1.8/day] =162

Simple tourists : $135 \times 1/3 \times 3.6$ [$\lambda=135 \times 1/3$, W=3.6/day] =162

→ Therefore, the total number of customers is 324.

② How many guests are staying per business customer and simple tourist customer?

Among the daily average inflow of customers, there are 90 business guests with an average stay of 1.8 days and 45 simple tourists with an average stay of 3.6 days, so the average stay time of all guests is (90 × 1.8) + (45 × 3.6) /135 = 2.4 days

③ What is the average income per room?

Multiply the number of guests' inventory of each type by the cost they pay, then divide by the total inventory.

[(162 people x 250$ = 40500$) + (162 people x 210$ = 34020$)] / 324 people = 74520$ / 324 people = 230$

Company A and Company B produce the same product. Therefore, the raw materials used and the production process are similar.

However, the factory manager of company A not only has a deep understanding of the operating mechanism of the production process (i.e., the system), but also knows the mental models (linear planning, Little's law, constraint theory, etc.) for process optimization.

On the other hand, the plant manager of company B does not have this mental model compared to the plant manager of company A.

Which company's production process do you think will perform better?

Of course, it is Company A. The plant manager of Company A seems to have both a lens for looking at the production process (Pareto-based perspective) and a problem-solving tool (statistical thinking and application of Bayesian reasoning). It will make a huge difference, especially in times of crisis.

As we have seen, various mental models such as Linear Planning (LP) and Little's Law are applied to restaurants, hospitals, and factories. What are the implications for us? These techniques usually take numbers and data and analyze them using certain equations or statistics.

Therefore, those who know the know-how can solve the problem, while those who do not know the know-how have no choice but to live by rule of thumb. We need knowledge. And it reminds us that learning is necessary to form knowledge. This is why we are learning mental models now.

2. Mechanism of some Systems

1) A system called a fan

A system means a set of elements related to producing a desired result. And here, the minimal system is composed of tools, objects, and actions.

In other words, we can get what we want by changing the attributes of objects with tools.

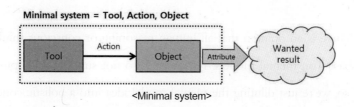

<Minimal system>

In order to change the properties(=attributes) of an object, an action must be applied to the object. A tool refers to a substance or object that acts to cause a property change of an object.

When you hit a nail with a hammer, the hammer is a tool, the nail is an object, and the properties are the diameter, color, material, and weight of the nail. Hit a nail (object) with a hammer (tool) when trying to hang a picture frame on the wall. Through hammering (action), the nature of the nail changes and the nail gets stuck between the wall and the picture frame. This changes to a new state (= desired result).

Actions for changing the attributes of objects can be made either naturally or artificially. When an action is applied to an object, the values of these properties change. A technical system is a collection of various components that enable a tool to operate.

We understand the minimal system as the picture above. This picture is, so to speak, a mental model that tells us what a minimal system is in an easy-to-understand way. Here I would like to point out one important point.

There is an opinion that all human reasoning or conscious thinking is based on mental models. However, I do not support this opinion. If so, we're just diluting the mental model idea into a holistic concept of thinking that encompasses almost all intellectual activity. Then this wouldn't be very useful.

Therefore, I propose three conditions that must be met in order to enter the realm of mental models among our mental activities.

① The mental model must be a system.
② Mental models should include possible state changes.
③ Mental models must include uncertainty.

Mental models relate to systems, state changes, and uncertainties.

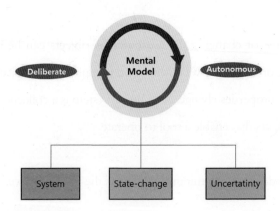

The above minimum system is above all a system, and shows the state change through the action between tool and object under uncertainty. Thus, this picture is well equipped with the three elements of the mental model.

Have you ever looked up at your ceiling fan as you're lying in your bed, and wondered how it was invented? The history of the electric fan is one that is relatively short, but one that has advanced extremely quickly in the history of time.

Through the Years…

① 4,000 B.C.: The Egyptians implored their servants to fan them with palm leaves, which became the first invention of the fan.

② 180 A.D.: The Chinese pioneered the mechanizing fan that was human powered.

③ 1830's: A doctor in Florida used blades to fan air from ice blocks to cool down sick patients.

⅛ H. P. ELECTRIC FAN
With Wire Guard and Switch for running fast or slow.

④ And the first electric fan using electricity was invented in 1882. Schuyler Wheeler applied electricity developed by Thomas Edison and Nicola Tesla to make a fan turn without human or horsepower. The first electric fan consisted of just two blades without a protective cage.

Tools play their part as part or all of the technical system. Fan blades and fans are tools. However, in order for any system to function effectively, there must be an energy source and an engine that converts this into usable energy within the system.

The energy converted in this way is transmitted to the working device (or tool) through the transmission in the system, and the energy transmitted to the working device is converted back into other energy or used as it is transmitted by the working device to act on the object. It is difficult to effectively perform work unless the control unit controls the entire process of the system that performs work through the flow of energy.

Soviet scientist Genrikh Altshuller insisted in TRIZ that there should be four essential components in this technical system: Tool + Transmission + Engine + Control Unit.

For reference, TRIZ is an acronym for Teoriya Reshniya Izobretatelskikh Zadatch, which means Theory of Inventive Problem Solving in Russian.

Here, the tool or working device is the subject that operates/acts on the object. Transmission is the transmission element of energy or force. Engine is energy or force. And the control unit plays the role of controlling energy(or force) or controlling tools.

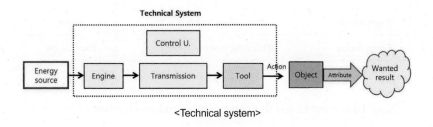

<Technical system>

Altshuller emphasized that a technical system must have four essential elements in order to survive and operate at a minimum. Therefore, when we consider the improvement of any technological system, we must first focus our activities on finding out whether there are any missing elements.

The technical system of an electric fan is shown in the figure below.

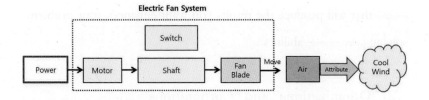

For example, the role of each component is defined as follows.

	role definition	component
Object	What will change?	Air
Action	What changes are taking place?	move
Tool	What does it do?	Fan Blade
Transmission	Through what is energy (power) transmitted?	Shaft
Engine	Where does energy (power) come from?	Motor
Control Unit	What adjusts (regulates)?	Switch
Energy Source	What is the source of energy?	Power Supply

Now I have explained the composition and mechanism of a system called an electric fan. Now you have a mental model of the fan system. There is good news. This principle is commonly applied to almost all engineering systems from steam engines to automobiles and airplanes.

There is a big difference between a person who has the picture presented above in his head and a person who does not have it in their understanding of mechanical and electronic systems.

Understanding how to construct a system (minimum system = tools, actions, objects) that will produce the results you want enhances your problem-solving (value-creating) abilities.

2) "Organizations" and "Corporations"

When someone sees an organization from a systems perspective, he gains important insight into how it works. Organizational theorists generally agree.

Organizational development (OD) theorist Peter Senge developed the concept of "organizations as systems" in his book <The Fifth Discipline>. He sees organizations as systems made up of parts that work together for a purpose as a whole.

From this point of view, the ultimate role of an organization is to continuously interact with the external environment for the survival and prosperity of the organization.

On the other hand, there are various perspectives looking at the essence of corporate. Traditional economics deals fragmentarily with the nature and function of capitalists and entrepreneurs.

According to this, a firm is a production function that produces goods by inputting factors of production. And an entrepreneur is understood as a manager who directs and supervises production.

Peter Drucker is considered the first scholar to view the corporation as an organization. A company is also a system in that it is a type of organization. The entire management system is divided into subsystems (HR, finance, production, marketing, etc.).

From this point of view, a systematic and analytical explanation of "management" becomes possible. The difference between economics and "management(namely, business administration)" is clearly revealed.

The conversion process from input to output is analyzed in detail. Business Administration empirically studies the suitability relationship between an organization and its environment using "management performance" as a dependent variable.

Nobel laureate in economics, Ronald Coase, understood business in terms of "transaction costs." A socialist in college, when he visited the Ford and GM automobile factories in the United States, he asked why it was impossible for the Soviet Union to operate as a single giant factory, when large American corporations were successful.

He theorized that businesses are similar to planned economies, but organized by people's voluntary choices, and that people organize businesses precisely because there is a cost to trading everything in a market.

Coase provided an economic explanation for why individuals choose to form partnerships, corporations, and other business entities rather than two-way transactions through market contracts.

Costs arise when economic entities transact. This includes all three costs:

① The cost of searching for the counterparty

② The cost of negotiating with the counterparty

③ The cost of actually implementing the transaction after the transaction is made.

In this way, all costs that must be paid in additional transactions other than the product price are included in "transaction costs." Coase saw that the reduction of this transaction cost is the reason why companies exist, that is, the essence of companies.

For example, if individual producers do not take charge of each stage of furniture production, but create a single organization and internalize the entire process from purchasing raw materials to producing finished products, the situation will be completely different. Not only does furniture cost much less to produce, but the final finished product costs significantly less.

It is a business that reduces transaction costs and produces and sells products at a low cost. Firms internalize market transactions into their organizations to lower transaction costs. Of course, entrepreneurs who set up companies aim for profit. Thus, companies will decide which to internalize and which to outsource on a case-by-case basis.

Human progress has been mainly achieved by technological innovation and reduction of transaction costs. Once you understand the concept of transaction costs (mental model), you will see that eBay, Amazon, Alibaba, etc. have grown their new businesses among their existing competitors through innovations that reduce transaction costs.

3) Business system

A business system is a set of defined principles, practices and procedures applied to specific activities to achieve specific results. Basically, it's about creating a series of shortcuts that make everything work correctly.

Benefits of business systems include greater efficiency, productivity, clarity, consistency and control. Systems can be implemented in many areas of the business, including sales and lead generation, payroll and management, and operational activity.

There are many businesses in the world. At first glance, Samsung Electronics (semiconductor and smartphone production), Amazon (various product sales), McDonald's (fast food franchise), Uber (transportation service), and Airbnb (accommodation) seem to operate different businesses.

However, considering that these various businesses are also systems, there will be certain components and operation methods. Fans and cars are different products, but just as you could understand them from the point of view of systems, various businesses have certain things in common in that they are systems.

Scholars study such things. There are concepts such as business model, business model canvas, value chain, 5 forces, and value network. These are what are usually called theories, models, etc.

With the help of these concepts (mental models), we can more easily and quickly understand seemingly disparate businesses through just a few lenses. So, when we have these models in our head, they greatly help us when we build our own business or understand the business of others.

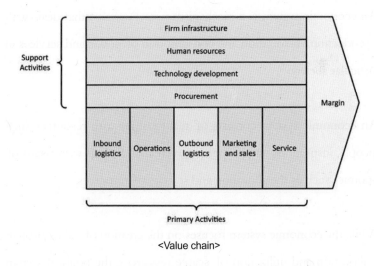

<Value chain>

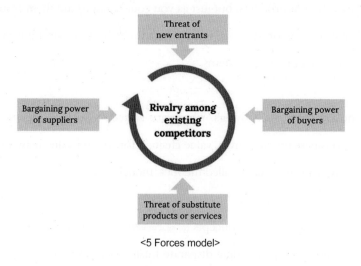

<5 Forces model>

4) System called "Capitalism"

An economic system is a mechanism (a social institution) that deals with the production, distribution and consumption of goods and services in a particular society.

An economic system consists of relationships with resources such as people, institutions and property agreements. It deals with issues of economics such as the allocation and scarcity of resources.

While the economic system focuses on the creation of value through the allocation and utilization of scarce resources, the political system focuses on the authoritative allocation of value.

The concept of "capitalism" as a representative economic system has evolved over time. Sub-elements of capitalism, such as markets, property rights, and investments, have also changed their concepts over time. The essence of capitalism is that it is a successful problem-solving system and a value-creating system.

In response, Adam Smith coherently explained three important properties that make the invisible hand (= price) so effective. It is the benefit of division of labor, specialization, and exchange. These three things are linked in such a way that each other makes each other possible.

(1) division of labor

Division of labor is about how much one worker does all the work necessary to produce something, and how finely the work is divided among the workers into specialized tasks.

When producing cars, there may be a way for each worker to complete one car from start to finish. On the other hand, there may be an assembly line method in which the entire work of making a car is divided into many tasks in small units, and one person performs each unit task according to a long sequential flow.

Adam Smith, in <The Wealth of Nations> of 1776, explains the productivity of the division of labor in a pin mill. An unskilled worker can make as many as 20 pins a day by himself.

However, when the work was divided into 18 units and 10 people divided the work, they produced about 48,000 units a day. In other words, each person can make 4800 pins per day. This is a 240-fold increase in productivity.

In addition to the case of Adam Smith's pin factory, 17th-century Baroque Belgian painters Peter Rubens and Henry Ford, and pop art master Andy Warhol also used division of labor to create greater value.

Author of the Black Swan, Nassim Taleb recommended the common people to the kingdom of the ordinary rather than the kingdom of the extreme. This is sensible advice. This is because even if someone is in an ordinary kingdom, he can create greater value if he makes good use of the division of labor.

(2) Specialization

This division of labor gives rise to two advantages of specialization.

① Each of us has things we do better than others, so if we specialize, we can do things better than others. As David Ricardo said, we can specialize in areas where we have a comparative, not an absolute, advantage over others.

Country A is inferior to Country B in the production of both cars and bikes. Country B has an absolute advantage. Country B does not seem to need to trade with country A.

Country A spends 10 hours producing 1 car. Country A can make 2 bikes in this time. Country A spends 5 hours producing one bike. Country A can make 0.5 cars in this time. Let's fill the table like this.

Labor hours (for producing 1 unit)	Cars	Bikes
Country A	10	5
Country B	8	2

Opportunity Costs (for producing 1 unit)	Cars	Bikes
Country A	2 bikes	0.5 cars
Country B	4 bikes	0.25 cars

Both countries have 2,000 labor hours available. If they both decided to allocate half of those resources to each product, country A could produce 100 cars and 200 bikes while country B could produce 125 cars and 500 bikes.

This would result in a total output of 925 units.

Opportunity Costs (for producing 1 unit)	Cars	Bikes
Country A	2 bikes	0.5 cars
Country B	4 bikes	0.25 cars

Total Outputs (for producing 1 unit)	Cars	Bikes
Country A	100	200
Country B	125	500
Total	225	700

Now, if country A specializes in the production of cars, and country B specializes in the production of bikes, their outputs will look considerably different.

In that case, country A will produce 200 cars and no bikes while country B will still manufacture 25 cars and use the rest of its time to produce 900 bikes. This results in an overall output of 1125 units which equals an increase of 200 units due to specialization.

Total Outputs (without specialization)	Cars	Bikes
Country A	100	200
Country B	125	500
Total	225	700

Total Outputs (with specialization)	Cars	Bikes
Country A	200	0
Country B	25	900
Total	225	900

② As experience accumulates, workers become better at what they do well. The more often someone performs a relatively small unit of work, the more proficient he becomes at it through repeated experience.

Nobel laureate in economics, Kenneth Arrow, said that productivity can be increased through this process, and called this "learning by doing." And Joseph Stieglitz, also a Nobel laureate, emphasized the importance of lifelong learning throughout society for growth and prosperity in the <Learning Society>.

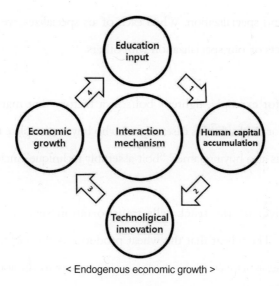

< Endogenous economic growth >

Related, the endogenous economic growth theory considers the formation and accumulation of human capital as one of the important factors of economic growth. Along with education and training, specialization in the workplace is often seen as a key economic growth factor in terms of increasing worker productivity.

Specialization is an important factor in the overall macroeconomy from the perspective of growth, but it is also an important factor in determining individual development and future income. Regarding these specializations, popular author Malcolm Gladwell argued that it takes 10,000 hours of practice to reach success. (I will explain later, but of course his claim is not true.)

(3) Exchange

The gains of exchange are merely the rewards of the gains of division of labor and specialization. When each of us specializes, we exchange the products of our specialization with others.

James, for example, tightens bolts in a factory that manufactures radiators for trucks. In this case, anyone who buys a complete truck with a radiator is also buying James' "bolt-assembly technique" included in it.

The driver of the truck sells transportation services to wheat producers. The wheat that the wheat producers sell (usually in the form of processed flour, the result of one specialized production) comes to the local bakery where James lives. James had just bought freshly baked bread there. This means buying from the most efficient suppliers.

The most efficient providers are those who have reached the most efficient state through the gains of specialization. Within an economy, many experts in any field conduct a multifaceted exchange, trying to be (or try to remain) the most efficient at what they do.

If we couldn't exchange our output with someone, each of us would have to do everything ourselves. Then there is no division of labor, no specialization, no learning by experience. Exchange creates a large market, from which a highly precise division of labor and specialization is possible.

No one else suffers a loss because I enjoy the gains of the exchange. In other words, the benefits of exchange are reciprocal, and everyone benefits. Of course, not necessarily everyone benefits to the same extent. Exchange completes the problem-solving and value-creating system. Each of us has problems to solve, needs to be met.

And we look for the person who can best solve each of those problems. Also, each of us decides which of the other people's problems we can best solve. James expertly tightened the bolts on the radiator.

It is the "freedom of choice" exercised by individuals that determines who solves the problem best. The chosen person is usually the one who best solves the problem at the lowest cost. Many of our customers who want to solve their problems will choose this person.

Customers do not choose people who do not solve problems well, who solve problems unsatisfactorily or at high cost. Freedom of choice is a powerful engine that rewards the world's best problem solvers (value creators) in every field and eliminates poor problem solvers.

Milton Friedman, author of <Free to Choose>, opposes "excessive government restrictions on freedom." Friedman talks about how the government's policy of achieving consequential equality undermines individual liberty.

Man has the right to pursue what he wants. That's freedom to choose. The government's deprivation of the people's right to choose for some purpose is most likely to be used for interest groups or only to increase the power of the government.

Modern society overlooks this point and constantly emphasizes the role of the government. Even America's Democrats and Republicans agree in their preference for big government, which is, in fact, a global phenomenon.

However, although the nation's prosperity in a learning society requires more intelligent people, the market does not play a sufficient role, so the role of the state is required. Therefore, we who live in the 21st century must think about the true value of freedom and the role of the state.

Two questions arise here.

Question 1: It takes a great deal of knowledge to solve each problem we face or to find problem solvers (value creators) that meet our needs. How is this issue handled?

Answer 1: When I have to solve the problem of buying a car, all I have to do is already solved by a lot of people who want to buy a car and a lot of people who want to sell it. This tremendous search process is summed up in a single piece of information. That information is the "price" of the car.

Chung Ju-yung needed only two things to change his job from selling rice to repairing cars. In other words, the income of farmers in Asan was very low, and the income of auto repair shops in Seoul was higher. He became the founder of South Korea's Hyundai Group, including Hyundai Kia Motors.

Question 2: How is the problem of incentives (i.e. motivation) necessary for these problem-solving systems to work?

Answer 2: The invisible hand solves the problem of motivation through a reward system that motivates voluntarily. Farmers and bakers reward truckers for the quick and reliable transport of their wheat to and from them. Chung Ju-yung repaired other people's cars and got paid. He then used the money he earned to pay others to buy the food he needed to support his family.

The core principle of the most successful problem-solving (value-creating) system in human history is surprisingly simple. The first requirement is that the private rewards that each individual receives for solving other people's problems must match the benefits others get from solving the problem—that is, the social rewards.

This social reward is revealed in the act of consumers voluntarily paying the price of bread when buying a piece of bread. The price of bread is also the baker's income per unit of bread (his social reward).

The baker, in turn, uses this income to purchase items important to him from others. Thus, the baker solves other people's bread problems and is rewarded for each piece of bread.

The second requirement is individual rights. The system should give everyone the right to choose which problem they solve. Then, problem solvers (value creators) seeking extremely efficient solutions will emerge from all corners of society.

The system helps people find the best solutions to their own problems and at the same time find the best roles for them to solve other people's problems. This is the "invisible hand" of the capitalist system.

5) The system of "Money": Compounding and Leverage

(1) Compound interest

It is very important that we understand how money works in a capitalist society. Let's learn about compounding and leverage to multiply and use money. Only three out of seven American adults are financially literate. For me, it's simple. Knowledge is power.

Albert Einstein once said, "compound interest is the eighth wonder of the world." Another one of my favorite quotes on the subject is Benjamin Franklin's "money makes money. And the money that money makes, makes money."

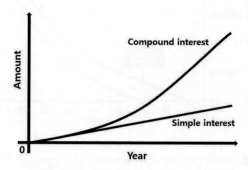

Simply put, if you have $10,000 and it earns 10%, you've got $11,000. That 10% you've earned was initially $1000, but now you have $11,000 earning 10%.

That equals $1100.00, so by that compounding effect, even without investing new money after 25 years, it's worth over $120,000. Again, the money initially invested is making money, and then the earned money is making money and compounding.

The chart below shows how a $200 a month investment over ten years can out-earn a $200 a month investment over 30 years. (with the same rate of return) All depends on how early those investments were made. This clearly shows the benefits of how important it is to start early.

IMPACT OF WHEN YOU START INVESTING (EVEN IF YOU STOP)

Jack invests $200 per month between the ages of 25 and 35. He contributes $24,000 total. By age 65, his portfolio is worth more than $520,000.

Jill invests $200 per month between the ages of 35 and 65. She contributes $72,000 total. By age 65, her portfolio is only worth about $245,000. By waiting ten years to start, she ends up with less than half what Jack accumulates.

Jack is able to stop contributing at 35 but still accumulate more than Jill thanks to the power of compounding. At first, Jack's $200 monthly contributions don't earn much interest: $14 in the first year and $30 in the second year. But by his tenth year of investing, his money is earning more than he puts in. In year 11, Jack contributes only $200 but earns $231. And it's only up from there: Over time, his earnings will exponentially exceed his contributions.

Jack's earnings will grow so large, they'll exceed all of his contributions combined. After 20 years of investing, Jack contributed $48,000 total. That same year, his $48,000 earned over $56,000. By year 25, his earnings ($103,000) are over 70 percent larger than his total contributions ($60,000).

This is why time is so important in investing: Given enough time, your earnings can compound to take on a life of their own. Even better is they can become self-sustainable. When your money is earning enough money that you no longer need to work, you've achieved financial independence.

Warren Buffett earned 99% of his fortune after his 50th birthday. In general, this doesn't seem to make sense. Buffett started investing at age 11, but essentially amassed nearly all of his fortune after age 50. Was the first 39 years of his investment years just a waste of time?

Not like that.

This is how compound interest works. Compound interest grows your wealth at an incredibly slow pace at first. Then it speeds up. And it gets faster and faster.

Compound interest is calculated on the **principal (original) amount** and on the **interest already accumulated** in previous periods.

$$A = P(1 + \frac{r}{100})^n$$

Where:
A represents the final amount
P represents the original principal amount
r is the interest rate over a given period
n represents the number of times the interest rate is applied over time

Imagine you invest $1,000 per month for 50 years at a 10% return. Here's how to increase your wealth. It will take you a very long time to build the first 30% of your fortune, but the other 70% will come much sooner.

If you look back 50 years from now, you would have accumulated 70% of your assets or 26% of your investments over the past 12 years. It's the classic 80/20 rule. (Not exactly an 80/20 ratio, but close enough to that number).

Of course, not everyone can invest for 50 years. But the point is this. If you invest for the long term, you can build wealth, as Buffett experienced. Some people may call you "lucky," but you'll find that it's math, not magic.

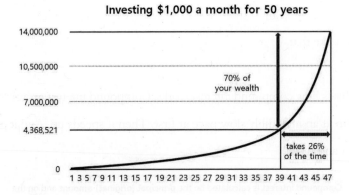

Investing $1,000 a month for 50 years

In summary, three things are needed to achieve "compound effect." It is time, consistency and patience.

(2) The Rule of 72

The Rule of 72 is a great mental model for estimating the effects of growth rates on everything from quick financial calculations to population estimates.

The formula is:

Years to double = 72 / interest rate

This formula is useful for understanding the nature of financial estimation and compound interest. Here are some examples.

- At 6% interest, it will take 72/6 or 12 years for your money to double.
- To double your money in 10 years, take an interest rate of 72/10 or 7.2%.
- If your country's GDP grows at 3% per year, the economy doubles in 72/3 or 24 years.
- If the growth rate increases to 4%, the economy doubles in 18 years.

You can also use the Rule of 72 for expenses like inflation and interest.

- If inflation rises from 2% to 3%, the value of money will halve in 24 years instead of 36.
- If college tuition increases at 5% per year (faster than inflation), tuition will

double in 72/5 or about 14.4 years. Paying 15% interest on a credit card doubles the amount owed in 72/15 or 4.8 years.

(3) Leverage

An easy way to express leverage is the power of the lever. And when such leverage is used as an economic term, it means "investment using debt."

Let's say you invest $10,000 and buy a $10,000 house. After a while, the house price jumped 10% to $11,000. This will give you a 10% return.

But suppose you bought a house for $100,000 with $10,000 and borrowed $90,000. The leverage ratio is 10:1. This is $1 in equity (your own money) for every $10 in assets.

How much would you have made if the price of your house rose 10%? You earned 10% of the total $100,000. The house is now worth $110,000, and after paying off the $90,000 debt, you have $20,000 left. That 10% increase turned into a 100% return on the initial investment (i.e. $10,000).

- **Leverage ratio = asset / equity**
- **return = leverage ratio x percent change**

Again, with 10x leverage, a 10% increase would be a 100% return on your initial capital. The price of the house only increased by 10%, but thanks to the purchase of a large house using debt, it made a profit of 100%. Taking advantage of debt in this way is called the leverage effect. Of course, if you buy with your own money, the leverage ratio is 1.

But now what about the other way around? The house price fell 10% to $90,000. You sell the house for 90,000, pay off the loan (90,000) and what's left... is 0!

Similarly, a 10% drop in price would result in a 100% loss of capital. If the price goes down, you lose 10x. House prices only dropped 10%, but 100% of your money was gone. And if house prices fall by 20%, you lose 200%. You lose the initial $10,000 and owe $10,000 more than that. (The house is sold for $80,000, but the loan is still $90,000).

If your investment falls to the 1/leverage ratio (in this case 1/10 or 10%), you lose your assets. If the leverage ratio is 25x, the investment will be wiped out after only 4% drop. Therefore, when investing with debt, it is important to keep in mind that there are both great benefits and risks.

Chapter 3

Improvement and Utilization of the System

Before started

A "system" is anything that has multiple parts that depend on each other. All machines and processes are systems at some level.

The capitalist society we live in is an economic system, and the democratic society is a political system. Organizations and enterprises are systems, and businesses are also systems.

When we understand how the system works, we can create value more effectively. Mental models identify the components of a system and how they interact.

So mental models allow us to better understand how systems work. And as we better understand how the system works, we can make better choices and create better value through better decisions.

When you see the world as a series of outputs someone has made, you only form opinions. However, when you see the world as a series of systems, you understand the system and form strategies to use it. These strategies will make your life better.

Now let's look at the improvement and utilization of these systems.

1. How to improve the system

1) One Level Higher

How do you know which systems in your life deserve significant improvement? To answer this we will use another mental model. This is the model often referred to as the "One Level Higher."

This is to start by identifying the highest leverage level to optimize when we are dealing with the system. Ask again and again if you are optimizing the cogs in the machine, not the system or machine itself. The higher the level of optimization, the greater the ROI(return on investment) in general.

Let's assume that you can expect a 25% pay increase if you change jobs, but you still work for a company for several years for a 15% pay increase. Then this means you are optimizing a cog (salary) in the machine (job).

Instead, you can reach your goal faster if you optimize your machine. In other words, you can look for another job. And those choices can lead you to a higher level of optimization.

The job market itself is like a cog in another machine. Having a job is about having financial security. But what if you could achieve financial security without struggling a 9-to-5? If your true passion lies outside the office, climbing the corporate ladder will fall victim to inertia.

Instead, a better way is to cut costs by moving to a cheaper city and living more modestly. You can pursue your passion by moving part-time for a fraction of the cost. Aren't these changes the high-level game you really want to optimize?

We always have problems. The One Level Higher model is a process of asking the following questions: Is it more leverage to optimize for a higher level (eg job transfer) than the level I am currently focused on (eg salary)?

This is a question most people find difficult to ask themselves due to inertia. People work hard without asking which job is better for them. This is a hidden form of laziness and stupidity. You can appreciate the beauty of what Mihaly Csikszentmihalyi called "flow" in what you do, but don't get addicted to it.

Think of it like this. Mental models are driven by information. The mental model generates various recommendations based on the updated information entered by the user.

So if you're in a flow state for a long time, you'll probably bury your head without consuming new data, advice, articles, etc. When this happens, your mental model will no longer function as a compass telling you what to do next.

A classic example is how teenagers are told to go to college. They go into a state of flow with the goal of getting into college, but they don't question themselves at any point.

Do you really have to go to university for your chosen degree? Or did you choose a degree "because it felt right" when you were 17 and haven't revisited that decision ever since? Can you make a compelling argument for why a degree is not a better option? If you can't make those arguments convincing, it's a sign that you're not thinking critically.

Once teenagers go to college, they fall into the rush to graduate. They play the low-level game of getting a high GPA, not the high-level game of learning useful skills to prepare for the job market.

Most college students aren't good at thinking about what's best for them. So college life is just 4 years of life that is treated like homework. And this applies to everything we do. What is your job like?

2) Theory of Constraints

Everyone is living with a limitation of resources. And even if someone doesn't know the economic term called opportunity cost, he wants the outcome of his choice to produce the maximum value. Because of this, we always live by distributing available resources for a specific result value in our daily life.

A similar situation always occurs in the production process of a company. "Theory of Constraints (TOC)" is a management innovation theory to solve these problems. It is a kind of IPO model.

Dr. Eli Goldratt, the creator of "TOC", argues that weak points (= constraints) in the production line lead to a decrease in overall productivity. He says that in order to raise the company's goal (Goal = profit), it is necessary to find and improve efficiency in this part that causes waste of resources.

In other words, the constraint theory is a system improvement method to discover the constraints that hinder the achievement of the company's goals and overcome them. Eli Goldratt argues that constraints are the key to increasing a company's output. This is the difference from the conventional theories that deal with the whole process of a factory or company-wide improvement activities.

For example, consider the entire business activity or "Supply Chain" as a chain. In this case, each activity from receiving orders, procurement of raw materials, production, delivery, billing, and collection corresponds to one link in the chain. Therefore, the profitability of the entire supply chain can be said to be the strength of the (whole) chain.

An important point is that if even one link in the chain is weak, the strength of the chain as a whole is equal to that of the weak link. This means that increasing the strength of any other link other than the weak link does not increase the strength of the connecting chain. Eli Goldlett says that the lowest level of ability (activity) is where the bottleneck occurs, that is, the constraint.

In other words, since the profit generated by the supply chain is limited to the section (activity) with the lowest ability, in order to increase the profit (= target amount), the weakest part must be strengthened. Let's take a closer look at an example of TCO application through the following example of a bicycle club.

There is a cycling club with 5 members. Riding courses do not only have bicycle-only roads, but there are many cases where you have to use automobile roads. Interference with vehicles may cause danger and inconvenience.

Due to the nature of bicycle riding, it is inevitable to ride in a single line, and the risk increases when the line is stretched. So how can we minimize the risk and inconvenience?

Since the bike club is not a race, all members must ride together and reach the destination. It means that someone cannot drop a member who is lagging behind. That is, the speed of the slowest person becomes the speed of the entire group.

These constraints are consistent with the core of the TCO theory: "Improvement of the least productive process is the most effective way to increase overall efficiency." Therefore, we can use the TCO theory to find improvements. The improvement steps are as follows.

Step 1: Find the bottleneck.

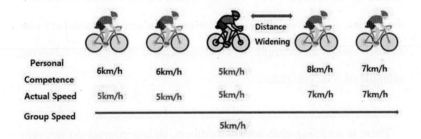

Personal Competence	6km/h	6km/h	5km/h		8km/h	7km/h
Actual Speed	5km/h	5km/h	5km/h		7km/h	7km/h
Group Speed			5km/h			

In the picture above, the speed of the middle rider is 5 km. This is slower than other riders. So, a bottleneck occurs from the rider, and as a result, the length of the line increases. Looking at this "distance widening phenomenon", you can find the bottleneck.

Step 2: Find a way to solve the bottleneck.

When you find a bottleneck, think about how to solve that bottleneck. There are many ways in detail, but there are two main ways.

① Change the order: Make the person with the lowest speed the leader. That way the line doesn't stretch. In the case of a production process, reversing bottlenecks improves the process. If the bottleneck occurs at the end of the process, reversing it will cause the bottleneck at the front. Then at least the factory doesn't have to keep a lot of stock initially.

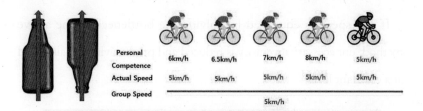

Personal Competence	6km/h	6.5km/h	7km/h	8km/h	5km/h
Actual Speed	5km/h	5km/h	5km/h	5km/h	5km/h
Group Speed			5km/h		

② Task division: The speed of the slowest person becomes the speed of the group. Conversely, when the leader speeds up, the speed of the entire group speeds up.

In order to improve the conditions of the slowest leader, it would be possible for someone to give him the best bike or for other colleagues to carry his luggage instead. In the case of the production process, the installation of an additional line (C') solves the bottleneck.

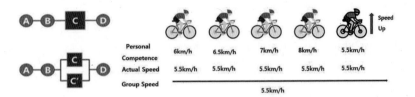

Personal Competence	6km/h	6.5km/h	7km/h	8km/h	5.5km/h
Actual Speed	5.5km/h	5.5km/h	5.5km/h	5.5km/h	5.5km/h
Group Speed			5.5km/h		

Step 3: After resolving bottlenecks, ensure that all processes are optimized according to the above decisions.

The length of the bike line is the cost of going through the whole process. The longer the line, the higher the cost of the entire process. The speed of the cycling club means the productivity of the whole process.

If the speed is equalized by solving the bottleneck in the above method, unnecessary inventory is reduced and productivity is maintained at a constant level.

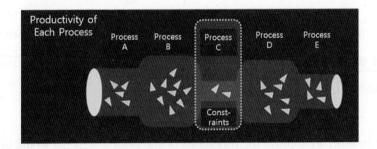

Therefore, in order to increase corporate productivity and reduce inventory, an approach such as the bicycle club's solution is effective.

First, find the process with the lowest productivity, and then match the overall productivity.

The process with the lowest productivity, this is called the "constraint." It is the same reason that the slowest person in a cycling club leads the group.

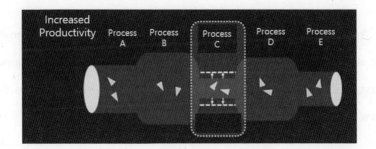

And just as the leader's condition was given top priority in bicycle riding, the condition of the constraints must be considered first in the production process.

If the productivity of the constraint-required process is improved through facility investment, manpower expansion, and employee training, the productivity of the entire plant can be increased in an optimized state.

Once you are faced with a system, you can start optimizing that system according to the constraint theory. At any given time, it is only one of the system's inputs that limits the other inputs to achieving a greater total output.

Therefore, if you want to continuously increase the system's output, you must iteratively identify and solve current constraints.

For example, if you want to pursue some new hobby, but you can't get started, first identify the underlying inputs like time, motivation, and knowledge of how to move forward.

And ask yourself. If I double down on any of these inputs, will I finally be able to pursue my hobby? If you know what it is, increase that input first. Then, if you get stuck again after starting, ask again. Perhaps the new constraint next time will be your time or motivation.

Constraint theory is particularly important in business. You may not get more customers because one of the inputs, such as lead flow, sales skills, product quality, or price, limits the other input.

Find the bottleneck, increase the capacity, and repeat this process over and over until you reach the desired location. One thing will be the most intrusive at any given time. Your job is to pause and remember to look for it.

Eventually you will reach the maximum potential of any system implementation. That's when it's time to break the bubble and move in a better direction by switching to "First Principle" or revisiting "One Level Higher."

3) First principle

If the system does not reach the desired level of efficiency even though you make iterative improvements using constraint theory, this is the time to discard your current approach to the system and re-examine the system "from scratch."

The first principle is a mental model used by Elon Musk to solve problems in complex systems. This is an approach like this:

What would be the most efficient way to solve a problem if you started from scratch? If you look back at humanity's attempts to solve it, what is the best approach if you reason from its fundamental principles?

Below is an interview with Elon Musk in 2015.

Usually we accept what already exists and try to innovate within that framework. When it comes to startups, the situation is not much different. Of course, this isn't all bad. Imitation helps prevent the worst. Because it is a proven method. However, in order to innovate, we must break away from imitation.

Don't take the situation as it is right now. Problems are there to be solved. Break down the problem in detail. You should always go back to the root of the problem. A better solution is bound to be there.

One might say "Car battery packs are really expensive and always are. Historically, it has cost $600 per kilowatt hour. It won't get much better than that in the future."

Even in this case, people who can't break the habit of copying think that the budget should be tight to $600. They do not intend to change the battery pack. They follow because all other companies do it.

Regarding this, you can ask: "What are the elements that make up the materials of a battery? And what is the market value of the components?"

Then you will easily find the answer that the material components of a battery are cobalt, nickel, aluminum, carbon, a polymer for isolation and a sealed can. And after this analysis on a material basis, you can ask, "What will it cost if we buy the individual components from the London Metal Exchange and assemble them?"

Then you get the surprising answer: "$80 per kilowatt hour." So now you can think of smart ways to combine these materials into

> the shape of a battery cell. In this way, you can use a much cheaper battery than anyone else.

Elon Musk challenged the existing assumptions, beliefs and stereotypes that "battery packs are expensive." Instead, he asked powerful questions that revealed the elements that make up the battery.

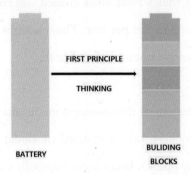

He did not think of the battery as a single loaf of bread, but after disassembling it into various elements that make up the bread, he stacked the elements as if making a sandwich.

Then he created an ingenious and innovative solution, literally from scratch. Musk described his own way of thinking as thinking based on first principle thinking. I think that even ordinary people are usually familiar with analogies. So, comparing the analogy and the first principle, it is as follows.

Analogy	Because batteries are expensive, electric cars that need to use batteries will be impossible.
1st principle	Purchasing individual components from cost-effective sources makes it possible to make much cheaper batteries.

SpaceX was founded in 2002 by Elon Musk. Musk succeeded when he applied what he said about car batteries to SpaceX in 2020.

One of the many things Elon Musk created was challenging NASA's practice of using one rocket per test. They thought it was either too difficult or too expensive not to do so, or both.

But Musk has challenged this assumption and developed a way for SpaceX to reuse rockets, saving millions of dollars per launch and helping his company SpaceX become commercially viable.

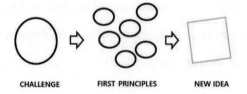

CHALLENGE   FIRST PRINCIPLES   NEW IDEA

How do you use first principles in practical problems? For all your future projects, ask:

• What systems will this project be based on?

• Is this system already efficient?

• If not, what are the iron-clad principles underlying it?

• Can we start again from first principles to identify a much better way to design this system?

We can efficiently explore the system using the above three models. First, use "one level higher" to identify the right level to optimize for. Second, optimize the system using "Theory of Constraints." If that doesn't work, use "first principles" to break out of the box and design a better system from the start.

2. Use of feedback loop

Feedback is where the output of the system affects the input. Consider a simple IPO model. Inputs go through a transformation process to produce results. However, the output value has a repetitive effect on the input value and reinforces or maintains the result(output). The diagram below shows what this means.

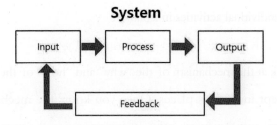

The feedback loop we are all familiar with is: Central heating systems with temperature control, refrigerators with temperature control, anti-lock brakes in cars, photo exposures in digital cameras, etc. But beyond these things, feedback loops appear very widely in our lives.

For example, at a place where a lot of people gather, such as a festival or event, a slight panic causes a few people to run away, which leads to a larger panic and more people to flee. This will result in a stampede, and eventually a minor panic will lead to major disaster.

We see this in bubbles and explosions in the stock market. And when a handful of bank depositors hear rumors (due to negative news) that the bank will go bankrupt, they will run to the branch to withdraw their money. The news that depositors flock to branches for money drives more depositors to follow. This ultimately leads to a bank run.

Nature keeps everything in balance. The food chain is one of the best examples. We face positive and negative feedback loops in our lives and investments. Because causality has a circular reference (from Microsoft Excel terminology), it is important to look at the system as a whole rather than looking at individual activities in isolation.

Let's look at the mechanism of the "why" and "how" of the feedback loop concept in various places. Once you know the mechanism of this concept, you can create value by incorporating the mental model similarly in completely new places.

1) Understanding feedback loops: some examples

(1) Example 1: All the apples are ripe in no time. → How to store fruits and vegetables smartly

One of the apples on the apple tree is starting to ripen. As apples ripen, they release a gas called ethylene through the skin. Ethylene gas also causes nearby apples to ripen. As more apples ripen, the total amount of ethylene gas released increases. More ethylene gas makes more apples ripen. In an instant, all the apples on the apple tree ripen.

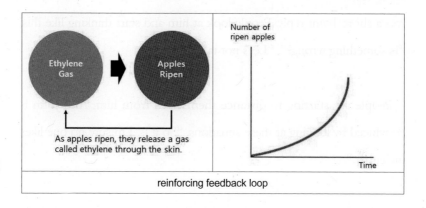

In this example, we can see how the effect provides repeated feedback to the cause. In fact, this is what feedback loops are all about. Instead, it is divided into a reinforcing feedback loop and a balancing feedback loop, depending on where the results of this repetitive feedback process flow.

The iterative feedback process in the example above contributed to the cause of ethylene gas. This process continues until all the apples on the apple tree are ripe.

This is called a reinforcing feedback loop (positive feedback loop). Reinforcing feedback loops continuously flow results in positive or negative directions unless there is a critical point.

(2) Example 2: The process of thoughts solidifying into beliefs→Listen to your thoughts.

John often thought that no one liked him. He seemed pretty cold and unemotional. When someone spoke to him, all he got back from John was a short, blunt reply. People look at him and start thinking like this. "Is something wrong?", "Let's not talk to John"

People are starting to distance themselves from him. And John is convinced by looking at these situations. "So it is. I'm sure no one likes me either."

This is an example of a reinforcing feedback loop. The iterative feedback process in the example above influenced the cause of "John's thoughts." As this process is repeated, his thoughts will become stronger and stronger.

(3) Example 3: How is body temperature maintained? →Feedback loops do not necessarily reinforce the results.

When our body temperature rises, our body starts to sweat. As sweat cools down, it causes evaporative cooling, which lowers the body temperature and keeps it normal.

Conversely, when the body temperature drops, the body begins to shiver (repeated contraction and relaxation of muscles). It generates heat energy by shivering, which raises the body temperature and keeps it normal.

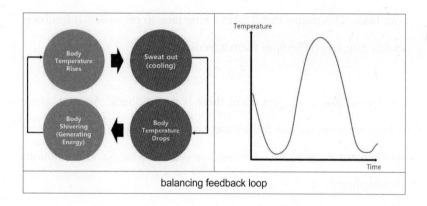

balancing feedback loop

This is called a balancing(negative) feedback loop. The balancing feedback loop maintains balance by sending results in the negative (-) direction when the result moves in the positive (+) direction, and in the positive (+) direction when the result moves in the negative (-) direction.

2) Use of feedback loop

(1) Example 1: Motivation to exercise steadily → Create intuitive and immediate feedback

It is easy to make up your mind to exercise, but it is very difficult to put it into action. Everyone knows that exercise is good for you. They are even convinced that positive changes will occur in their bodies if they "just do it consistently for a period of time."

So why is it so difficult to keep exercising?

If you exercise for a day or two, you won't feel dramatic changes in your body. This means that it takes a long time to get (or feel like) feedback. In this case, it is difficult to form a feedback loop.

Of course, that doesn't mean there is no feedback. As soon as we finish exercising, we can feel a variety of emotions including a sense of achievement (the feeling that muscles have been stimulated, pride, etc.). But emotions are temporary.

So it is not easy to influence us to exercise again the next day. At that point, feelings such as tiredness or annoyance may be felt more strongly.

At times like these, when we need a stimulus to urge us to exercise, can't we intentionally create new feedback?

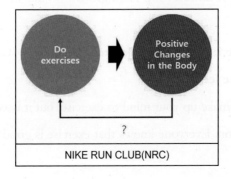

That's how exercise apps like NIKE RUN CLUB (NRC) appeared. You can get a variety of feedback even if you exercise for just one day with NRC. Such intuitive feedback affects the next exercise, creating a reinforcing feedback loop.

In fact, there is no causal relationship between the changes that occur in the body and the feedback the NRC gives. Unlike a ripe apple that releases ethylene gas from its skin, making other apples ripen faster, I can't say that receiving so many badges at Nike has changed my body in a positive way. Instead, this feedback definitely affects the cause of "doing the exercise."

Normally, feedback loop systems work naturally. However, as shown in the case of the NRC, feedback loop systems can also be intentionally designed. This is very important. And the longer you exercise, stimulated by the NRC, it is bound to cause positive changes in your body.

(2) Example 2: How they take my time → make it easier and faster to get feedback

What is the reason for the rapid growth of the short video service (TikTok, Reels, Shorts, etc.) market in a short period of time?

The point at which a user falls into a service is the point at which he or she obtains something through the service. If you can't achieve anything and get nothing out of the service, there's no reason to use it any longer.

Users want to get that very thing (information or knowledge or fun) as quickly and easily as possible. The time and effort spent on searching is only a factor that hinders such users from achieving their goals.

Therefore, a more precise configuration of the "recommendation algorithm" affected the success or failure of the service.

The short video quickly and repeatedly delivered the reward the user wanted. This iterative feedback process has influenced the cause of "new content discovery." As this process is repeated, users will consume more and more content. The longer it takes to get feedback, the more difficult it is to form such a feedback loop.

A well-designed feedback loop can steer you towards positive or negative outcomes without you realizing it. The faster you receive feedback, the more intuitive the comparison and measurement, the more natural it is, and the more it stimulates your instincts, the tighter the feedback loop can be made.

3) What well-designed feedback loops have in common

A well-designed feedback loop has four things in common:
① Speed: Feedback must be made quickly.
② Measurability: It should be possible to show abstract feedback in numbers.

③ Context: Feedback should be given according to the flow.

④ Motivation: It must be instinctive or something you want.

Let's take the case of NRC (NIKE RUN CLUB).

① Speed:

As soon as the exercise is finished, feedback (achievement record, badge, rank) is provided.

② Measurability:

You can compare last week's record with this week's record at a glance through the data chart.

③ Context:

Feedback, like badges, is related to the workouts you've done up to this point.

④ Motivation:

At the base is your desire for body and health.

Feedback is important for learning, practice and job improvement. We learn, practice something, get feedback, adjust our methods based on the feedback, and do it again. This loop helps reinforce and improve learning.

In particular, "deliberate practice", suggested by Professor Anders Ericcon, has a feedback loop at its core. See Chapter 7. The more we learn, the higher level ideas we will be able to understand, which snowballs over time into tremendous intellectual advantages.

There is a "network effect." For example, we use Facebook because many people are on it. As more users participate, the network becomes more useful and thus more users participate. Another example is eBay. Customers go there because most suppliers are there. Most of the suppliers are there because most of the customers are on eBay.

You can actively utilize these feedback loop systems to naturally propel you towards a specific goal or outcome. Think about what actions you are repeating on a daily basis and what results those actions are aiming for.

If you are aiming for a negative outcome, think about how you can break that feedback loop. Also, if there is a result you want to achieve, but it is difficult to act repeatedly, think about how you can create a feedback loop.

This can be effectively used in a wide variety of areas, such as not only developing your own capabilities, but also bringing out the capabilities of your subordinates as a leader, or eliciting consumer purchasing behavior in sales and marketing. You have now learned that you can create value by leveraging feedback loops in your life.

3. A system called "Luck"

I think every event that happens to me is also a kind of system. So good luck and bad luck are also a kind of system. The reason I came to think this way was after I came across the impromptu poems of Buckminster Fuller, who is regarded as today's Leonardo da Vinci. He was an American architect, writer, designer, inventor, and poet.

He invented the "Geodesic dome" in the 1940s, a geometric shape that provides maximum strength with minimal structure without internal supports.

Large exhibition halls were constructed economically with a prefabricated construction method using minimal materials. He created a new value called "do more with less" at the construction site.

Buckminster Fuller gave the following impromptu poem to Russell Schweickart. Shuwaikat is an astronaut who circled the Earth 151 times aboard Apollo 9. He is said to have been very surprised when he received Fuller's impromptu poem. I also had a great realization. Fuller's poems are given below.

For each individual, the environment must be everything that exists "except me." In contrast, the universe (i.e. system) would be everything that exists "including me." The only difference between the environment and the universe is "I"…me who sees, does, thinks, loves, enjoys.

1) Magic potion

If there was a magic potion that made people lucky, it would be very expensive. Nonetheless, people will be happy to buy it. Because we all want to be lucky. But we don't have such a potion. Is there no other way in the world to make us lucky?

2) 4 stages of luck and "luck surface area"

Luck is an uncontrollable event that leads to positive or negative outcomes. We cannot force it because we cannot control it. However, you can increase (much) your chances of getting lucky. To do this, let's first define luck better. Because not all luck is the same. There are four levels.

① There is blind luck.

This is what most people mean when they talk about luck. Where you were born, who your parents are, winning the lottery, and more. It's completely random.

② Hard work brings good luck.

You work hard enough to bring good fortune. Even if you tweet 5,000 times, nothing happens. However, the following tweet gets "likes" from big accounts and goes viral. You gain thousands of new followers. This kind of luck finds you because you've worked hard to reach it.

③ You find good luck.

When you have deep knowledge in a field, you begin to see fortunes that no one else sees. Millions of people watched an apple fall from a tree, but only Isaac Newton knew how to turn an apple into a great discovery.

Trend spotting, investing and "information arbitrage" opportunities are other examples of finding luck with knowledge. Information arbitrage is trading that takes advantage of the knowledge gap between you and others. Accountants who know how to save money can trade their information and knowledge with potential clients.

④ You attract luck.

This is the ultimate state of being lucky. You don't have to look for luck at this stage. Luck always comes to you. Good examples include having a personal brand with a large audience, being known for what you do, or being in a position of power.

Imagine lucky events with random arrows flying around. They are like the arrows of Eros. You want to be hit by an arrow.

The best way for you to hit a random arrow is to increase the surface area of your target. The larger the surface area of your "luck surface area," the more likely you are to get lucky.

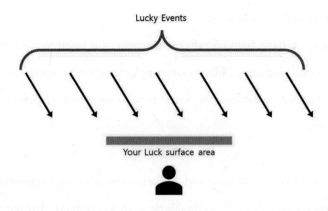

Now let's connect the 4 levels of luck and the "luck surface area". Then you will see your "luck surface area" expand from level 1 to level 4. Now let's go tactical!

3) Improving the luck system: 5 ways to increase your "luck surface area"

① Do and say

Everyone knows that "doing" and hard work are important. But most people miss the "telling" part. Whatever you do, share it with the world. Your chances of luck increase every time someone new hears about your work. Marketing your work is just as important as doing it.

② Follow your curiosity

As adults, we become adept at curbing our curiosity. But your childlike curiosity allows you to go deep into new subjects and connect with others you know. So you may be in a position, like Newton, to be able to discern luck no one else can see (or understand). The Greek philosopher Seneca said that luck is what happens when preparation meets opportunity.

③ Allow for serendipity

Go to parties, join digital communities, and meet friends of friends. And hang out with people who know more than you know. Think of the "weak ties." Each new person you meet expands your luck surface area.

④ Build your personal brand

Create useful value to the world. Create value, especially for people. Be famous for something. Build your reputation. A personal brand is a "competitive advantage." Luck will start looking for you more often in unimaginable ways.

⑤ Take luck as a skill

Now you know you could be luckier. There are magic potions. So, start seeing "luck" as a "skill" that can be improved upon. You will see how it works. Be the one who brings good luck to yourself while others innocently wait for luck.

Chapter 4

Decision-making methods for value creation

Before started

Enthusiasm, diligence, fighting spirit, and luck are important to the success and prosperity of people and organizations. Most of those things actually affect "success."

However, the road to success that people think is different from the road to actual success. People think the path to success is "linear," but in reality it's like a tangled thread. And it is uncharted, treacherous and maddening road.

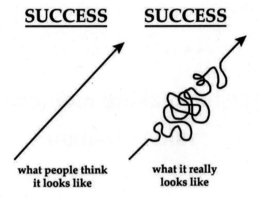

SUCCESS   **SUCCESS**

what people think   what it really
it looks like   looks like

But the most important thing in life is what happens inside your head. Because "quality of thinking" is more important than anything else in order to achieve an excellent and prosperous life.

Quality of
Relationships

Reinforcing
Engine of
Success

Quality of
Results

Quality of
Thinking

Quality of
Actions

Your thoughts (especially decision-making) determine your direction. This will either lead you to success or lead you away from success. This is a very simple but very powerful fact.

1. Making a decision

Good decision-making is an exercise in quelling your "instincts" and turning them into mental models. Remember the "Five cognitive dimensions of Mental Models" in Chapter 1. You can leave the "gut decisions" when you play sports for now. But when you play life, try to avoid it.

Most of us work like carpenters with only a hammer. To a man with a hammer, every problem looks like a nail. Whatever his job, people will pull out a hammer and try to make it work.

A hammer can often get the job done eventually, but it comes at a cost. A hammer wasn't enough and more tools were needed. We can use appropriate mental models to make decisions.

1) Long-term: Regret Minimization

We are often overwhelmed by events and things that seem big at first glance. The "big decisions" in life are also among the "big things." However, we can break things that seem big into small units and solve them one by one. The first thing you need to do is to establish the perspective you need to make a decision.

That's what happened to Amazon founder Jeff Bezos. In 1994, Jeff

Bezos was working at the hedge fund D.E. Shaw&Co. At the time, he told his boss about his startup idea. It was about Amazon. But the boss said, "The idea seems more suitable for someone without a job. Think seriously and deeply for 48 hours."

When Bezos heard this, he fell into the agony of "a decision that seemed big." He realized that before making such a decision, he needed a perspective to form "how to look at that decision."

With that perspective expressed in the phrase "Regret Minimization," Bezos says, "the decision to quit the company and start Amazon was very easy."

The "Regret Minimization Framework" can be defined as: Assuming that you minimize the number of regrets in your life when you are close to death at age x, which of the alternatives in your decision minimizes your regrets the most?

Jeff Bezos said,

I knew that when I was 80 I was not going to regret having tried this. I was not going to regret trying to participate in this thing called the Internet that I thought was going to be a really big deal. I knew that if I failed I wouldn't regret that, but I knew the one thing I might regret is not ever having tried.

And he became a billionaire by founding Amazon. This view is indirectly supported not only by Jeff Bezos, but also by other studies.

Australian nurse Bronnie Ware published a book about her conversations with cancer patients. Here is a list of "The top 5 regrets of the dying."

① I wish I'd had the courage to live a life true to myself, not the life others expected of me.

② I wish I hadn't worked so hard.

③ I wish I had the courage to express my feelings.

④ I wish I had stayed in touch with my friends.

⑤ I wish I had let myself be happier.

Among her list, the thing patients regret the most right before they die is "not living the life they wanted in life." In other words, the patients regretted not having had the courage to be more honest with themselves.

A long-term perspective of looking at the present from a point close to death (of course, we do not know when death will come) allows us to focus on the part of "what choice does not create more regrets in the long run?"

Through this perspective, when people stand in front of death, they can lead a life that allows them to face death without regret.

Bezos used Regret Minimization to prioritize his space exploration company away from his Amazon business. Like Elon Musk, he used First Principles to revisit spaceflight from scratch. His space company Blue Origin competes with Musk's SpaceX for NASA contracts.

Musk and Bezos loved to break their flow to use mental models. Thus they unlocked the creator's hidden locks in the game of life. Austrian-born British philosopher Karl Popper preached that "All Life is Problem Solving." Musk and Bezos gain the wisdom to solve problems by using mental models.

2) Medium-term: Pareto Principle

Now here's another decision-making mental model. This helps in allocating resources. The Pareto principle states that 80% of the effects come from 20% of the causes. Expressing this as the "IPO model," 80% of the output comes from the top 20% of the inputs. Also known as the "80/20 principle."

(The Pareto Principle is so important that it will be covered separately in Chapter 6.)

For example, 80% of the value you get from socializing comes from your top 20% of friends. So, strengthen your relationship with those friends first and forsake much of the rest. Recognize cultivating friendships that actually matter.

Use the Pareto principle to make medium-term decisions. To maximize ROI, prioritize investing in the 20% of the inputs that produce the most output. This is how you optimize for a year or a decade of your life. Who to spend time with, what skills to train, and what business to build.

In particular, the Pareto principle provides a standard for us to see the probability as 80/20 rather than 50/50 when we have to make important decisions. This allows us to focus on the 20% that we need to focus on the most.

3) Short-term: ICE

When faced with many options that require prioritization, we can use a scale of 1-10 to score each of the three variables. And we make decisions within a day or as quickly as possible.

① Impact: If the option succeeds, how much will it have a positive impact (on my business or activity)?

"How much does this contribute to the goal?"

The goal, in this case, is anything you're trying to achieve. For example increasing customer retention, getting more customers, increasing the authority of your website, etc.

Choose one of the following options:

1 for No Impact, 3 for Very low Impact, 4 for Low Impact, 6 for Medium Impact, 8 for High Impact, 10 for Very high Impact.

② Confidence: How confident am I about the viability of this option?

When answering this question, think about previous similar tasks, how impactful they were but also see what others tried and worked.

Choose one of the following options:

1 for No Confidence, 3 for Very low Confidence, 4 for Low Confidence, 6 for Medium Confidence, 8 for High Confidence, 10 for Very high Confidence.

③ Easiness: How easy it is to pursue this option (low resources, little time).

In software development, it's often easy to misinterpret this and think only about the development effort. But coding is not the only thing you do to deliver features. Make sure you think about the task as a whole, how difficult it is for all parties involved.

Choose one of the following options:

1 for Extremely hard, 3 for Hard, 5 for Medium, 7 for Easy, 10 for Very easy.

```
ICE SCORE = Impact X Confidence X Ease
```

The final ICE score is calculated by multiplying Impact, Confidence and Ease and you will end up with a score between 1 and 1000. Higher the ICE score, higher in priority the task is.

Project Idea	Impact [0-10]	Confidence [0-10]	Ease of Imp. [0-10]	ICE Score [I × C × E]
Community tab	7	2	8	112
Update submit flow	5	5	3	75
Add PayPal billing	8	1	5	40
Fix receipt issue	1	4	3	12

Each item is rated on a scale of 1-10, added, then divided by 3 to obtain the average. The average value is ICE. Repeat this exercise for each option under consideration, then rank all options by ICE score.

Options at the top of the list have the highest expected values and should be given priority over other options. This is how you plan your life on a time scale of weeks or months.

4) Immediate: Eisenhower Matrix

When many things are pouring in at the same time, we get nervous. The Eisenhower Matrix helps you make day-to-day decisions.

Create a 2x2 grid marked "Important" and "Urgent". Categorize your daily tasks into four quadrants and prioritize them in order of important and urgent, important but not urgent, unimportant but urgent, and neither important nor urgent.

According to the Eisenhower Matrix, the work given to us can be divided into four types.

	URGENT	NOT URGENT
IMPORTANT	DO THIS NOW	DO THIS LATER
NOT IMPORTANT	DELEGATE THIS	DELETE THIS

For example, what if we apply mailing to the Eisenhower matrix?

For important and urgent cases, it should be sent by registered express mail. If it is important but not urgent, you can just send it by registered mail. For urgent but not important cases, you can send it by express mail. If it is neither important nor urgent, you can send it by regular mail.

What insights does this give us?

When you apply these principles to your daily work, you become wiser. You are more likely to achieve better in school, work performance, and life in general.

2. Systems thinking

Systems Thinking is a way to understand the complexity of the world by looking at it in terms of wholes and relationships rather than dividing it into parts. The figure below shows how to think about society through systems thinking.

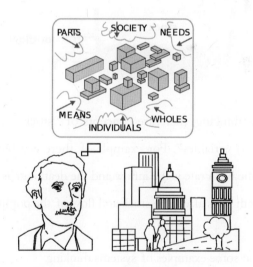

There are many elements that make up society. Analytical thinking divides the whole into parts and analyzes each one. In contrast, systems thinking looks at the whole, encompassing each component.

Systems thinking looks at the connection, interaction and also feedback between each component overall. And the system becomes self-powered, when it has additional feedback loop.

On the other hand, the core of systems thinking is causation (i.e., the relationship between cause and effect). Systems thinking thinks in terms of inputs, transitions, and outputs. Below is a picture of the bathtub. Systems thinking is thinking like a bathtub.

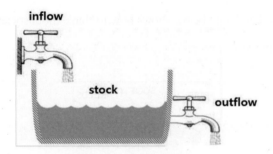

In systems thinking, there are concepts of "stock (level) variables" and "flow (rate) variables". For example, if there is a bathtub called population, the birth rate is the inflow and the death rate is the outflow. Birth and death rates affect the stock and flow of the population.

Let's look at some examples of systems thinking.

① New York police strengthened crackdown on drug trafficking, and drug-related crimes decreased, but then increased again. This is because when drug trafficking is caught and confiscated, the supply of drugs is reduced, which in turn increases drug prices and crimes to get money. Systems thinking takes the view that current problems are the product of past solutions.

② If a city creates an employment program for the poor and builds housing for the low-income, will this project succeed?

At first, it was successful, but as poor people from nearby and other cities moved to this city, it was necessary to expand the program, which would increase fiscal expenditure and increase taxes. As a result, companies leave the city, which reduces the tax revenue source, which in turn can lead to a vicious cycle of reducing investment in the poor.

③ John is worried that his performance is not coming out properly. This may not be because he did the job wrong, but because he did it wrong in the first place. That is, it was a matter of choice. Doing the right things is more important than doing things right.

Then, how is it possible to make the right choice, which is a prerequisite for the challenge? It comes from right assumptions. And correct assumptions are possible through correct understanding and reflection on the world and changes.

Harvard Business School professor Chris Argyris suggested double loop learning, which reexamines the basic premises and assumptions that determine current behavior (or a company's business model, etc.) when problems arise.

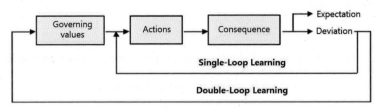

<Single-loop and Double-loop learning>

Double-loop learning is not limited to error checking and correction of any apparent issue (single loop learning), but analyzes the entire system. In this respect, it is also connected to the 5th principle advocated by Professor Peter Senge of MIT Sloan Business School.

The fragmentary causal way of thinking of A→B does not reflect the complex reality. Instead, a systems thinking bites tail after tail to clarify the core of the issue and suggest a solution to the problem. In his book <The Fifth Discipline>, Peter Senge demonstrated the importance of systems thinking through his "Beer Game."

Participants in the Beer Game play a part in the entire distribution process from production to consumption through wholesale and retail. One person is in charge of a production plant, another a wholesaler, and another a retail store owner. Each person has to use their best judgment about the order and then decide.

- There are 4 players in this game. A factory, a distribution center, a wholesaler and a retailer.

- Each order takes 2 weeks to be delivered, and beer production takes 2 weeks as well.

- A cost of 1 point is incurred each time inventory is held, and 1 point is deducted even when an order is received but inventory is insufficient.

- Each player does not know the entire order status, and the quantity is determined by the demand in the previous step.

The game usually unfolds in the following story.

- When consumer demand increases, a retailer increase order volume.

- A wholesaler also increases order volume, and factory receives orders to increase production.

- Ordering and production take time, and delivery is delayed due to the rapidly increasing logistics volume.

- Consumer demand remains unsatisfied, so an impatient retailer anticipates higher order volumes and increases order volumes.

- Demand for beer decreases after the season, but there is a time lag between ordering and production, so all chain companies suffer from inventory processing.

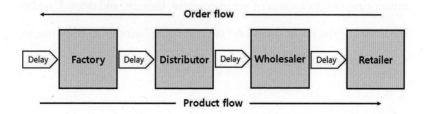

Almost always the same result in this game. That is, huge inventories accumulate in a factory and a wholesaler. Each of us judged and worked to the best of our ability, how could that happen?

The problem is not in the lack of sincerity, but in the fact that the participants did their best without understanding the whole process, that is, the beer distribution system. Usually, participants think, "Since customer demand has increased, we have no choice but to increase the order volume accordingly." This is thinking in terms of individual "events."

But an individual can never exist alone. In the system, individuals exist while being affected by the system and also influencing the system. Therefore, in order for individuals or companies to effectively use their capabilities to create value, they must understand how the system works. How should you think in the system? You have to think, "How will each chain behave?"

The picture of systems thinking in the beer game is as follows.

Everyone in the system affects each other in some way. Here, the influencing factors consist of reinforcement, balance, and delay. Usually, the actors in the chain focus on "strengthening" actions in response to the demand they feel.

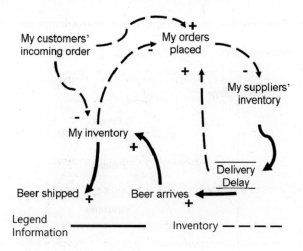

My customers' incoming order

My orders placed +

My suppliers' inventory -

My inventory -

+

+

Beer shipped +

Beer arrives +

Delivery Delay

Legend
Information _____ Inventory — — — —

If the retailer had been aware of his order volume, factory inventory and order backlog, and delivery delays, and adjusted his order volume, the outcome of the game would have been different.

The discipline of systems thinking attempts to help people construct useful mental models. Lesser leaders reduce complex systems to individual components and events. They do not fully grasp how the different components interact. Systems thinkers, on the other hand, look for what lies beneath the surface. The deeper you reach, the higher the leverage for lasting change:

- Events: what happened
- Patterns: what has been happening (finding trends)
- Structures: why has it been happening (finding relationships between trends and events)

- Mental models: how do we think about what is happening (finding blind spots, assumptions, and beliefs)

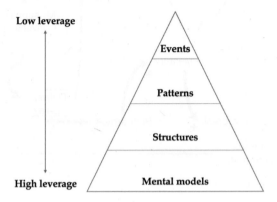

The key to systems thinking is to appreciate any complex system as an interconnected whole. The components of the whole - the companies in the supply chain, the organs in the body, or the employees in a company - are interconnected and influence the behavior and emergent properties of the system.

These components are not just connected but also interdependent: each part of the system depends on some other part for its effect on the whole. In the example of the human body: your brains need your heart and lungs to function and vice versa.

In commerce, every finished product is the result of countless people and companies collaborating in a complex supply chain system. To appreciate just how complex, it is worth reading <I, Pencil>, a delightful story about the coordination required to manufacture the humble pencil.

Way back in 1958, an economist named Leonard Read wrote an essay called <I, Pencil> which points out that no one person knows how to make a pencil. On the surface, the pencil seems like a simple invention. In reality, it is the result of a vast range of specialties which are not centrally coordinated:

I, Pencil, am a complex combination of miracles: a tree, zinc, copper, graphite, and so on. […] millions of human beings have had a hand in my creation, no one of whom even knows more than a very few of the others. There isn't a single person in all these millions, including the president of the pencil company, who contributes more than a tiny, infinitesimal bit of know-how. […] There is a fact still more astounding: the absence of a master mind, of anyone dictating or forcibly directing these countless actions which bring me into being.

The pencil collaboration is a testament to highly-distributed processes in diverse disciplines collaborating to solve problems. Said more simply, it shows that loosely coordinated networks of people can produce concrete results.

Of course, this isn't limited to a pencil but is true of virtually every invention and of society in general. The Nobel-prize winning economist Milton Friedman used a similar story to illustrate how the free market system promotes cooperation and harmony among those with no common interest. It's not much of a leap from the pencil collaboration to decentralized autonomous organizations.

The pencil collaboration also reminds us that, no matter how indispensable we think we are, everything we do is dependent on others. The modern version of "no one is an island" might be "we are all nodes in the network."

These thoughts will be of great help to you in understanding Chapter 9 "Value creation based on Plus-sum mindset" and Chapter 10 "The Impact of Social Networks on Success and Prosperity" in more depth.

3. Game theory

(Credit: Shutterstock/Crystal Eye Studio)

"I think that you think that I think."

This is the easiest expression of the essence of game theory. This is a decision based on the existence of the other party. To put it simply, it is a psychological warfare in rock-paper-scissors. It is easier to understand if you replace the word "think" with "expect" in the above sentence.

The Prisoner's Dilemma is a very important concept in strategic decision making. The Prisoner's Dilemma deals with:

Two prisoners who committed a crime together are isolated. They are advised of the following outcomes.

① If prisoner 1 testifies and prisoner 2 remains silent, then prisoner 1 will walk free while prisoner 2 will get 10 years in prison.

② If prisoner 2 testifies and prisoner 1 remains silent, then prisoner 2 will walk free while prisoner 1 will get 10 years in prison.

③ If both prisoners betray each other and testify, they will each get 6 years in prison.

④ If both prisoners remain silent, they will each get 1 year in prison for the lesser charge.

These four outcomes can be displayed in a payoff matrix. How would the prisoners behave in this situation?

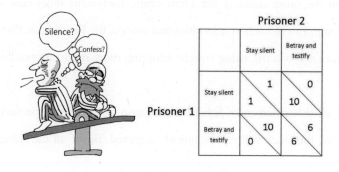

The best option is for both to remain silent, but no prisoner chooses to remain silent in the absence of trust in the other. If one confesses, the other is forced to do so to avoid the harsh sentence that will be returned to the accused who did not.

The price war between companies is no different. When Shell gas stations lower prices, Exxon Mobil gas stations also lower prices. If one side keeps the price high, the other side can attract customers by lowering the price. But if both sides lower their prices, neither side makes any money.

If the Republicans only care about the wealthy right while the Democrats are promoting certain policies to appeal to the floating vote, the Republicans will probably lose the election.

On the other hand, if the Democratic Party only takes care of its core supporters, such as minorities and unions, the Republican Party can capture and win the swing vote by adopting more moderate policies.

If all fishermen catch fish in moderation at a level that protects the species, the stock will not be quickly depleted. But if all the fishermen are fishing aggressively and only one fisherman is trying to catch the right amount, that person will be looked upon as a fool. This leads to overfishing and extinction of fish.

But is it possible to change the current game? If we could change it, what game could we change it to and how? Let's find answers to these questions that marketing strategists are constantly struggling with through game theory.

The players in the company's game are the company, its customers, suppliers, substitutes, and complements. A supplier is a player who supplies physical and human resources necessary for business activities to a business.

A substitute is a purchase target that customers consider an alternative, or a player that suppliers can sell a resource to as an alternative. Complements are companies that can purchase complementary products from the customer's point of view, or purchasing companies that can sell complementary resources from the supplier's point of view.

Tactics are the actions that the player perceives the game and creates the way it is played. Here are four tactics that companies can use to reshape their current games into the best ones for them.

① Change the player

You can reorganize the game in your favor by changing the players in the game. Take, for example, the case of changing complementors.

3DO, a video game company, had the hardware and software technology for next-generation 32-bit CD-ROM games.

Hardware and software are traditional complements. In order for 3DO to sell software, it first needed people to buy hardware. However, early adopters were reluctant to purchase hardware because there was not enough software on the market.

3DO solved this "chicken and egg dilemma" by bringing new players into the game. 3DO made new hardware manufacturers such as Panasonic and LG enter the game by providing hardware production rights free of charge.

In 1993, 3DO released the software with aggressive marketing. Because 3DO's software runs on all types of 3DO's hardware, 3DO's hardware competes only on cost, as 3DO intended. 3DO succeeded in significantly lowering the price of hardware, a complementary product of software.

② Reduce the bargaining power of other players by lowering their added value.

Companies can take the lead in the game by adjusting their bargaining power by increasing their own added value or lowering the added value of other players.

For example, by developing its own game character called Mario, Nintendo blocked the unique value creation of famous cartoon characters such as Spider-Man and Mickey Mouse. Rather, Nintendo made huge profits by selling the rights to use Mario to comics, board games, cereals, and toy companies.

③ Change the rules of the game

Korea's Seoul Milk has reorganized the rules of the game regarding how consumers buy milk. To purchase fresher dairy products, consumers used to subtract the purchase date from the expiration date and calculate freshness with the difference.

However, because each manufacturer has a different expiration date, it was not easy for consumers to choose fresh milk in this way. Seoul Milk understood the psychology of these consumers and added the manufacturing date to the existing expiration date.

In 2009, the introduction of Seoul Milk's date of manufacture increased consumer confidence. After the labeling, average daily sales of Seoul Milk increased by 25% from 8 million to 10 million.

Considering that the total milk production in Korea at the time was 23 million, it was a large volume of 44%. As Seoul Milk marked the date of manufacture, the rule of the game for purchasing milk changed to how quickly the product was distributed after production. It completely reorganized the competitive landscape of the market.

④ Reset the scope of the game

In the early 1990s, Goodyear and Michelin suffered from fierce technology development competition. When one side developed a 20,000-mile tire, the other released a 30,000-mile tire. It was like the arms race between the US and the Soviet Union during the Cold War.

The problem is that these new products prolong the product purchase cycle, which paradoxically has a serious negative impact on sales and profits. However, it was an embarrassing situation where there was no choice but to respond to the other party's new technology development.

To get out of this trap, Goodyear decided to expand the scope of tire's "longevity race" game. And this strategic decision was reflected in a new product called Aquatread, which reduces the braking distance and improves driving stability in rainy weather. The two companies were able to escape from the suffocating longevity race.

4. Second-order thinking

Things are not always what they seem. Often when we solve one problem, we unintentionally create another, worse problem. The best way to examine the long-term consequences of our decisions is to use second-order thinking.

Howard Marks, a leading value investor in the United States and the chairman of Oaktree Capital Management, explains the concept of second-order thinking in his book <The Most Important Thing>.

First-order thinking is simple and superficial, and almost anyone can do it. What a first thinker needs is an opinion about the future, such as "the outlook for the company is favourable, meaning the stock price will go up." Second-order thinking, by comparison, is deep, complex, and complex.

First-order thinking is quick and easy. It happens when you look for things that solve immediate problems without considering the consequences. For example, this is a thought like, "A chocolate bar makes me feel good, so I'll have a chocolate bar whenever I'm tired or in a bad mood."

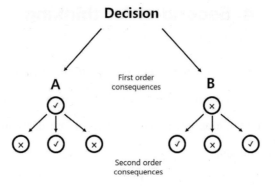

Decision

A

B

First order consequences

Second order consequences

Second-order thinking is more cautious. It understands that despite our intentions, our interventions often do harm. So it is to think in terms of interaction and time.

Second-order thinkers ask themselves the question, "And then what?" They think about the consequences of repeatedly eating a chocolate bar when they are hungry and use it to make decisions. This way, you are more likely to eat healthy food.

In 1955, after seeing a flock of sparrows pecking at grains of rice, Chinese President Mao Zedong immediately declared war on the sparrows, saying, "That bird is a harmful bird." It was believed that the food shortage could be solved to some extent by exterminating the sparrows.

But this turned out to be a fiasco. When the sparrows disappeared, the number of pests increased, resulting in a significant decrease in rice production and the miserable end of tens of millions of people starving to death.

Convenience stores in Korea have been pasting opaque sheets on the outside glass walls of convenience stores since July 2021. This is to prevent outsiders from seeing cigarette advertisements in convenience stores.

The Korean government believes that it can prevent the increase in smoking desire among teenagers and general consumers caused by indiscriminate exposure to advertisements.

Eventually, the inside of the convenience store could not be seen from outside. A robber broke into a convenience store for cash and stabbed and killed an employee with a weapon.

Convenience store owners are now equipped with stun guns and gas guns. Officials in the South Korean government couldn't see an inch ahead.

The mistake of the Mao Zedong government and the South Korean government was the lack of second-order thinking.

They made decisions based only on the primary outcome (decrease in sparrows = increase in yield, decrease in advertising exposure = suppression of smoking), which eventually led to disaster (starvation due to reduced rice production, increased violent crime at convenience stores).

The ability to think about problems to second, third, and nth order (or what we call second-order thinking for short) is a powerful tool for strengthening thinking skills. You will be faced with many decisions in life that at first glance seem like easy decisions. Don't rush your decision. Think about the consequences and ask yourself several times, "So what?" Only after applying second-order thinking can you draw more deliberate conclusions about which options are right for you.

Use the questions below to identify the secondary consequences of your decisions.

- What is the range of possible outcomes?
- Which outcome is more likely?
- What are the possible influences of other factors (social, financial, emotional, etc.)?
- How does this decision fit into the bigger picture?
- How will you feel in 10 minutes, 10 months, and 10 years? (10-10-10 rule)

You could move to a new city in the future, consider a job offer, or start a new business. Or you may be a politician or civil servant who decides laws and policies that have a huge impact on the people. Use second-order thinking for important decisions. It eliminates blind spots so you can make the best decisions for yourself.

5. Marginal thinking and sub goals

1) Marginal thinking and holistic thinking

All people act for maximization. A wise person will make a choice only if the marginal benefit of that choice is greater than the marginal cost.

Everyone has their own goals and strives to maximize them. Swimmers want to maximize swimming speed, professors want to maximize students' knowledge, and restaurant owners want to maximize profits.

In economics, it is assumed that the goal that consumers seek to maximize is utility, and that the goal that firms maximize is assumed to be profit.

Net Benefits = Benefits - Costs

When a consumer or a company engages in any action, benefits and opportunity costs occur at the same time. The difference between this benefit and the opportunity cost is called the net benefit.

Consumers and businesses make decisions to maximize the net benefits of each activity. Of course, the specific benefits and costs depend on the type and content of the activity being considered.

For example, in the case of a firm's activities related to production, the total revenue earned from selling the goods produced would be the production benefit.

And the opportunity cost of producing that item will be the total cost of the firm. And the net benefit of this firm is the difference between total revenue and total cost.

We must make decisions "marginally." Everyone has to think marginally to maximize net benefits. Thinking marginally means comparing the size of additional benefits (marginal benefit) and costs (marginal cost) that increase according to one's choice. So what are marginal benefits and marginal costs?

Marginal Benefits and Marginal Costs

"Marginal" means to change some behavior little by little. The word "marginal" means "additional." Marginal benefit is the additional benefit we get from doing one more action. Marginal cost is the additional cost of doing one more action.

If the satisfaction I get from eating one more hamburger is the marginal benefit, then the price I have to pay to buy another hamburger is the marginal cost. The marginal benefit is the revenue a firm earns from producing one more computer, and its marginal cost is the cost of producing one more computer.

This explains why we need to take a closer look at soda size and McDonald's size. The 6-ounce bottle of Coke was the king of soda when an upstart company called Pepsi-Cola sold a 12-ounce bottle for the same price.

The year was 1934 and the price was 5 cents. Pepsi's competitive strategy has been called brilliant because its biggest costs were advertising, bottling and distribution. For Pepsi, an extra 6 ounces did little to their cost but must have delighted consumers.

21 years later, Coca-Cola finally started selling 10- and 12-ounce "King-Size" bottles. McDonald's though stuck with its 7-ounce Coke during the 1950s, offered a 16-ounce Coke in the 1960s and the 21-ounce size in 1974. Once "normal," the 8-ounce serving has become a small or "mini" because of what we are used to.

The place we are going here is "the margin." Cost and calories are a perfect way to see how firms and consumers think at the margin when they decide whether to add or subtract a little extra.

Below, you can see how the "margins" for soda size have monumentally changed:

My bottom line?

Economists like to point out that decisions usually occur "at the margin" where, based on cost and benefit, consumers and businesses make decisions about a little more or a little less.

Everyone wants to maximize the net benefit. So how do you maximize the net benefit? In this case, the marginal principle or law of marginal decision-making should be applied. The marginal principle can be summarized as follows.

If the marginal benefit of doing one extra activity is greater than the marginal cost, you should do that activity more. If the marginal benefit is less than the marginal cost, the activity should be reduced.

The net benefit is maximized when the marginal benefit equals the marginal cost. This seems so natural. However, this logic becomes the basic principle of decision making.

Marginal principle: Example 1

Suppose Paul's father's car company has a marginal benefit of $10,000 and a marginal cost of producing one more car of $9,000. Paul's father is thinking about whether he should produce more cars. What should he do?

If the company produced one more car, it could increase its net benefit (i.e., profit) by $1,000. So the company has to produce one more car.

Applying this logic, we can see that if the marginal benefit is greater than the marginal cost by even one cent, the company should increase production of cars. This is because net profit increases.

Now suppose that the marginal benefit of producing one more car is $10,000 and the marginal cost of producing one more car is $11,000.

If the company produces one more car, it loses a net benefit of $1,000. Conversely, the company could increase net benefits by reducing car production by one. If the marginal cost is greater than the marginal benefit by even a fraction of a cent, the company can increase net benefit by reducing car production.

Combining the above two cases, the company can find a way to maximize net benefits. The firm can maximize net benefit by increasing or decreasing production until marginal benefit equals marginal cost. This is the limiting principle discussed above.

Marginal principle: Example 2

There is a laundry with 30 employees. Total labor cost is $600,000, and gross sales are $800,000. In this case, ignoring other costs, the profit is $200,000. On average, each employee produces $26,667 and earns $20,000 in wages, so the net profit per employee is $6,667.

Hiring one additional new employee brings total sales to $825,000 and total labor costs to $620,000. In this case, the average profit per employee is only $6,613.

Profits per employee fell. Therefore, this may be seen as a poor choice. But this is the right choice. This is because the owner gets the gross profit, not the average profit. Gross profit is $205,000, $5,000 more than before.

To find the right answer, you need to compare the marginal cost of hiring a new employee ($20,000) with the marginal profit that employee earns ($25,000).

On the other hand, marginal thinking is a frame of thought that is meaningful only in a microscopic and static situation in which we devise how flowers can grow well when all conditions in a greenhouse are given. This is thinking about how to optimize the combination of greenhouse temperature and humidity to produce 10% more flowers.

However, in order for organizations such as corporations and governments, which are living organisms, to adapt and develop to environmental changes, a total concept that transcends marginal thinking is required

Holistic thinking is decision-making, such as how to deal with a pandemic like Covid19 or bird flu. Holistic thinking requires more systematic thinking than marginal thinking.

2) Sub goal

Shlomo Breznitz, a psychologist at the Hebrew University of Israel, conducted an interesting experiment. He had two groups of soldiers equally march 40 km. But he spoke differently to each group. He told Group A that the distance to march was 30 km and actually had them march 40 km.

Meanwhile, he told Group B that the distance to march was 60 km and actually had them walk 40 km. After the march, he took blood from both groups and measured the levels of stress hormones.

As a result of the measurement, the level of stress hormone was determined according to the idea of how much more to walk in the future, regardless of the actual distance traveled (=40 km).

Both groups of soldiers walked the same 40km, but the levels of stress hormones in the 30km goal were significantly lower than those in the 60km goal. Soldiers who walked thinking it was a 60km march actually showed much more fatigue. In other words, the bodies of the soldiers did not react to reality, but to the images they viewed as real.

Marathon runners divide the entire 42.195 km into several sections and set a target time for each section. Exercise physiologists call these broken down goals "subgoals."

This principle applies equally to whatever you do. Even the toughest goals can be easily achieved if you break them down into smaller ones. What you need at this time is "Atomic Habits."

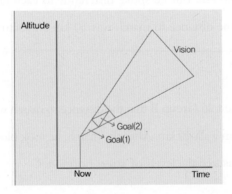

Setting small goals can seem trivial and shabby at first glance. However, rather than being overwhelmed in front of a huge goal or frustrated in the process of moving toward a goal, it is preferable to set up, practice, and achieve sub-goals that can be achieved more easily in a short period of time.

In the shallow stream, there are stones that we can put our feet on, all the way to the other side. In this way, place the stones in front of you one by one.

Just as someone looked across a stream and laid stones, you must look at your vision and set small goals. If you set goals that have nothing to do with your vision, you will never get to where you want to be.

Also, stepping stones must be placed to the point where the stream ends, so that you can reach the destination without falling into the water.

If you don't give up and create small shapes similar to your vision, each small piece will come together like a fractal structure to form the overall desired shape. This is the secret to achieving your goals. The sum of the parts is not the whole. But remember, the whole is made up of parts.

6. Numeracy and Analytical Thinking

Why did PlayPump fail?

The Playpump is a technological device conceived from amusement equipment, and when children turn the merry-go-round-type amusement equipment, the power is used to raise groundwater so that people can use water whenever they need it.

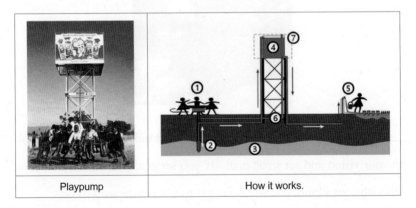

| Playpump | How it works. |

Ronnie Stuiver, who was running a business digging wells in South Africa, came up with an amazing idea when he saw children enjoying a merry-go-round in a playground. The idea is to use the energy of these frantic children to raise groundwater deep in the ground.

Many countries in Africa have had to draw groundwater from deep underground due to water shortages. To do this, the villagers had to pump hard all day long. However, wouldn't this difficulty be solved if the energy of children playing Merry-go-round was used to raise groundwater? Ronnie took this brilliant idea straight to the 1989 Agricultural Fair.

Advertising executive Trevor Field was impressed by the pump at an agricultural show. Trevor immediately decided to invest in Ronnie's idea and started working on a business idea together. Trevor added the idea of earning advertising revenue by attaching a billboard to a water tank that stores water pumped by children.

The idea was that two sides of the four-sided water tank would be sold as billboards to businesses, and the other two sides would be sold to the government or public institutions with public service announcements such as AIDS prevention.

Ronnie and Trevor established a company called Roundabout Outdoors and started to commercialize the idea in earnest. Under the name of Playpump, a trade name was registered and a patent was applied for. However, when they started the business, people's interest was colder than expected. "It's a great idea, but why are people indifferent?"

They blamed the indifferent and believed that one day their brilliant ideas would see the light of day.

Then one day, South African President Nelson Mandela visited the new school and toured the school facilities, which was featured on TV and news. President Mandela looked around the school and turned the Playpump that Ronnie and Trevor had installed as pilots with his own hands. As the scene spread across Africa, calls inquiring about the Playpump suddenly started pouring into Ronnie and Trevor's offices.

Once exposed to the media, Playpump began to attract the attention of numerous investors and non-profit organizations. The smiling faces of African children and the video of water spouting from the water tank were perfect for promoting Playpump. Numerous charities praised this idea and flocked to see the Playpump, as it could provide laughter and water to Africans suffering from thirst at the same time.

In 2000, the World Bank awarded the Playpump the World Bank Development Marketplace Award as one of the most innovative ideas. Subsequently, Case Foundation, a representative non-profit organization in the United States, shows interest in Playpump and decides to invest. In the end, the Case Foundation established PlayPumps International, a non-profit organization that installs Playpumps in Africa through charitable funds, and started to recruit investors around the world.

Steve Case, the CEO of AOL, an American internet company, also fell in love with Play Pump belatedly. The rich man started a charity that installed thousands of Play Pumps across Africa. One Water for fundraising was launched and was a huge success. The media also helped with reports such as "The Magic Roundabout" and "Pumping Water is Child's Play."

Former U.S. President Bill Clinton praised it as "an outstanding innovation." Laura Bush, first lady of then-president George W. Bush, contributed $16.4 million, or about a quarter, to a campaign to raise $60 million to install 4,000 Play Pumps across Africa by 2010. Thanks to this heat, about 1,800 Play Pumps were installed in South Africa, Mozambique, Swaziland, and Zambia by 2009. It really became a "Miracle Roundabout."

However, in 2009, the British weekly Guardian published a skeptical article about the Playpump. The Guardian reporter visited the village where the Playpump was installed, but there were no children playing. A Guardian reporter found that there were no children around the wheel that was supposed to be spinning, and that it was rusting as if it hadn't been used for a long time. The reporter who met the villagers and asked what the hell was going on received a ridiculous answer.

"If our villagers want to drink water from that pump, the children can't go to school and have to run Merry-Go-Round all day long."

What does this mean?

A shocking story began to be heard from all over Africa that the Playpump, where underground water had to rise even when children were having fun, had become a forced labor camp for children. Playpumps have become an abomination all over Africa. It was a scene that once again confirmed the uncomfortable truth that good intentions do not always produce good results.

As with all failures for a reason, there were several problems with the Play Pump. The biggest problem that caused the business to close was the lack of efficiency and practicality. The exact calculation was not done in the first place.

How many revolutions does the playpump have to make to obtain the recommended water consumption of 15 liters per person per day for the villagers? How many kids in town are there to run the Playpump? And for how long can children run the Playpump up to the recommended water capacity? It turned out that even these very basic calculations hadn't been done at all.

According to a survey by The Guardian, the Playpump must run non-stop for 27 hours a day to supply 15 liters of water to 2,500 villagers. However, since there are 24 hours in a day, this is an impossible figure. In other words, no matter how hard the children work, it is impossible to cover the supply of drinking water with this alone.

Also, the play pump does not increase speed because a large part of its rotational power is used to lift the water. Therefore, unlike the equipment that uses rotational force, it did not function as a "play" equipment at all. Spinning round and round like that all day is not only not enjoyable, but also quickly tiring. In the end, running the Play Pump became the responsibility of an adult woman, not a child. The children lost their playground and wandered around looking for a place to play, resulting in an absurd situation.

Citibank Success Story

Until the mid-1970s, the revenue model of the US credit card business was to raise funds at an interest rate of 9% (funding rate), and to provide good customers with less than a 1% chance of becoming bad credit at a rate of 13% (credit rate).

Of the 4% difference between these two rates, 1% is used for business operating expenses, 1% for bad credit provisions, and 1% for marketing expenses to acquire and retain good customers, leaving a net profit of 1%.

Accordingly, credit card companies raised their credit loan interest rates to 22 percent. Therefore, the 4% interest rate differential remained unchanged, and the profit structure of the credit card industry was not significantly affected.

In 1981, however, the situation reversed and the funding rate fell to 12%. However, there was no need to lower the loan interest rate for customers who were accustomed to the 22% interest rate, so the credit card industry reaped huge profits.

At this time, a young Citibank executive asked himself the timely question: "What must Citibank do to become a leader in the credit card business?" And while he was looking at market yield data, he had another pertinent question: "Why should we focus only on customers with less than 1% bad credit probability?"

So the idea that came out was to issue credit cards to customers with a bad credit rate of 1-2%, which no other card companies were interested in. Citibank's strategy was a huge success.

If other conditions are the same, and assuming that the number of customers doubles and the amount of loans doubles as the number of customers issuing cards increases, the net profit will increase by 100%. In fact, thanks to this, Citibank will rise to the top of the credit card industry.

John S. Reed, the protagonist of this exciting story, graduated from the MIT Sloan School of Management and became the CEO of Citi Financial Group and later served as the Chairman of the New York Stock Exchange.

7. Optimization: Linear Programming

Optimization is the process of obtaining the best result while satisfying given requirements within the limits of the allowed resources. Optimization is to create a state that the economic agent making the decision considers the most desirable. Assuming human rationality, etc., we seek the solution of maximizing utility for consumers and maximizing profits for companies.

Linear programming is the most popular method among current optimization methodologies. It means performing optimization by expressing the alternatives (decision variables) that we have to choose as linear equations or inequalities.

The Soviet Union's Leonid Kantorovich devised linear programming in 1939 while working on the optimization of production for the plywood industry. Plywood is made by stacking several veneers of thinly sliced wood into a single board. He struggled with how to produce a large number of high-performing plywood under given constraints.

This was eight years before 1947, when the American mathematician George Bernard Dantzig published the method of linear programming. Due to the ideological conflict that divided the world into two after World War II, the two men agonized over the problem of resource distribution in their own ways without knowing anything about each other's research.

Leonid Kantorovich was awarded the Order of the Defense of Leningrad and won the Nobel Prize in Economics in 1975 for continuing his optimization studies after the end of World War II.

Linear programming is largely composed of decision variables, objective functions, constraints, and sign restrictions. Here, the "decision variables" refers to what the decision-maker has to decide. In other words, it refers to a variable whose value is not yet known, but which we want to determine (know) through optimization.

Suppose there is a toy manufacturing company that produces soldier toys and train toys. Then the toy company must decide how many soldier toys and train toys each week it should produce. Therefore, the decision variables can be defined as follows.

x_1 : **number of soldier toys that need to be produced per week**
x_2 : **number of train toys that need to be produced per week**

The "objective function" represents the goal that the decision maker wants to achieve, and it is expressed mathematically. An objective function is subject to maximization (sales/profit, etc.) or minimization (cost, etc.), and the function to be maximized/minimized is defined as an objective function.

"Constraints", as the term implies, are conditions that limit our ability to achieve our goals. In the absence of realistic constraints, the value of the objective function can increase or decrease indefinitely. "Sign Restrictions" are the range of values that a decision variable can have. It mainly has positive conditions and negative conditions. A toy company cannot produce toys in negative numbers.

A simple example of linear programming is as follows.

Richard sells two types of bread. To make chocolate bread, he needs 100g of flour and 10g of chocolate, and to make wheat bread, he needs 50g of flour. After deducting the material cost, if he sells chocolate bread, he has 100 cents left over, and if you sell wheat bread, you have 40 cents left over. Today, Richard has 3000g of flour and 100g of chocolate as ingredients. Assume that he can sell all the bread he makes and he no longer receives the supply of ingredients.

Richard can use linear programming to calculate what kind of bread and how much he should make to maximize his profit.

Target : $\max\limits_{\mathbf{x}} 100x_1 + 40x_2$

Condition : $100x_1 + 50x_2 \leq 3000$,
$10x_1 \leq 100$,
$x_1, x_2 \geq 0$.

Here, x1 is a variable that means the number of chocolate bread and x2 is the number of wheat bread. Referring to the picture, the way Richard makes the most profit today is to make 10 chocolate bread and 40 wheat bread, and the profit he can get is 2,600 cents.

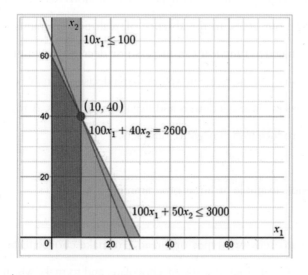

Linear programming is incorporated into life and industry around us. Now let's look at where linear programming is applied. If it is not applied, let's think about whether there is room to apply it. No matter what you expect, linear programming will always give you the gift of an optimal solution for the current situation.

8. Probabilistic Decision Making

According to the National Transportation Safety Board (NTSB), the odds of a plane crash occurring are only 1 in 120,000 flights, and the odds of dying in a plane crash are 1 in 11 million.

And according to a study published by a research team at the University of Michigan, the probability of dying in an airplane accident is only 1/65 compared to a car accident.

There is a chance that someone will die in an airplane accident, but there are not many people who do not fly because they are afraid of the possibility. When analyzing a situation like this, if we calculate the probability, we can make a very reasonable and correct decision.

Probabilistic reasoning is a mental model that can be useful when making decisions. This is a decision-making process that allows us to predict, based on logic and mathematics, what the outcome will be when a particular event occurs.

For example, a certain stock price of a certain company is formed at $100. However, unconfirmed rumors are circulating that the government will announce measures to reduce the value of the company. If this is true, let's assume that the company's intrinsic value drops by 50%.

The very next day, the company's share price in the market fell to $60. In this situation, a smart investor can use probabilistic thinking to make decisions such as whether to buy more stocks or sell stocks. Investors who have analyzed and diagnosed the situation make the following probabilistic assumptions.

There is a 20% chance that the company's intrinsic value will fall by 50%. (worst case) There is a 30% chance that the company's intrinsic value will fall by 30%. There is a 50% chance the government will not issue this regulation. Therefore, the intrinsic value does not decrease. (best case)

When calculated as a weighted average of the results of each probabilistic estimate, the intrinsic value of the company is approximately $81 per share. ($21 per share higher than the market's response the next day).

The world is uncertain. We can never know 100%, and even if we did, it would be too late if we put off making a decision until then. Although we cannot make decisions with 100% chance, probabilistic thinking allows us to make efficient and rational decisions based on several possible outcome scenarios.

In this scenario, you might conclude that this is a 35% chance ($81) from the current stock price of $60, or an opportunity to create an internal rate of return of 16% over two years.

"Thinking in bets" is a decision-making framework developed by former professional poker player Annie Duke. Because of luck, bad decisions can lead to good outcomes. Or, good decisions can make bad decisions.

And people judge the quality of decisions by their outcomes. However, this is a flaw that creates dangerous illusions about future decisions.

The world runs randomly, so you shouldn't ignore the large role that luck plays beyond the range of decisions you make. Instead, we can think of every decision as a "bet" by taking into account "luck (and therefore probability)" and calculating an expected value.

I'll give you two real-world examples here of how people "mistakenly" evaluate decisions based on their consequences. You will know why it is wrong. Then you will know how to take your luck into account by thinking like a poker player.

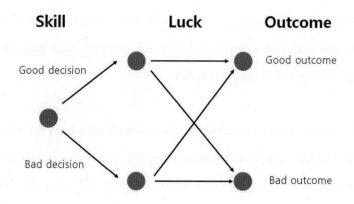

1) Bad Decisions but Luck vs. Good decisions but bad luck

Mike was excited when he heard about the new cryptocurrency from his close friend. Everyone was talking about the growth potential on Reddit. He thought he had come early enough to finally reap huge returns in a short amount of time. And he was so sure. He invested all his savings into it.

Two weeks later, his dream came true. His investment was 10 times higher and he cashed out. Mike said to himself: "It was the best decision of my life."

Jane was working in the marketing department of a consumer products company. One day she received a job offer in the tech industry. The offer was good. Promotions, stock options, team leaders and more. After thinking about it for a week, she decided to accept her offer. It was a great opportunity and the tech industry was better for her future.

But five months later, a recession set in. The tech industry has been hit hard and stocks have plummeted. Her new company went through her restructuring and decided to fire her.

Since she is her new employee, she wouldn't have been fired if she had stayed at a consumer products company. And during the economic downturn, finding a new job was impossible. Jane said to herself: "It was the worst decision of my life."

2) Think Like a Poker Player

Life is a decision game. Investments, projects to work on, career changes, and more. The better decisions you make in the long run, the more successful you will be.

But people make a common mistake when evaluating their decisions. They judge the quality of a decision by the results. And this is a flaw that creates dangerous illusions about future decisions. Because life is poker, not chess. Luck plays a bigger role than you think.

Mike risked all his savings and made a terrible decision, but was lucky. Jane made a good decision by taking a chance on better terms, but her luck wasn't on her side. When you think about bets, you take into account luck (and odds) and become a better decision maker in the game of life.

3) How to think of betting in three steps

(1) Imagine a bet with a friend

Suppose you want to buy real estate. You expect to get good returns in 3 years. But imagine your friend makes a bet against your predictions. "Are you going to bet?"

This makes you think what your friend knows about something you are missing. So you can find blind spots in your thinking before you make a decision.

(2) Calculate the expected value

Professional poker players calculate the expected value of their bets to decide which hand to bet on or not. Suppose there is $300 in the pot. That's the total money you can earn. You need $50 to call your opponent's bet and assume a 25% chance of winning.

So the expected value of that bet is 25% of $300, or $75. Since the expected value ($75) is higher than the bet amount ($50), it makes sense to bet $50 on that hand. Do the same with your life decisions.

Compare the expected value to "your bet" by estimating:

① The potential reward of the decision — not just money, but joy, freedom or time

② Probability of getting it — You cannot know the exact probability, but estimate it in the best possible way (remember the bet with your friend).

③ The resources (time, effort, money) you bet on to get the reward — consider the opportunity cost as well

If the expected value is higher than the bet, it is a good decision. This will also help overcome "loss aversion." Here, loss aversion refers to a psychological state in which suffering from losses is greater than pleasure from gains when seeing the same gains and losses.

(3) Analyze your past decisions

Another way to make better decisions is to review past choices. But remember "regardless of the consequences". Why have you been so successful in that investment? Your good decision or luck?

Was it a good decision to start the business despite the failure? If you don't find your mistakes, you risk repeating them. There are exactly two things that determine the outcome of our lives. It is the quality and luck of our decisions. Learning to recognize the difference between the two is what "thinking in bets" is all about.

9. Backwards reasoning

We usually look to the future from the present. We are used to the way we plan for future goals in the present. Retrograde analysis, on the other hand, is looking backwards from the future.

Backward analysis is a powerful way to solve difficult problems by working backwards. Like a game of chess, the problems of future life can be solved by looking backwards. This is a mindset that requires us to do the opposite of what we normally do.

"If you can watch the last game, you won't waste your youth." - Maurice Ashley, master chess player

Let's solve the following simple problem.

Bacteria double every 24 hours. If bacteria take 30 days to fill a lake, on what day was the lake half full?

Reversing the above problem gives you the answer. For example, in the figure, the small circle in the middle represents the final result.

In the case of bacterial growth, after 30 days, the lake was full of bacteria. Then, from that end result, think about when the lake will be half full. It takes 24 hours (a day) for half to double, so by day 29 half of the lake would have been filled with bacteria.

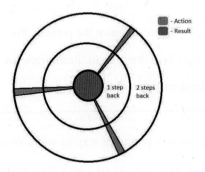

Backward (final version) inference is an informative and convenient method. Think of the center of the circle above as the end result or goal you want, and step out from there backwards one step at a time.

However, it is not easy to practice because it is an inference that goes back in time. Inference becomes very difficult, especially when the number of variables to be considered increases.

But without this kind of thought process, we cannot make optimal choices. You can make this reasoning a habit for a variety of everyday decisions, such as doing your favorite sport, driving home through rush hour, or trying to get to the airport on time.

Usually, when we want to arrive at the airport on time, we automatically start inferring from past experiences. You should estimate how long it will take to check-in and get through security, keeping both yourself and other passengers in mind.

If you drive your car, add the time to park in the parking lot, the time spent in traffic jams, etc. When taking a limousine bus, calculate the time the bus arrives at the bus stop you want to board and the time it takes to get from there to the airport.

You make your decision based on a number of factors related to your choices with others, such as what time of day the traffic is, what day of the week it is, and how close you are to traffic near the airport.

And you have to anticipate how crowded check-in and security will be. You have to put all of these factors together and choose a time to depart for the airport.

If you expect strict security checks or heavy traffic, you may want to leave a little early. You can roam on your smartphone at the airport, shop for gifts for someone, and stop by the lounge for a meal.

You have a meeting with a customer at the Four Seasons Hotel in Palo Alto at 18:00 on May 22nd. In this case, you will reverse the schedule of when and how you will move from Korea to San Francisco.

All of this comes from your Last Version. Starting from this last picture, we will check whether the current selection meets the conditions.

An inexperienced person can expect too much or too little time to get to the airport on time. This is because it is not easy to imagine future situations and make current choices in the absence of experience.

The airport example is an example of the final version inference that we practice in our daily lives, but in addition to that, we also obtain values or properties that we do not directly know by calculating them backwards.

For example, inverse operation. It is usually used when problems with sequential calculations or when the first value can be inferred through the resulting value.

We are accustomed to thinking of effects (future) from causes (past). However, it is also very beneficial for us to think in terms of inferring causes from effects.

10. The 3 stages of decision making and simplification

Making decisions is tiring. The more decisions you make, the less willpower you have. This is called decision fatigue. Zuckerberg and Jobs understood this. We can guess why Mark Zuckerberg and Steve Jobs preferred to wear the same clothes.

This is a great example of simplifying life. They used "Occam's Razor/Oakham's Razor" to cut out the need to waste mental energy every day on unnecessary elements. It is often called the principle of economy or the principle of parismony. It can also be said that the simple is the best.

Ockham's razor is a method of choice named after William of Ockham, a 14th-century English logician and Franciscan monk. Ockham's argument is, so to speak, "If something can be explained in many ways, we must explain it using the fewest number of assumptions among them."

In fact, building a latticework of mental models is nothing more than a way to "simplify" the decision-making process. What could be simpler than going through a mental model checklist while solving a problem? Here are three tips for "simplifying" based on the advice of Warren Buffett and Charlie Munger.

① Avoid the unknown and unimportant.

The first step in simplification is to understand the futility of chasing after the unknown and unimportant. Buffett explains.

"There are two questions you should ask yourself when making a decision. First, is it knowable? Second, is it important? If it is unknowable, as there are all sorts of things that are important but unknowable, I just forget them. And if it doesn't matter, it makes no difference whether it is knowable or not. I don't care."

For example, where interest rates are going, what the stock market will do next, etc. all matter. But we don't know these things.

Stephen Covey emphasized in <The 7 Habits of Highly Effective People> that we should focus our efforts on "circles of influence" rather than "circle of concern." Focus most of your time and energy on areas you can control.

Simplification starts with avoiding activities that are heavily influenced by the unknown. Similarly, before attacking a problem, ask if it is worth solving. Now regarding "Simplification" I want to tell you something very important.

Everyone has their core values in life. Core values are the fundamental beliefs of an individual or organization. As a kind of guiding principles, they guide people to act and help people understand the difference between right and wrong.

What is important to you? Core values determine the answer to this question. Your core values emphasize "what you stand for." Core values guide your decisions and behaviors. Like this, when you know what you value, you can live by those values.

I have three core values. The first is Health & Wealth. Health cannot be overemphasized. A healthy soul resides in a healthy body. Second is Truth & Responsibility. This is being true to myself and to others. Self-reliant, acting independently and taking responsibility for results.

And the third is Achievement in Peace. I pursue a peaceful life without quarrels. Of course, the world does not just move according to my will. Life is full of sudden misfortunes and disputes. However, through life experience, I have learned to forgive, love, and try not to blame the world.

I seek a simple life. My life in 3! (Three Factorial) is a milestone. 3! = 3 × 2 × 1 = 6. I pursue a simple life of home, work and religion. Family harmony is the starting point. If there is only one more place to care about, 4!(=24)→5!(=120)→6!(=720)→7!(=5,040) becomes a complicated and war-like life. A person without family reconciliation cannot guarantee the completion of the plan, no matter how good the plan is.

② focus, focus, focus

The second level of simplification is focus. If you try to accomplish too many things at the same time, you end up not getting everything right. Decision-making becomes simpler when we focus on one thing at a time.

Studies have repeatedly shown that the human brain is not optimized for multitasking, especially when performing complex and unfamiliar tasks.

Here's what Buffett said about focus in a 1997 letter:

"..serious problems arise when the management of a great company neglects and neglects a good business foundation by acquiring a so-so business or another business that is lesser than that.... Loss of focus is usually what Charlie and I worry most about when we're trying to invest in a business that looks great. Don't forget the Pareto principle. 80% of your revenue comes from 20% of your activities."

③ Invert, always invert

Charlie Munger, Warren Buffett's business partner and vice chairman of Berkshire Hathaway, attributes some of his and Buffett's success to skill and knowledge, but he often cites the way they think about problem solving is crucial to their success.

Munger suggests that thinking and planning the exact opposite of what you want can give you a competitive edge in everything you do. So the third trick to simplification is to invert. This thinking technique has been used by some of the greatest thinkers, scientists, and innovators throughout history.

Success equals good decisions minus bad decisions. The most powerful benefit of using inversion techniques is that they help you avoid making poor decisions that hinder you from achieving your goals.

Munger said he was amazed at how much he benefited in the long run by constantly trying not to be stupid instead of trying to be smart.

Buffett and Munger emphasize that they focus on not losing money (rather than, like most business leaders, focusing on how to make more money).

They suggest using inversion thinking as follows:

① Think about what you want to do.

② Then switch it to the opposite scenario.

③ Brainstorm "counter-solutions" that help achieve what you don't want to do.

④ Brainstorm "preventive solutions" to prevent these "opposite solutions" from occurring.

Here is an example.

① What you want to happen.: "How can I become a better leader?"

② Inversion of what you want to do: "What will stop me from becoming a better leader?"

③ Opposite solutions: Blame the people you lead for everything that goes wrong and take all the credit when things go well. Ask your team what they would prefer you not do. Don't let the team contribute.

④ Preventive solutions: Lead by example. Listen 80% of the time and speak the other 20%. Reward and recognize team effort. Encourage new ideas and open criticism.

We tend to look to the future to achieve our goals. However, this may not be the most effective way to avoid making bad decisions that hinder our progress. Instead of focusing on what you want to happen, you can use the inversion technique to think about what you don't want to happen and make a plan to avoid it.

Part II.

Competence
and Performance

<Wanderer Above the Sea of Mist, by Caspar David Friedrich, 1818>

The back of a man standing tall on top of a rocky mountain is impressive. A strong wind blowing from the top of the mountain blows his short blond hair.

The fog seen under the feet breaks white like a raging wave, and as if representing the psychology of the main character, it elicits a curious visual pleasure.

What is the man thinking as he gazes at the vast sea of fog? Although he was thrown into an unknown harsh world, he seems to have a strong spirit to practice his convictions without being intimidated by this.

How can you make the most of your current abilities? What can you do to make your skills shine even more? What must you do so that your hard work is not in vain and bears abundant fruit?

★★★★★ Chapter 5. ★★★★★

Meta-cognition and Circle of Competence

1. Value creation and Competence

We live in a fierce competition. That's why Jack Welch, former chairman of GE, said, "If you don't have a competitive advantage, don't compete." What is Competitive Advantage?

"Competitive advantage" is a unique advantage developed by a company to give it superior performance compared to its competitors. Let's look at this picture. Companies acquire "distinctive competences" based on their "resources" and "capabilities."

And through this, the company has a "competitive advantage" of cost

A Model of Competitive Advantage

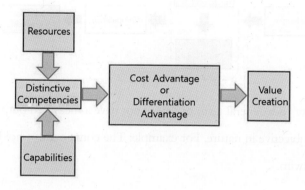

advantage or differentiation advantage in the market. And through this, it creates "value" for the market(customer). Of course, this principle applies equally to individuals.

Samsung Electronics and Apple are competing in the smartphone market. They strive to make the most of their resources and capabilities in order to have a "competitive advantage" over their competitors.

Perhaps you want to create value and, if possible, increase that performance. Then, what determines the performance of value creation?

Above all, the "performance of value creation" depends on your "competence." And competence, as we have seen, are the combination of your resources and capabilities. Therefore, we must clearly understand the meaning of these terms.

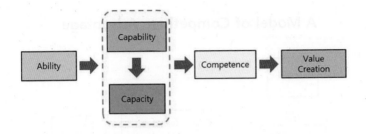

"Ability" is a general term that does not have a measured output. It is purely subjective in nature. For example: The container can hold water. / I can swim.

"Capacity" is a quantifiable description. Capacity is always dependent on the ability or inability of an individual or thing. For example: The container holds 100 ml of water. / I can swim 200 m in 50s.

"Capability" is the penultimate(=last but one) level of evaluation which defines if the capacity can be increased further, or not. For example: The container can hold 200 ml of water. I can improve my capacity to swim 200m in 40s with suitable practice/training.

The gap between Capability & Capacity is initially latent. The purpose of training programs is to improve the capability (& competencies) of individuals. Not always, the capability improves capacity immediately, but continuous effort & practice will result in rewards.

When someone has a driver's license, we expect him or her to be able to drive. But that doesn't mean he's a good driver. Whether his driving level is as good as that of a car racer cannot be determined by whether he has a driver's license or not. The word "capability" here means how well someone can drive, not whether or not they have a driver's license.

Professor David McClelland of Harvard University first used the word "competence" in his paper "Testing for competence rather than intelligence" in 1973.

He interviewed successful people and analyzed what made them successful. And he defined "competence" as the enduring stable behavioral characteristic of successful people.

Let's look at the word "competency" in English. Then the meaning becomes apparent. This word is a noun of the verb "Compete." Therefore, "competency" is, in a word, the ability to win in "competition."

Competence is the ability that Bill Gates and Usain Bolt were able to succeed by competing with others. This is the difference between competency and capability.

Businesses must create value to survive and prosper. Businesses need employees who do their jobs better. John and Paul are salespeople for the Chinese market. John is more fluent in Chinese than Paul.

However, Paul's sales performance in the Chinese market is higher than John's. Then, as a salesperson for the Chinese market, Paul is a more competent employee. John has the capability to read, write and speak Chinese. However, this is not a sufficient competency as a salesperson.

"Competence" is the competitiveness that wins the competition, so it is not an individual ability, but a comprehensive ability. This is like the fact that in order for a country to win a war, its overall capabilities, including not only military power but also economic power, must be stronger than its opponent.

In this regard, Professor Ray Klein, who served as deputy director of the US Central Intelligence Agency(CIA), presented the Formula for National Power Measurement.

$$Pp \text{(Pp=perceived power)} = (C+E+M) \times (S+W)$$

He calculated "national power" by multiplying the tangible factors such as Critical Mass (C, territory and population), economic power (E), and military power (M), and the intangible factors like national strategy (S) and people's will (W).

The most distinctive feature of this calculation method is that the national strategy (S) and the people's will (W), which are intangible elements of national power, are added together to give a number based on 1, and this is multiplied by the tangible national power factor.

He gave 1.5 and 1.4 to Switzerland and Israel, where the national strategy is well established and the people are united, and Bangladesh, which has poor national strategy or people's will, was given 0.4. If there is no strategy(S) and will(W), the total national power may become zero.

The Vietnam War is well described by this equation. At the time, the United States overwhelmed Vietnam in terms of economic and military power, but the strategy (S) and public will (W) for war were weak. The will and strategy of the United States toward Vietnam was close to zero. On the other hand, the fighting spirit and strategy of the Vietnamese people to achieve independence were very strong.

Let's keep in mind the case of Paul, a salesman with poor language skills but better sales performance, and Vietnam, which won the war with the United States with its weak national strength.

In the end, "competence" is the power to win in competition, and mental factors such as "beliefs", determination, and drive are more important than knowledge and skills.

(Source: https://iaocr.com/competence-and-clinical-research/)

In general, "competence" is often expressed as shown in the figure above. Knowledge and skills are accumulated through experience. You do some behaviors based on this. As a result, you get some performance against your goals. At first glance, this model looks cool. But, it's actually crappy.

First, it's not clear what "competence" is. Second, there are no resources, circumstances and beliefs here. Third, there is no consideration for "value creation."

Your "competence" is your "comprehensive competitive advantage," which includes your resources, beliefs, attitudes, knowledge, skills and experience, and different levels of activity such as learning and working.

Therefore, a new "mental model" that comprehensively expresses the relationship between "competence" and "value creation" is needed by reflecting all of these points.

2. Competence and Meta-cognition

So I liken each of us to a "House" as shown in the following picture. Just as we can look outside and look into a house, we can see ourselves outside and inside. It's like we can see our outer appearance through a mirror, and we can see our inner side through reflection.

Just as we can imagine the inside and outside of a house as vivid images, recalling ourselves as images provides a completely different experience from vaguely thinking about ourselves.

I call this house the "Temple of Success." This is a kind of model house, as we saw in the mental model. This picture shows what each of us is made of.

This house is largely composed of floors, pillars and a roof. The Floors(=post stones) are stacked in order from bottom to top with three floor stones: first environment and resources, second beliefs and attitudes, and third knowledge, skills and experiences.

The Pillars consist of a series of four Pillars: Learning, Work, Fellowship(=social networking) and Others(=rest, religious activities and meditation, etc..) Finally, the roof consists of vision, mission and goal.

I will now assume that this house is yourself and explain its meaning. First, the Floors will be explained. The environment is literally the environment in which you were born. When and where you were born is the key. Resources include your natural intelligence, appearance, size, body type, and temperament. As you go through life, you develop certain beliefs, values, attitudes, and perspectives. You also gain knowledge, skills and experience.

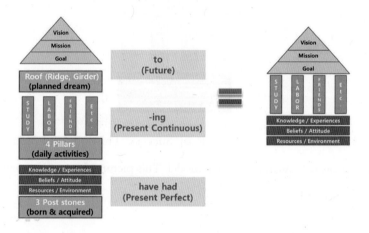

These are things you were born with or built up to a certain point in time, say, the present. Therefore, when expressed in English tense, it can be said to be present perfect.

The four Pillars are a set of activities. As a living being, as you go through life, you engage in certain activities. As representative activities, I divided them into four categories: study, work, fellowship, and others. These activities can be expressed in English tenses as present continuous because they are what you are currently doing.

The roof is made up of vision, mission and goals. Since vision points to a certain direction and future point, it can be expressed in the future tense in English.

We humans are made up of past, present and future. We are not made up of the past, and if we do not live only in the present, we move on to the future. Life on earth ends with death, but life in space continues without end.

The "temple of success" is you and the universe. What kind of masterpiece will you build using this model house and how? Let's build your own "temple of success" based on this model house. You are not a house fixed to the ground, but a house that flies freely through space.

The painting below is Le Château des Pyrénées (1959) by Belgian surrealist artist René Magritte. I think you can draw a more dynamic and wonderful image than this picture.

"There is but one temple in the universe and that is the body of man."
German poet Novalis (1772-1801)

According to the Bible, God created human beings from clay in the image of God. Build your own breathing Temple of Success. However, this castle is not a castle built with these hard stones.

Let's look at the molecular formula of water. H2O. Water can be of any shape. Water can contain anything liquid, gaseous or solid. Water can go anywhere. There are no boundaries, no limits. You must build a castle equal to Water. You can be of any shape and anything like water.

The Temple of Success represents each of us. So we can put Warren Buffett in the temple of success. Of course you can be in this position too.

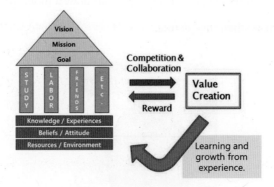

We can make better decisions and create better value through mental models. And we learn and grow through the experience of value creation. Success in creating value increases our resources. Our knowledge and skills change. What really matters is that our beliefs change. We grow into more capable and competent people.

However, there is one very important issue here. In a word, there can be a difference between "your competence that you think of yourself" and "your actual competence." Most people overlook this point, repeat trial and error, and end up in great frustration.

For value creation, the (actual) size of your competence is important, but it is more important that you have a good understanding of the reality of your competence.

For example, let's assume that two people A and B are high school students, job seekers, or entrepreneurs who are facing problems and goals to solve, such as college entrance exams, employment, or investment attraction.

In this case, the magnitude of the competence that the two people have is actually the same as the number 50, but A may think (overestimate) that it is 70 greater than it actually is, and B may correctly evaluate it as 50. In this case, B, who knows himself well, is evaluated as a person with high "metacognition."

	Actual competence	Perceived competence	**Metacognition**
A	50	70	Low
B	50	50	High

"Metacognition" is a term coined by American developmental psychologist John Flavell in 1970s. It refers to "the ability to make judgments about one's own thoughts." It is a cognitive activity in which one looks at one's resources and level of competency. For example, if you have ever thought about why you made certain decisions in the past, you are engaging in metacognition.

"Behaviorism" saw humans as stimuli and responses. However, according to the "theory of cognitive development", there is a process of mental activity between input and output.

External information undergoes processing in our brain. So our brain remembers and uses schemas, mental models, knowledge and skills. This is a cognitive process.

And based on this knowledge, we plan, execute, and reflect. This is called metacognition. Simply put, if "shopping list" is cognition, "making a shopping plan" is metacognition.

Socrates said to know yourself, but it is very vague whether we really know ourselves or not. We are at a loss as to how we can know ourselves.

It is here that the Temple of Success I devised becomes a very powerful tool.

At this time, you can think of the temple of success. You can look into each of your base stones, pillars and roof. And you can look at your entire value creation process. This is a lot more powerful than you might think.

In 1999, David Dunning and Justin Krugger, professors and psychologists at Cornell University, studied the relationship between "actual competence" and "perceived competence."

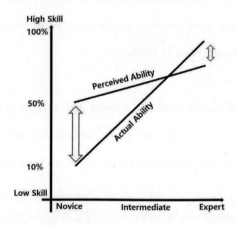

The two tested the participants' logic, grammar, and sense of humor. They found that those in the "bottom 25 percent" generally self-assessed their skills as well "above average." It is from this study that the "Dunning-Kruger effect" is derived.

The Dunning-Kruger effect has two components.

① People who are incompetent at something do not recognize their own incompetence. And they are likely not only unaware of their own incompetence but actually convinced that they are competent. They will also perceive themselves as superior to others.

② On the contrary, highly competent individuals may mistakenly assume that tasks that are easy for them to do are easy for others to do, or that others will have a similar understanding of a subject they are familiar with.

The trigger for Dunning and Kruger to conduct this experiment is interesting. They were inspired by the stupid and brave robber who robbed a Pittsburgh bank in 1995.

McArthur Wheeler stole the money and ran away with his face uncovered. Because he did not cover his face, he was captured very clearly on CCTV and was caught by the police an hour later.

When the police show Wheeler the CCTV, Wheeler says something. "I put on lemon juice...?" He believed that his face had become transparent because he had smeared it with lemon ink, which children use to write secret letters.

Competence is on the X-axis, and confidence is on the Y-axis. It is okay to substitute the words knowledge, skill, and experience instead of

Dunning–Kruger Effect

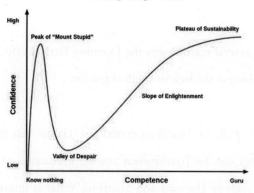

competency. You can also replace it with the word "mental model."

Looking at the graph, at first, as competence grows, so does confidence. A bank robber who smeared lemon juice on his face falls into this category. However, after reaching the "peak", the competence increases, but rather the confidence decreases. Because people generally realize that the more they know, the more they don't know. So there is the "Valley of Despair."

Then, as people progress through the valley, their confidence begins to rise slowly in proportion to the amount of knowledge, following a normal learning curve as their competence increases.

A person who has read one book pretends to know everything in the world. Then he meets a person who reads a lot of books and gets frustrated with his lack. Then, little by little, he grows up reading and learning.

There are several reasons why the Dunning-Kruger effect occurs. But the biggest thing is the lack of meta-cognition.

Thomas Sowell, an American economist, claims that the Dunning-Kruger effect can be found even among graduates of prestigious universities such as Harvard and Stanford. What is interesting is that they tend to mistake a degree from a prestigious university as if it were knowledge.

Metacognition entails awareness of one's strengths and weaknesses, self-awareness and self-reflection. Therefore, if you have a high metacognitive ability, you can more accurately identify your abilities and limitations and appropriately invest your time and effort where necessary, increasing your efficiency.

However, if you do not know your competence well, there is a high possibility that you will jump into a field you do not know well and pay a large tuition fee.

3. Competence and Circle of Competence

1) What is the circle of competence?

IBM founder Tom Watson said, "I am not a genius. But I am smart in a certain area and stay around that area." He emphasized that he has skills that anyone can easily learn, one of which is knowing the boundaries of one's capabilities.

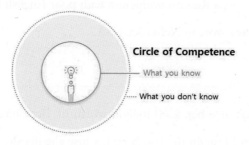

Warren Buffett called these areas where someone can be wise the "Circle of Competence(CoC)." This area is what you know, and outside of it is what you don't know.

The key here is to know the boundaries of the "circle of competence", not the "size." In order for you to make smart decisions, you must move away from the realm of making stupid decisions.

As long as you are inside the "Circle of Competence" area, you are safe. This is the safety zone. Because you know very well that you don't know, there is little reason to take a risky gamble. But if you pretend to know when you don't know, you are likely to be in great danger.

Since Tom Watson is a businessman and Warren Buffett is an investor, it's easy for you to misunderstand that this only applies to the realm of business and investing. But the circle of competence also applies to fields other than investment.

Buffett describes the circle of competence of one of the business managers (Mrs. B), a Russian immigrant with poor English who built the largest furniture store in Nebraska, USA.

> I couldn't give her $200 million worth of Berkshire Hathaway stock when I bought the company because she doesn't understand stocks. She understands her cash. She understands furniture. She understands real estate. But she doesn't understand stocks, so she has nothing to do with stocks.
>
> If you deal with Mrs. B, she will buy 5,000 tables this afternoon if the price is right. She plans to buy odd lots of 20 different carpets, and this is because she understands carpets. Everything else will be the same. But she wouldn't buy even 100 shares of General Motors, even if it was 50 cents a share

There was nothing wrong with her that she had such a narrow range of competences. In fact, I could argue to the contrary. Her rigorous dedication to that area (ie her circle of competence) allowed her to focus on it. Because of that focus, she was able to overcome her own handicap and achieve tremendous success.

Value creation depends on your capabilities and competences. However, there is a difference between what you think of yourself as your capability and your actual capability.

So you should keep in mind the concept of metacognition. It's important that you size up your competence, but it's even more important to know the boundaries of your "circle of competence."

Buffett says he doesn't know stocks like Amazon, but he knows Coca-Cola. And he says he only invests in a few companies he knows well. All in all, he invests 80% in five companies.

A similar story appears in the documentary <Becoming Warren Buffett> aired by HBO in 2017. It's a passage where Buffett is quoting legendary hitter Ted Williams from <The Science of Hitting>. Ted Williams is the last 40% hitter in the major leagues. Since Ted Williams hit .406 in 1941, a .400 hitter hasn't reappeared in the majors.

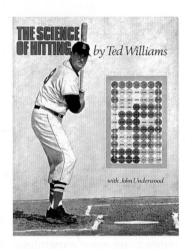

Ted Williams divides the strike zone into 77 small areas and only aims for balls that come into the center (sweet spot). Ted Williams analyzed that if he hits a ball coming into the middle, he can hit 40%, but if he hits a ball coming into a low outside corner, his batting average drops to 0.235.

And he patiently waited for the ball to come in the middle. The result is legendary. Ted Williams recorded a career batting average of 0.344 in 2292 games over 19 years. He was inducted into the Hall of Fame in 1966 with 93.4% of the vote.

There are two types of hitters in a baseball game. First, there are hitters who hit all kinds of balls. They go all out to hit a home run every time. This also requires a lot of strength and stamina, so some athletes take banned drugs.

On the other hand, there are also smart hitters. Innate physical condition may be bad, but they are wise. They only hit probable balls. They don't even try to hit a home run. They just want to hit the right ball where there are no defenders. Most of the players in the top 10 are the latter, and Ted Williams is a master among them.

Buffett says investing is far more lucrative than baseball. Because there are no strikeouts. All you have to do is wait for a strike, and when the opportunity finally arrives, swing the bat as hard as you can. If people are jeering, "Swing, You Bum!", Buffett advises ignoring it. No matter what others say, wait until the ball you want to hit comes in.

2) If so, how can you find your circle of competence?

The most important thing when it comes to figuring out the scope of your competence is to be honest with yourself. As Buffett said, the size of the circle is not very important. More important is defining the limits of the circle. The wiser you are, the better you know your competence.

Charlie Munger is a colleague of Buffett and the vice chairman of Berkshire Hathaway. He presents two principles in investing.

"Take a simple idea and take it seriously."

And Munger applies this concept beyond business to the realm of life in general. The essential question he wanted to answer was this. "Where should we devote the limited time of our lives to achieve the greatest success?"

Charlie's prescription is:

If you want to become the best tennis player in the world, you probably start your efforts with hope. Unfortunately, however, you will soon discover that there is little hope of accomplishing anything there.

But if you're going to be the best plumbing contractor in any small town, two-thirds of you can. It requires a strong will. Some intelligence is also required.

But after a while you gradually learn everything about the plumbing business and master the craft. It is an achievable goal given enough discipline.

And those who can never win a chess tournament or stand on center court in a great tennis tournament can rise to great heights in life by slowly developing a range of competences.

This stems partly from the environment they were born with and partly from what they steadily develop through their work.

Think of an area where you have an advantage over most people. This can come from study, work or simply life experience. This is similar to a hint applied when someone is trying to figure out their "aptitude."

In other words, when someone tells you you're good at something or bad at something, that's your chance to snatch it. Ask him questions very gently. "What made you think so?"

It is very difficult for someone to discover their aptitude on their own. Perhaps that's why Johann Wolfgang von Goethe gave us the advice to do whatever comes your way. But with this one simple question, you have the opportunity to see your aptitude through the eyes of others.

Each of us has a range of competence. For example, a lawyer who has been studying and applying his or her knowledge in court for decades will have a range of competences in law. It is highly specialized and gives him a clear advantage when it comes to that domain. When he is there, he has an extreme advantage. But if you invest outside the circle of competence, you either take a big loss or the returns will revert to the mean at best.

What experiences and knowledge do you have that give you an edge over the average investor? It is important to identify this and define your "Circle of competence."

If you are an avid gamer, investing in a gaming company would be wise. If you work as a software developer, you could probably use that knowledge to pick software stocks with huge upside potential.

This is why Buffett doesn't want to invest in tech stocks. Simply put, it is outside his circle of competence. And once you've defined your circle of competence, you can work on expanding it if you want. We will look at this in Chapter 8.

4. Negative capability

We think of capability as a positive term—it's active and additive rather than passive and subtractive. It's about proactive action, getting things done, leading the way, and delivering on results and desired outcomes.

But this pre-occupation with action and results can also mean an inability to handle more complex, unknown situations where actions and outcomes might not be as clear. As we know, we operate in complex and uncertain conditions.

How do we go about correcting this imbalance? How can we better position ourselves to operate effectively in uncertain conditions?

One place to start is to develop "negative capability." When I explained hard mental models and soft mental models in Chapter 1, I briefly mentioned this term without any detailed explanation. Now let's take a closer look at this term.

The English poet John Keats coined the term in 1817 in a letter to his brother George:

At once it struck me what quality went to form a man of achievement especially in literature and which Shakespeare possessed so enormously— I mean Negative Capability, that is when man is capable of being in uncertainties, mysteries, doubts, without any irritable reaching after fact and reason.

"Negative" here is not pejorative. Instead, it implies the ability to resist explaining away what we do not understand.

Rather than coming to an immediate conclusion about an event, idea or person, Keats advises resting in doubt and continuing to pay attention and probe in order to understand it more completely. In this, he anticipates the work of Nobel laureate economist Daniel Kahneman, who cautions against the naïve view that "What you see is all there is."

Relatedly, the great genius of mankind, Leonardo da Vinci, left a saying, "Learn how to see!" He was an artist as well as a brilliant scientist. He discovered one day that moisture and dust in the atmosphere diffused light and made the outlines of distant objects blurry. He applied these principles to his works and expressed everything in shades without using any clear lines.

In a word, this is a technical method of softening the boundaries between colors in painting without clarifying them. This is called the sfumato technique. Here, sfumato is a word derived from the Italian word sfumare, which means hazy or foggy. Of course, it was first invented and named by Da Vinci. The secret of Mona Lisa's mysterious smile is right here.

The Sfumato principle, like negative capability, describes a person's ability to accept both the unknown and confusion as opposed to clinging for philosophical certainty.

Sfumato is also akin to the concept of Socratic Wisdom (paradoxically the same as Socratic Ignorance), which is the wisdom that knows just one thing: that it knows nothing. Socratic Wisdom is accepting your ignorance and claiming that you don't know anything without reasonable doubt.

The great playwright wrote in the space beyond what we know — that's where he found beauty, hope, and a new way of thinking. But for most people, fear of the unknown is one of the greatest fears of all. We like to know how things will end — at the beginning.

As shown in the picture below, there is always an Unknown between Known and Known. However, Unknown makes us uneasy because it is unstable by its nature. So most people instinctively try to resolve uncertainty quickly by heuristics. As a result, people often end up failing that they shouldn't have.

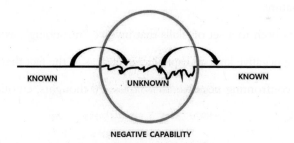

NEGATIVE CAPABILITY

Keats tried to capture the thought processes of literary geniuses, but the concept is equally applicable to the lives of us ordinary people today. Because today we operate in a complex environment where ambiguity and uncertainty prevail.

And this also applies to leaders. People want their leaders to be omniscient, but those external expectations prevent leaders from functioning effectively in that kind of environment. What is needed is an openness to ignorance and staying with the anxiety it creates.

Negative capability has two paradoxical aspects:

① Of "being in"/"being with" : "capable of being in uncertainties, mysteries, doubts" and

② Of "being without" : "without any irritable reaching after fact and reason"

Capability at first glance is a positive term. Keats combined it with negative thus capturing its paradox. It's a capability that goes against human nature.

It refers both to a set of skills that involve "not-doing", as opposed to doing-a negative kind of capability-as well as to the fact that this skill involves confronting negative (as in "unpleasant") thoughts, emotions, and situations.

What defines negative capability

Operating in uncertainty requires a different set of skills in contrast to known situations. Negative capability is a way of operating in conditions of uncertainty defined by an ability to stay with the discomfort and anxiety of doubt and not-knowing.

Capability, like capacity, derives from the Latin word capax. It means "able to hold much." It is grounded in the idea of "containing" or "spaciousness." Imagine the space inside an enormous shipping container. Its internal space, how much it can hold, determines its capacity. As Lao Tzu said in <Tao Te Ching(道德經)>, "It is the emptiness within that makes it useful." Keats used "negative" to describe the space beyond what we know.

We can either rush in to fill it with what we already know, or let the empty space create something new. Do we rush in to resolve a situation with habitual activity, emotions, and thoughts, or do we stay with the discomfort long enough to yield different answers?

It is also a good idea to take the time to look at matters from multiple perspectives. Shakespeare's comedies are full of mistaken identities and misconceptions, including mixed-up genders. Keats reminds us that we are most likely to gain new insights if we can stop assuming that we know everything we need to know about people by neatly shoehorning them into preconceived boxes.

Negative capability also testifies to the importance of humility, which Keats described as a "capability of submission." As Socrates indicates in Plato's "Apology," the people least likely to learn anything new are the ones who think they already know it all. By contrast, those who are willing to question their own assumptions and adopt new perspectives are in the best position to arrive at new insights.

Iinformation technology seems to give everyone instant access to all human knowledge. To be sure, the internet is one gateway to knowledge. But it also indiscriminately spreads misinformation and propaganda, often fueled by algorithms that profit off division.

This, it goes without saying, can cloud understanding with false certainty.

And so our age is often described as polarized: women versus men, Blacks versus whites, liberals versus conservatives, religion versus science – and it's easy to automatically lapse into the facile assumption that all human beings can be divided into two camps. The underlying view seems to be that if only it can be determined which side of an issue a person lines up on, there's no need to look any further.

Uncertainty can be uncomfortable. It is often quite tempting to stop pondering complex questions and jump to conclusions. But Keats counsels otherwise. By resisting the temptation to dismiss and despise others, it's possible to open the door to discovering traits in people that are worthy of sympathy or admiration. They may, with time, even come to be regarded as friends.

Why do we need negative capability in "negative" situations?

Ironically, we need negative capability the most in situations where there is a lack of something. Peter Simpson, a professor in organization studies at Bristol Business School, identifies three key types of situations in which we need to use negative capability:

① Not knowing what to do
② Not having adequate resources
③ Not trusting or being trusted

How to practice negative capability.

To reach a similar state of mind, start with these simple principles:

• Embrace your ignorance. According to John Keats, false certainty is a form of arrogance which should be avoided. Become comfortable saying "I don't know"—it is a form of courage and humility.

• Suspend your judgement. Instead of rushing to form and express a definitive opinion, refrain from trying to find a solution for a little while. Keep on being a neutral observer, collect more information, consider various perspectives. Finding the truth is not a race, it's a journey.

• Sit with your doubts. Because they make us feel uncomfortable, we often brush our doubts away, dismissing them as inconsequential, and focusing on our cosy certainties instead. Take a bit of time to get familiar with your doubts. In the same way some people make a list of their beliefs.

• Question your assumptions. All of our opinions are based on assumptions. That's fine, as long as we are aware of them. What are the underlying assumptions behind your opinions? What are these assumptions based on themselves?

• Revisit your ideas. It is okay to change your mind! Even when you have formed an opinion, don't let it cement and become part of a fixed mindset. Regularly revisit your ideas to see whether they have evolved, or whether new information should contribute to a shift in position.

Negative capability is more philosophy than science — it's an art which needs to be practiced to improve, and which can probably never be fully mastered. But through this process we can connect deeper with ourselves, with each other, and with the world.

Chapter 6

Pareto's Principle

Episode: Reverend John Maxwell

John Maxwell is a leadership master and best-selling author who has trained more than 6 million leaders in 180 countries around the world over the past 50 years. His books have been translated into over 50 languages and sold over 34 million copies.

John Maxwell was born in USA in 1947. After graduating from Ohio Christian University, he received a master's degree from Azusa Pacific University and a doctorate from Fuller Theological Seminary.

Here is an interesting story about Reverend John Maxwell. Let me quote some of the contents of his book <Leadership Gold>.

I still vividly remember the frustration I felt when I first took on the leadership role as a pastor. It was a time when I was working hard but not being efficient.

I spent most of my time counseling believers and had to take care of minor administrative tasks. I put a lot of time into it, but with little positive results. It was a worthless waste of time.

When I was taking a business management lecture at university, I wanted to shout "Eureka" to myself. The professor was lecturing on the "Pareto Principle", also known as the "80/20 rule." As I listened to his explanation, I opened my eyes again.

According to him, 20 percent of salespeople account for 80 percent of sales. And 80% of decisions are made with only 20% of the information gathered.

Isn't it amazing?

That means the 20 percent are 16 times more productive than the other 80 percent. If someone wanted to simplify his life while

---

increasing his productivity, he had to focus on the best 20 percent.

In that class that day, I realized two things. One was that I was doing too much, and the other was that I was doing the wrong thing. So I had no choice but to live inefficiently.

1. Non-linear: efforts and results

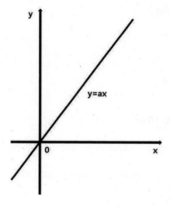

We often tend to think that the relationship between "input and output" is linear. In fact, if you double the raw materials in a bread factory, twice as much bread is produced.

So we think of the relationship between "input (X) and output (Y)" as if $Y = aX$. And we even think it's fair that the "inputs and the results" are proportionate.

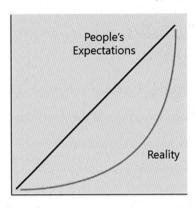

But if you double the effort, do you reap twice the output? If you were a student, would your score double if you increased your study hours from 4 to 8 hours a day?

Not like that.

Why would this happen?

This is because many "variables" are involved between "input and output." The relationship between inputs and outputs is "non-linear."

The world (= system) often does not simply move in a "linear" fashion. We think it is linear, but the data suggest otherwise. So we need to think about how to control these "variables" in our lives and workplaces.

Vilfredo Pareto, an Italian economist, realized that 80% of a nation's wealth was in 20% of the population. Joseph Juran, an American management consultant, took note of Pareto's research and applied it to the field of quality management. He found that most quality problems (typically defective products) are due to a small number of causes.

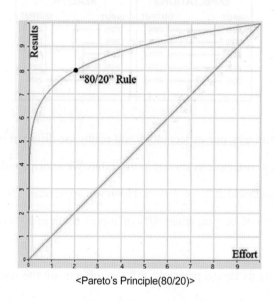

<Pareto's Principle(80/20)>

He defined a rule that 80% of results are produced by 20% of causes. By announcing this fact to the world, along with Joseph Juran, Vilfredo Pareto also gained great popularity. And more and more people have learned that the Pareto Principle applies in many areas through research, observation, and analysis.

So, here are some examples:

20% of a companies products represent 80% of sales

20% of customers generate 80% of sales

20% of employees are responsible for 80% of the results

20% of students have grades 80% or higher

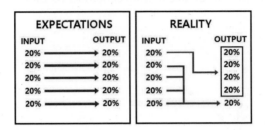

The reason why our expectations and reality are different is explained by the Pareto principle as shown in this table. We anticipate that 20% of resources will yield 20% of results. However, sometimes 20% of inputs result in 80% of output, while 80% of inputs result in 20% of output.

According to Pareto principle, 80% of effects are the result of 20% of causes. It refers to the inherent imbalance of cause and effect in all aspects of life.

Pareto principle reminds us of the need to sort things in order of priority. We live in a world where time and resources are limited. Whether learning or decisions, the important deserves to be treated as important as the less important as the less important.

2. Pareto Principle and Performance

From the Pareto principle (80/20), 80% of 80% is 64%, and 20% of

20% is 4%, thus implying the "64/4" principle. Similarly it means "51.2 (about 50)/0.8 (about 1)". In other words, 1% accounts for half of the total performance of 100%.

It's like "Fractal". A fractal is a geometric shape in which "some" small pieces are similar to "the whole."This is also called self-similarity. "Self-similarity" means that when a part is magnified, it shows a resemblance to the whole, including itself.

On the other hand, if this is expressed as input, output, and "relative value", it is shown in the table below.

	INPUT	OUTPUT	RELATIVE VALUE
A time Magic 1%	1%	50%	200
B Time 4% Sweet Spot	4%	64%	64
C Time Leveraged 20%	20%	80%	16
D Time 80% Mass	80%	20%	1

The table shows surprising results. Compared to the low efficiency 20/80, the "Pareto region" 80/20 has a relative value 16 times higher.

This is what John Maxwell realized. And the 64/4 area has a result with a relative value of 64 times, and the magic area of 50/1 has a 200 times higher relative value. Applying the Pareto Principle to education and knowledge, it can be expressed as "20 percent of knowledge produces 80 percent of results."

A prosperous life depends not only on your innate intelligence and inherited wealth. It doesn't just depend on your efforts. It depends on how much "intellectual life" you practice.

But if your head is filled with entertainment and sports news of little value, your future won't be bright either. At least economically prosperous life starts with how efficiently your brain is equipped with useful "mental models" and knowledge related to "value creation." And, of course, you are the one using it.

There is an example introduced by Gǔdiǎn, known as the best self-development coach in China with 2 million Weibo followers. He tells how ordinary instructors have been able to produce their own content more quickly or succeed in certain fields.

He surveyed more than 100 highly qualified teachers and lecturers at universities, secondary schools, and various educational establishments. As a result, he identified five core competencies. Excellent teachers had all five of the following items.

① Professional knowledge: Systematic, scientific, and verified knowledge within the lecture area

② Composition of lesson plan: Ability to compose a reasonable lesson plan tailored to the needs of different students

③ Technique development: Teaching skills using language, movement, educational software and multimedia

④ Personal charm: Instructor's unique personality

⑤ Positive mind: Positive psychological state and mindset

Gǔdiǎn designed an instructor training system based on five core competencies. And through this system, he cultivated the ability of an instructor and achieved a clear growth effect.

However, even in the same training process, there was a group that showed an extraordinary growth rate compared to other groups. This was a very interesting point. They didn't grow faster because they were smarter than others or because they worked harder. They were able to grow faster because they took smarter learning methods.

Most instructors feel that their own expertise is lacking when they are taught by an excellent instructor. Then they usually immerse themselves in the acquisition of large amounts of knowledge for a year. They continue to study, feeling that they have more to learn by taking various classes.

Two years later, they return to the field, but despite spending all their time trying to replenish their expertise, they still feel they have a long way to go.

On the other hand, wise instructors apply the Pareto Principle.

They first invest 20 percent of their time, bringing their expertise up to 80 percent. And they focus on designing the syllabus, only until they get to the 80% level, not 100%. Next, they cultivate their teaching skills and research ways to develop their personalities, and finally, they examine their own learning models and status quo.

How would the results of the two groups differ in this way?

Instructors who have raised a field to 100% level over the same period become 100% instructors. However, instructors who divide 100 percent of their time and energy into five items over the same period and achieve 80 percent in each become 400 percent instructors.

Harvard University recommends "speed reading" to students. JFK read a lot of books even after graduating from Harvard University and becoming president. He is said to have read over 600 words per minute. For reference, the average person reads 200 words per minute. However, there is a more effective way of reading than speed reading.

Let's apply the Pareto principle to reading. There are far better ways than blindly reading a book from cover to cover.

For example, if you read the author's preface and table of contents first, the author's intent and emphasis will be revealed. And the whole structure of the contents of the book is drawn in your head. After doing this, it is efficient to start reading or learning from the important part.

In the case of a 300-page book, the table of contents of the book is about 2 to 3 pages, which is about 0.8% (about 1%) of the total. According to the Pareto principle, 20% of the input produces 80% of the output, and 1% of the input produces 50% of the output. If someone only reads 1% of a book and tells you that he has read half (=50%) of this book, you'd think that would be an exaggeration or a leap.

However, if you have a good understanding of an author's usual beliefs and arguments, you can easily guess what the author will say without reading the entire contents of the book. Or, it is easier to predict what conclusion it will end up with.

What about John Maxwell? The subject of his book is almost "leadership." Humans generally predictable.

Tom Peters, called the management guru, wrote dozens of books in his lifetime. However, even though his books have different titles, their arguments and conclusions are almost the same. He worked on "Excellence" all his life.

Below are the titles of his books. And his other books not listed below are almost all about "Excellence", except that "Excellence" is not included in the book name. His research subject is the same.

<In Search of Excellence(1982)>, <A Passion for Excellence(1985)>, <Re-imagine! Business Excellence in a Disruptive Age(2003)>, <The Little Big Things: 163 Ways to Pursue Excellence(2010)>, <The Excellence Dividend(2018)>, <Excellence Now: Extreme Humanism(2021)>, <Tom Peters' Compact Guide to Excellence(2022)>

This stems from the limits of human interest and cognition.

People have their own worldview and beliefs. And there comes the consistency of perspective and argument. Because of this, human words and actions are largely predictable. Moreover, if the words of yesterday and today are different, he is no longer an intellectual.

I read some books by John Maxwell and Tom Peters. I'm still interested in their new books. But I don't read their new books from cover to cover unless it's a special occasion. In this age of information overload, we need to become more efficient. I recommend that you read books as follows from now on.

First, read the book title and table of contents to guess the author's intent and conclusion. Next, read the author's foreword, testimonials, etc. And if there is something unfamiliar in the table of contents, find it and read it. That's it!!!

ChatGPT and Reading

Generative AI, represented by ChatGPT, will have a great impact on education and learning. Generative AI specializes in "summary" functions, such as summarizing the content of books or papers. Let's take a look at how ChatGPT affects reading.

When we read a book or a paper, we can read it as a summary by asking ChatGPT to "summarize." But summary is a double-edged sword. When you really need to digest a lot of information in a short amount of time, a summary may be better because you won't be able to see it all anyway. When we are short on time, i.e. in special circumstances, it is useful to read even a summary. And it's also a generally useful approach because we live in constraints.

In this case, a person with a lot of prior knowledge can guess the entire contents of a book just by looking at the title, book review, and table of contents. If the reader has a wider and deeper background and related knowledge than the author, he can have richer and more profound insights than the author just by reading the summary (even the table of contents). Such a person has reached a level where, when he learns one thing, he understands two things and applies five things.

But to the general public, on the other hand, reading the entire book and only seeing the summary are completely different. Readers who only read someone's summary may not learn the rich knowledge and experience of the author.

If someone reads only the summary of ChatGPT without prior knowledge, he will be entirely dependent on ChatGPT's point of view. It is easy for him to uncritically accept the claims of ChatGPT rather than his own subjectivity and conclusions.

This is the road to slavery where the thinking function of human intelligence is subordinated to artificial intelligence. In fact, we can't trust human summaries, so can we trust artificial intelligence summaries?

3. Focus on High-value areas!

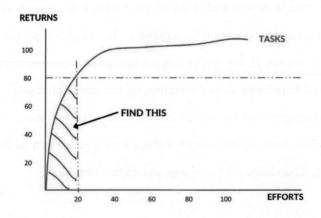

According to the Pareto principle, the hatched area in the above figure is the "high value area." It is a place where a small investment of effort and resources reaps great results. What did Warren Buffett learn from Ted Williams?

He learned the "Circle of Competence." Buffett doesn't invest in areas he doesn't understand. Buffett was conservative in investing in tech companies such as Amazon, saying he did not know the business of high-tech companies. Instead, he says he knows Coca-Cola well.

He invested intensively "about 80%" in around 5 companies he knew well. As a result, Coca-Cola stock, which was $2 in 1988, exceeded $60, giving him a return of 1,200%.

The Coca-Cola CEO was paid about $10 million USD in 2017. Warren Buffett earned $592 million USD in dividend income. Warren Buffett seems to be making very good use of mental models such as the circle of competence and the Pareto rule. He is in the high value realm.

Many people ask me where the "high value areas" are. Most of the "self-help" books on the market urge people to start anything in areas where they have their "strengths."

It sounds like the right thing to say, but this is bad advice. It is "competence", not capability, that matters. In other words, it is the strength and competitiveness in the field of competition. If you don't know where you're competing, how do you know who you're competing against and what "strengths" you have?

Above all, someone must have their own competitiveness to occupy a "high-value area." However, each competency is different. Therefore, the term "high value area" that applies to anyone may be absurd.

For example, lions and cheetahs have different competitiveness and have different living environments. Areas of high value to lions may not be areas of high value to leopards at all. So you need to think about "value", not just strengths. After identifying your high-value areas, think about your strengths.

Here is an email I sent to the son of a close acquaintance about this. I advised an acquaintance's son (PhD in Economics) to go to the emerging market. I would advise him to enter the market first and build up later, even if his skills are somewhat lacking in the market at this point.

I was actually against you starting a business. I think you remember this too. Of course, I guess you might be very sorry about leaving your business. But I consider it very fortunate that even now you handed over your business to your cousin.

As I always emphasized to you, there is a flow(trends) in the world. There are relatively sinking ones, while there are floating ones. The invention of paper, for example, was a remarkable innovation. So did the invention of printing that followed.

In the meantime, the paper business began to stagnate little by little. Of course, in the meantime, the publishing business was a decent business compared to the simple printing business.

This is because the printing industry is the price-taker, while the publishing industry is the price-maker. Today, however, all paper-related businesses, whether printing or publishing, are on the decline. The paper newspaper business is no exception. At a time like this, if someone decides to engage in paper business, he has a hard road ahead.

But if he goes to a booming market, he can achieve great results with little effort. pigs can't fly However, said Léi Jūn, founder of Xiaomi in China. Even pigs can fly if they are in the path of a storm.

I told you two floating markets symbolized by one color. They are "White gown" and "White chalk". The former is a market related to health and medical care, represented by occupations such as doctors and nurses wearing white gowns.

Due to advances in anti-aging technologies and treatments for diseases such as cancer, life expectancy is projected to increase from less than 80 today to 100 by 2030. In 2030, South Korea will reach an era of 100 years of average life expectancy. South Korea overtakes Japan to become the world's longest-lived country.

As life expectancy increases, people become more concerned about their health and spend more money. No wonder these markets are growing.

And now the era of lifelong education has come. In the past, after people had completed a certain level of education, they would have jobs, work, and then retire and rest.

However, now it has become such an era where people study, work and rest at the same time throughout their lives. No wonder this market is growing. These are the two markets that are definitely growing.

And man does not live in a vacuum. We are not Robinson Crusoe on an uninhabited island. Whether people like it or not, they are in a competitive situation.

Therefore, relative ability in a situation competing with someone is important, not ability when living alone on a deserted island. This is called competency.

Therefore, if someone wants to live a prosperous and happy life in society, he must look at two key points. First, they need to see what the emerging market is. Then they have to see if they have the right capabilities for that market.

Ordinary people start with their current abilities. They align with their current skill level and try to go to a market that wants that level of skill. This is what normal people do.

Extraordinary people don't do this. They look first at what is a rising market. They look first to see where there is a relatively high value. And they decide to go there.

If their capacity is not enough to get there right now, they think about how to fill the gap. And they move there little by little. Market is far more important than ability. This is what I want to emphasize.

Currently, the most emerging market is the education market. And fortunately, you are best prepared for that market. You have a PhD in Economics.

And your father is also involved in the education market. And I'm with you too. You are still in your early 40's. You are still young. I advise you to stay focused on this market from now on.

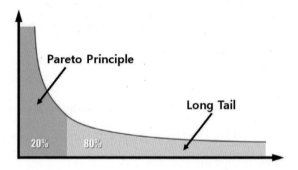

Meanwhile, there is a "long tail phenomenon" associated with the Pareto principle. As you can see on the left in the picture above, the Pareto principle states that "small numbers" create "large values."

On the other hand, "long tail" refers to the 80% part that forms a long part like a tail when the Pareto law is graphed. The "long tail" is a phenomenon in which the unnoticed majority creates greater value than the core minority. As shown in the figure, 57% of Amazon sales are sold online.

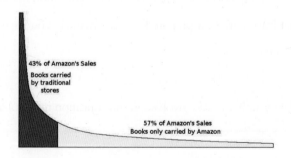

Most MBA courses teach the "long tail phenomenon." However, almost all students do not know its true meaning. They just acquired fragmentary knowledge about the long-tail phenomenon.

What really matters to us is that through the acquisition of knowledge we form a "latticework of mental models" in our heads and use them to make better decisions for value creation. And "better decisions" lead our lives to "excellence and prosperity."

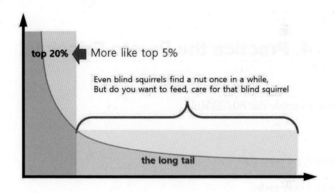

Let's take the case of "Telecom Company A." First, let's look at the Pareto principle. It shows that the top 5% of aligned partners are creating 95% of the value. This is a number that even transcends 80/20.

Effort and money are being spent on the unproductive 95%. Money and energy is wasted in finding, managing, or promoting unproductive partners.Even blind squirrels occasionally find walnuts. But do you want to feed and care for a blind squirrel? Of course, the choice is yours.

Please remember! Amazon is only possible because it is the Internet. It is difficult for us as individuals to create value through the long tail in our lives. It is desirable to focus on Pareto.

Finally, I would like to ask you two questions. What is the reason for the Pareto zone, the high value area? How can you find the Pareto zone? Please think deeply about this. When you think in this way, the grids of your mental model become very profound.

4. Practice the Pareto Principle!

Steps to apply the 80/20 Rule

Identify all your daily/weekly tasks
Identify key tasks
What are the tasks that give you more return?
Brainstorm how you can reduce or transfer the tasks that give you less return

Create a plan to do more that brings you more value
Use 80/20 to prioritize any project you're working on
Set a plan to focus on activities that produce the most result

First, we must keep in mind that our lives are path dependent. "Path dependence" refers to the phenomenon that once a certain path is formed, we cannot get out of that path even if it is inefficient.

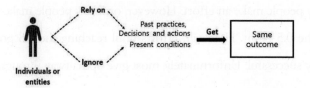

The past leads to today, and today leads to the future. When we rely on past practices and decisions, we don't get to perform better, we end up with the same outcome.

Albert Einstein said about this.

"Insanity: doing the same thing over and over again and expecting different results."

We don't know much about the "system(=self, others and the world)." Therefore, we should always examine our beliefs, assumptions, and "mental models."

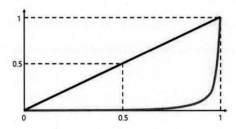

Second, as shown in the "compounding" graph, we must keep in mind that our performance is farther away than we expected.

Many people make an effort. However, ordinary people make efforts up to the 0.5 point. However, efforts until reaching the 0.8 point are not very successful. Unfortunately, most give up halfway through. They enjoy no fruit.

In this regard, let me tell you a short episode when I asked for directions in Vietnam. A taxi driver told me "Looking is near, walking is far."

This is broken English. However, it applies very precisely to performance, success, and our lives. Our success lies farther than our expectations.

So, what's the point?
I'm not telling you to "be patient!" as some self-help books say.

First, I am giving you a rationale(=logical basis) for "why" we should be patient. Second, and I'm saying that if we have patience, we can definitely succeed. The data says so. Now you should know exactly "what" to do.

★★★★★ Chapter 7. ★★★★★

A Critical Review of the 10,000-hour rule

1. 10,000-Hour rule

In <Outliers> published in 2008, the phrase "10,000 hour rule" appears. In other words, it is said that one must invest 10,000 hours in order to be successful in any field. The "10,000 hour rule" has become popular all over the world. Rather, it has become more famous than the title of the book <Outliers>.

It was so popular in Korea that lectures, articles, and books related to the 10,000-hour rule overflowed. However, as the 10,000-hour rule was promoted, misunderstandings arose. It created a misconception that anyone can succeed if they put in 10,000 hours of hard work.

If we calculate 10,000 hours arithmetically, it is "10 years of 4 hours a day" or "5 years of 8 hours a day". In any field, if anyone finds their talent and puts in 10,000 hours of effort, they become a master in that field. It touched the hearts of the public. This rule has become persuasive. This is because the absolute amount of effort was clearly presented in numbers. It is necessary to know the 10,000 hour rule in more detail and accurately so that your efforts are not in vain.

2. Original source of the 10,000 hour rule

In 1973, Nobel Prize winners Herbert Simon and William Chase first proposed the "10-year rule" for acquiring professional skills in a paper comparing international chess masters and beginners. A chess master's long-term memory contains between 50,000 and 100,000 game notes, and it takes about 10 years to acquire them.

In 1976, Professor Anders Ericsson of Florida State University, based on Simon's research results, conducted an extended study focusing on chess masters and published a paper jointly with Simon.

And in 1993, Ericsson and two colleagues published a paper titled "The Role of Deliberate Practice In the Acquisition of Expert Performance."

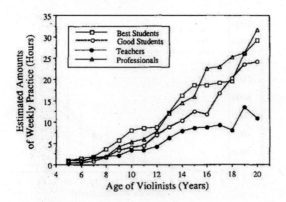

There were several differences between Best students, Good students, and those who aiming to music teachers. The biggest difference was revealed in the amount of practice these students had by the age of 18, before entering music school. It was 7,410 for the Best, 5,301 for Good students and 3,420 hours for the teacher candidates.

In 2008, journalist Malcolm Gladwell wrote in <Outliers>:

People think that the reason geniuses are outstanding and extraordinary is not because of extraordinary efforts, but because of natural qualities. However, if you train for 10,000 hours, anyone can become extraordinary.

"Effort" is undoubtedly a necessary condition for achieving "success." But 10,000 hours is not the true path to excellence.

Professor Brooke Macnamara analyzed in 2014 the time spent practicing by the age of 20 by dividing the performers into three

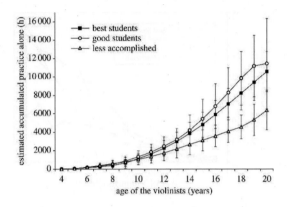

groups. Both really good players and players with some level of skill have practiced for 10,000 hours. After that, skill is determined by other factors. She argued that "practice" was not the main determinant of skill.

McNamara also analyzed the results of 88 existing studies on the relationship between "deliberate practices" and "performance."

"Consistent training" was found to explain only 12% of "performance." By field, games, music, and sports accounted for 26%, 21%, and 18% respectively, but only 4% in education and 1% in professional occupations.

"Practice" makes perfect?

"Consistent practice" is important. But it is less important than what people know. The age at which practice begins, intelligence, personality, and working memory ability may be important factors.

If these factors are not supported, it is risky to invest 10 years. McNamara stressed the importance of people understanding the "limits of practice."

Meanwhile, Ericsson discovered that his theory was being misread by people, and published a book called <PEAK> in 2016. In this book, Ericsson emphasizes that there is no set time to become an expert.

The basis Ericsson presented in this book is not the 10,000 hour rule. Conscious effort, natural talent, and practice method showed a high correlation. However, "constant practice" at a low level, even for many hours, was of no use.

The papers by Simon, Ericsson and McNamara are primary sources of information. This is the source of knowledge. However, most of the information we encounter on the market (e.g., the 10,000 hour rule) is tertiary information. And these low-level information are often the cause of lowering our cognitive efficiency.

Malcolm Gladwell's message is wrong. There are criticisms that the author intentionally simplified the contents of the book or caused misunderstanding to the readers. Gladwell is a journalist, not a psychologist, educator, or researcher. He is more of a storyteller. He tells the story the public wants, and there are parts that appear to have hidden or omitted difficult and complex stories.

"Effort" is undoubtedly a necessary condition for achieving success. But 10,000 hours is not the true path to excellence.

3. In-depth review of the 10,000 hour rule:

1) When effort and performance are not related. (Luck)

There are definitely areas of "luck" in the world that we don't know about. Randomness is inherent in any selection process (even presidential elections).

The odds of winning first place in the US Powerball are 1 in 292,201,338. Even compared to the odds of winning the lottery in Korea, which is 1/8,145,060, it is an extreme probability that is 35 times more difficult. But even so, there are people who win.

In 2012, a man named Mark Hill from Missouri won $588 million in Powerball. He donated half of his winnings to the community to help build the town's fire station. He has taken steps as a philanthropist, such as donating scholarships or building a playground and sewage plant in the town.

Most self-development books describe "success" as if it were a foregone conclusion if you followed what it says. But it seems to me this is the author's delusion, a lie to sell the book. They pretend to be guru giving readers the secret to success. We need to go deeper into these areas, not just skim the surface.

Because, contrary to their claims, the road from efforts to success can be very arduous and difficult, while success is easily achieved through just "luck."

As we have seen, the "paths to success" are very diverse and can even be determined simply by "luck." Perhaps this is the difficulty of living in a world where there is no set right answer.

We do not know whether God throws the dice or not. But only this is clear. We inevitably live in a probabilistic world. That's why you need to increase your odds to achieve what you want. And that is why, as I stated at the beginning of this book, we must live intellectual lives.

So, in order to win the competition, you have to participate in several competitions, and if you want to get a job, you have to send your resume to many places. If you want to play a leading role in a play or musical, it's good to try as many auditions as possible.

Imagine lucky events with random arrows flying around. You want to be hit by an arrow. The best way to hit a random arrow is to increase the "surface area of the target."

The larger the surface area of your "luck surface area," the more likely you are to get lucky. You don't know from which cloud the rain will fall, so it's best to poke at several places.

The "winner effect" is a term used in biology to describe how an animal that has won a few fights against weak opponents is much more likely to win later bouts against stronger contenders. It applies to humans, too.

If you win once, you win again. Once you win, you can keep winning after that. This is also proven by data. Success begets success. The probability of success increases in proportion to the number of attempts. So don't give up and keep trying!

2) If the aptitude is not right for you

The 10,000-hour rule doesn't apply to work that doesn't fit your "aptitude." It is very difficult to achieve results with efforts that do not fit the "aptitude". That is why many studies emphasize that we must first find the aptitude that suits us.

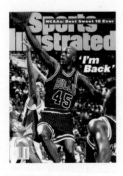

As a basketball player, Michael Jordan won "2 Olympic gold medals in 1984 and 1992", "5 regular season MVPs", "6 championship MVPs", "1st place with 30.2 average points per game", and "1st place with 23 consecutive points per game."

He has won almost every award a basketball player can receive, such as "Rookie of the Year", "Best of the Year", and "Top Scorer."

However, Michael Jordan as a baseball player was a minor league player, not a major league player, and was demoted from Triple-A to Double-A in the minor leagues.

The results from 127 games of Double-A are as follows.

He had a .202 batting average, a .291 on-base percentage, three home runs, and 114 strikeouts. His fielding percentage was 95%. This means 5% mistakes. The players average is less than 2%.

Sweden's Stefan Holm won a gold medal in the high jump event at the 2004 Athens Olympics. Holm started high jumping at the age of 6 and took 20,000 hours of training before winning a gold medal. The training time he has reminds us of the "10,000 hour rule."

But in 2007, it was Bahamian Donald Thomas, who had just started the high jump, to win over Stephen Holm. Until a few months before the competition, Thomas had never done the high jump. Thomas won the world title eight months after starting his high jump.

And over six years, Thomas practiced thousands more hours, but his record didn't go up an inch more. What happened to the 10,000 hour rule?

There are examples in Korea that show that aptitude is important.

Seongbin Yoon started playing "skeleton" at the recommendation of his high school physical education teacher. He developed into a world-class athlete in just three months of starting his sport and eventually won a gold medal at the 2018 PyeongChang Olympics.

A study of chess in 2007 suggests that this number of "10,000 hours" may just be an "average." The average time it took to become a master at chess was 11,000 hours. However, some people became masters in 3,000 hours, some took 23,000 hours, and some did not become masters even after investing more than 25,000 hours.

Psychologist Phillip Ackerman says that the effectiveness of "practice" depends on the "type of task."

When it comes to simple things, practice makes everyone alike. Driving a motorcycle is a simple exercise and everyone can become a driver at a similar level. But when it comes to complex tasks, practice widens the gap between people. Being a high-tech fighter pilot is not something anyone can do.

Meanwhile, science tells us that many of these differences are due to "genes." Edward Thorndike found that the effect of practice differs from person to person. David Wechsler said that people's physical and mental abilities vary from 2:1 to 3:1.

David Epstein, author of <The Sports Gene>, explained the relationship between "aptitude" and "effort" by saying,

Find a field that suits your "gene" first through various experiences. Then train to death.

3) When the amount of effort is not enough

Ericsson's paper analyzed the practice time and skill of violin students. The highest grade students practiced 10,000 hours, the excellent grade 7,000 hours, and the average students stayed at 3,000hours.

And Gladwell focused on 10,000 hours, a number that appeared in this paper, and considered the amount of practice to be the factor that had the greatest impact on skill, and created the 10,000 hour rule. 10,000 hours, which is the most attractive to the public, is just a symbolic number. Therefore, even if you find a job that suits your aptitude, 10,000 hours is not enough time. Because there may be jobs that require 12,000 or 15,000 hours to build a competency.

Above all, our aptitudes are diverse and there is a difference in their level. And the fields we challenge are diverse and the time required to become a master is also diverse. Therefore, there is no reason for us to be buried in the number of 10,000 hours.

Ericsson advocated "Deliberate practices." According to him, the amount of mere "effort" is not proportional to the "performance." "Practice" in "Deliberate practices" is neither work nor play. The challenges of these practices should be moderately difficult. Practice should enable learners to continuously develop.

The elements are as follows. There should be room for improvement through mistakes or failures. Also, appropriate "feedback" is needed.

Ericsson was wary of the idea that people just had to work hard. He said it wasn't "how long" that mattered, but "how right" it was. He stressed that carefully planned practice is never easy.

4) When quality is more important than quantity of effort

In the case of chess or baduk, the improvement of skills varies greatly depending on which teacher (mentor) you meet. In general, the area of arts and sports is the area where the effect of "feedback" including mentoring and coaching by mentors is greatly exerted.

A representative example is Fernand Gobet's study in 2007 of Argentine chess players. Of the 104 players, some took only 2 years to reach the top level, while others took 26 years. Even after practicing all their lives, there were not a few cases where they could not reach the highest level.

A very important part of deliberate practices is "feedback". Learners need someone who can give them feedback on the direction and performance of their efforts. This allows the learner to review and correct the practice process. "Competence" is developed only when this process is accumulated.

For Yuna Kim to practice her Triple Lutz, it is difficult for her to practice enough by looking at textbooks and filming and supplementing her practice.

There is a know-how in the jumping movement that cannot be explained in textbook text and requires a coach's demonstration or direct correction of the movement.

4. A more realistic alternative for us

In order for learners to receive "feedback" (especially in 1:1 lessons), they must pay the teacher (or mentor) a price proportional to their time. Only a few can afford to pay such a cost.

In the case of certain areas such as arts and sports, we must recognize that there are "limits" to the level of practice we want due to this situation. That way you can avoid making wrong choices.

For deliberate practices, not only "perseverance" but also "economic resources" to spend 10,000 hours must exist to achieve results. In other words, the "social conditions" in which an individual lives can greatly influence the development of an individual's "competence." This is depressing news.

But we also have good news. We can overcome these environmental limitations to some extent through metacognition. Through metacognition, we can create the effect of "deliberate practices" alone.

In the case of study, if you repeat the process of "exploring the part that is lacking → learning that part repeatedly → accepting feedback", you can get help from the 10,000 hour rule alone. Nevertheless, the help of a mentor is always welcome.

Benjamin Franklin was a scientist and one of the Founding Fathers of the United States. He is ranked as the number one person most admired by Americans.

He is the only person to have signed the Declaration of Independence(1776), the Treaty of Alliance with France(1778), the Treaty of Peace with England(1782), and the United States Constitution(1787).

Ben Franklin's practice of improving writing skills is a good example of deliberate practices. He reads a certain text and writes down only the meaning, and after some time passes, when the original text is forgotten, he writes his own writing referring to the written meaning only.

He was able to improve the composition and vocabulary of his writings by comparing his writings with the original writings based only on the meaning. He repeated this tedious process countless times with a large amount of text, compared it to the original text, and got "feedback" straight away.

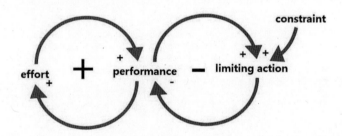

When someone puts in "effort", his "performance" grows. However, certain "constraints" lead to performance-limiting activities. If you do not consider this point and make an "effort" recklessly, you may encounter futile "results" like pouring water into a bottomless pot.

Part III.

Mindsets

Chapter 8

Expansion and Strengthening of Competence

Before Started

Warren Buffett said that the area where someone can be wise is the Circle of Competence(CoC).

This area is what you know, and outside of it is what you don't know. It's comfortable when you're in the "circle of competence." It is a "comfort zone."

It's also safe, at least in the sense that you won't make the mistake of putting yourself at risk. It is a "safety zone."

However, life there is like a squirrel running on a treadmill. Life is monotonous and uninteresting. You feel like you are always stuck in one place.

Is there anything wrong with Warren Buffett's advice? If so, what could be the problem? Will your life continue to be comfortable and safe?

1. What's wrong with staying in your comfort zone?

1) If you settle in your comfort zone, there is no growth, but rather stagnation.

The term "comfort zone" was coined by management thinker Judith Bardwick in her 1991 book <Danger in the Comfort Zone>. She defined comfort zone as "a behavioral state where a person operates in an anxiety-neutral position."

Meanwhile, Professor Brené Brown defined the comfort zone as follows. "It is a place where our uncertainty, scarcity and vulnerability are minimized—a place where we believe we have access to enough love, food, talent, time, and admiration. Where we feel we have some control."

Thus, within the "comfort zone," there are not many incentives for people to reach new levels of performance. The comfort zone is where people perform risk-free routines so that progress stagnates. However, this concept can be traced further back to the world of behavioral psychology.

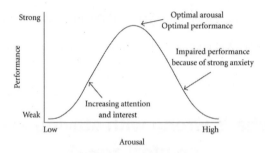

In 1907, American psychologists Robert Yerkes and John Dodson conducted one of the first experiments to establish a link between anxiety(arousal) and "performance."

They saw that the mice became more motivated to complete the maze when given electrical shocks of increasing intensity. Above a certain threshold, it started to hide rather than perform. And corresponding behavior has been shown in humans.

According to this law, peak performance is achieved when people experience moderate levels of arousal(stress). Too much or too little arousal lowers performance, sometimes severely, but when arousal reaches a certain level, performance can peak.

The key idea is that there is a Goldilocks arousal zone in our nervous

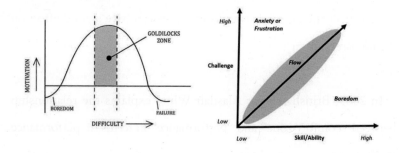

system. This means that we need pressure (appropriate tension and stress) if we want to perform better.

Goldilocks is the name of the blond girl in the British fairy tale "Goldilocks and the Three Bears". The "Goldilocks Zone" refers to the most appropriate place that is neither too big nor too small, neither hard nor soft, neither hot nor cold. So, this term is also used in the same sense as the "Habitable Zone(HZ)", which means a space where life outside the Earth can live.

This has also been shown medically. Dr. Thomas Luckey showed that low doses of radiation had this effect in 1970.

He studied the "effects of long-term cosmic radiation exposure on astronauts" conducted by the Apollo program, and revealed that low-dose radiation has the effect of improving immunity, suppressing aging, and preserving a young body.

This is called hormesis because it acts like a hormone. In other words, even a small amount of harmful substances can have a good effect on the human body.

In 2009, British scholar Alasdair White explains the relationship between "comfort zone" and "performance" in terms of performance management.

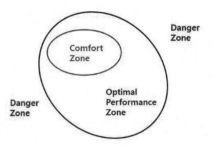

According to him, there is an "optimal performance zone" where performance can be improved by some degree of stress. Beyond the zone is the "danger zone", where performance deteriorates rapidly due to excessive stress.

According to this, in order to manage optimal performance, it is necessary to maximize work (or study) time in the "optimal performance zone." The main goal is to expand the comfort zone and optimal performance zone.

2) Comfort zone and safety zone are not the same. And the safety zone changes.

People think it's dangerous to be out of their comfort zone. Therefore, people think that "comfort zone" and "safety zone" are interchangeable terms, or that comfort zone is included in safety zone. These two zones were also considered to correspond with the "Circle of Competence."

We feel comfortable and safe when we are in the circle of competence. Because it is a place we know well and we do things we know well over and over again. We don't challenge ourselves to create something new, and even if we do, we've historically done well there.

In <The Icarus Deception>, bestselling author Seth Godin distinguishes between a safety zone and a comfort zone. The comfort zone is a concept we already know. Meanwhile, the "safety zone" is an area where your business runs smoothly in a favorable environment.

In simple terms, this is an area that is a "cash cow" for us. A cash cow is a concept that appears in the BCG matrix developed by the Boston Consulting Group. It is a business that has good profit or cash flow due to high relative market share (=cash generation), but is difficult to grow due to low market growth rate.

Our life is a process of adjusting our comfort zone and safety zone. Until now, we have been taught that we are safe only when we are inside the fence. The comfort zone and the safety zone have coincided.

However, as times have changed, the safety zone has also shifted accordingly. The industrial society that surrounded us has now collapsed.

We cannot afford to make sure we are in our comfort zone every time we make a decision. So, we gradually forgot about the "safety zone" and started paying attention to the "comfort zone" instead. In other words, we have come to value only "the feeling of being psychologically safe."

Even though the safety zone has shifted, your comfort zone may remain the same. The things you used to think were safe, like executive offices, diplomas from top universities, and full-time jobs, are no longer so.

Successful people match their armchairs to their safety zones. It is dangerous for you to stay in your "comfort zone" even though your "safety zone" has shifted.

Some say that the salary that comes out on a fixed date every month is a drug. When you get high on that drug, new challenges start to scare you. Is the armchair you are sitting in safe?

2. Get out of your comfort zone?

The image above is quite known to people. But when people come across the sentence "the magic happens outside of your comfort zone.", they misunderstand it to mean that we have to "step out" of our comfort zone in order to be successful.

What's interesting is that people may have different ideas when looking at "the place where magic happens."

Perhaps for self-directed and adventurous people, "the place where the magic happens" feels so close they can reach it. They are willing to go through hardships to get there.

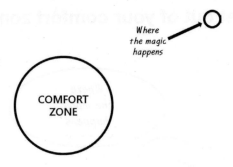

Where
the magic
happens

COMFORT
ZONE

However, for most people who are passive and complacent, "the same place" must be very far away. No matter how attractive the place may be, they consider it beyond their abilities to reach it.

That's why we need to know what lies outside our "comfort zone." That's because we can predict what path we'll be able to take once we get out of our comfort zone. It is for the same reason that we need compasses and maps in unexplored lands. There are two "mental models" that can help you do this.

1) Model 1: comfort zone → fear zone → learning zone → growth zone

See the diagram below. There are several zones outside your comfort zone. And as shown in this picture, we can move from the comfort zone through the fear zone and the learning zone to the growth zone.

It takes courage to step out of your comfort zone into your fear zone. Without a clear roadmap, there is no way to build future plans on

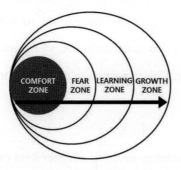

previous experience. This can cause anxiety. But if you persevere long enough, you enter a learning zone where you acquire new skills and become adept at meeting challenges.

After a period of learning, a "new comfort zone" is created, which expands the ability to reach higher places. This means that you are in a "growth zone."

If you lack some degree of self-awareness, it becomes more difficult for you to move into growth areas. This is true of most behavior change attempts as well.

So, if you want to move out of your comfort zone and into your growth zone, you should consider the following.

① How big is your comfort zone? Remember that it is not its size that matters in the circle of competence, but its boundaries. To get out of your comfort zone, you have to recognize your outer limits. And

② What are your strengths? Suppose you are currently in comfort zone A. This means that your strengths, weaknesses and capabilities are appropriate there. Otherwise you won't be able to stay comfortably there.

However, if you want to move to a higher level of comfort zone B, you will have to level up your current strengths and competencies. (Of course, as I emphasized, you may need to move to emerging markets before you have all the strengths you need in place.) This is also true when you lead someone.

2) Model 2: comfort zone → "Stretch zone" → panic zone

American educator Karl Rohnke developed a "comfort, stretch, and panic model" based on the Yerkes-Dodson law. He argued as follows.

Too little pressure causes people to stay in their comfort zone, where boredom sets in. But if there are too many, people go into a "panic zone" and progress is delayed.

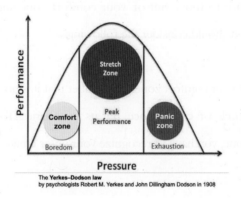

The Yerkes–Dodson law
by psychologists Robert M. Yerkes and John Dillingham Dodson in 1908

In the picture below, he added three zones, including the comfort zone, on top of Yerkes-Dodson's original graph. So he set up the "stretch zone" in the middle of the comfort zone and the panic zone.

In the "model 1", we must first pass through the fear zone in order to grow. Most learners fear this.

In contrast, in this model, we gradually build up confidence in our body and mind, just as we stretch.

3) Synthesis of the two models

I redrew the Rhonke's model like the following picture, in the form of a circle. The innermost comfort zone, next the stretch zone, and the outermost the panic zone. You might find this model much more comfortable than the Model 1.

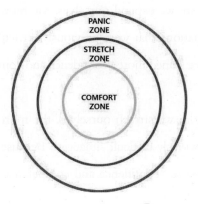

Why?

Perhaps this is because in "Model 1" the "Fear Zone" lies just outside the comfort zone, whereas in "Model 2" the "Stretch Zone" lies just outside the "comfort zone."

When we get into the habit of "stretching" in healthy ways that allow us to recover, rest, and revitalize, we not only reach our achievable goals, but we also manage to grow our "comfort zone." You can see that the area of the comfort zone (center) has increased.

In fact, the more we expand ourselves, the more comfortable we become with situations that were previously difficult. Because in the meantime, we have gained more "confidence and competence."

In fact, the more we stretch ourselves, the more comfortable we become with previously difficult situations. Because in the meantime we have gained more "confidence and competence". In this respect, providing opportunities for children, learners, and employees to experience "small wins" is very useful. On the flip side, small losses or setbacks can have an extremely negative effect.

For this reason, it is also necessary to divide large goals into "sub-goals" and provide them. And success brings success. Those who have experienced success are likely to succeed again. This is the "winner and loser effect." As far as I know, people with high metacognition behave wisely in this way in life.

We can achieve greater "performance" by growing our "circle of competence." In order to grow the circle of competence, we must accept discomfort and fear. And we must learn. We must learn lifelong. In particular, we need to learn "how to learn on our own."

In comfort zone 1, performance levels are low. From here, the learner begins to experience a rapid increase in performance levels as they adjust to the growing level of anxiety.

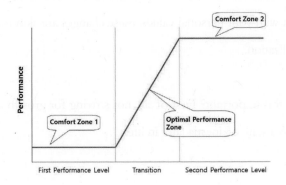

The learner moves from comfort zone 1 to zone 2. He has moved from a lower performance level to a higher level. His competence has grown in size. You have a higher performance level.

This means that the learner has grown in terms of his competencies by the height difference between these achievements. The result of this growth is revealed to the outside (outside people). He will create greater value in Comfort Zone 2 for the time being. He will get higher pay.

As you expand your circle of competence, you have a performance boost. You will be able to create more value and higher value in learning, work and business.

Beyond this, there are many less direct benefits of expanding your circle of competence (whether by stepping out of your comfort zone or increasing the size of your comfort zone).

For many people, self-actualization is a powerful motivator to leave their comfort zone. As long as the decision to leave your comfort zone is consistent with your personal values, these changes are akin to a bid for self-actualization.

Why is this important? First of all, not striving for growth can mean falling into a state of inertia later in life.

The statistician Nassim Taleb (2012) introduced the concept of antifragile systems that "thrive and grow when exposed to volatility, randomness, disorder, and stressors".

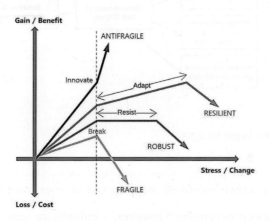

Fragile(elastic) systems return to the same level after an impact, while antifragile systems learn to reach new heights from this.

Life is not exactly predictable. Everyone faces adversity. The habit of expanding your comfort zone is intentionally cultivating antifragility as long as you don't fall into a panic zone.

As described by Albert Bandura (1997), self-efficacy is the belief that one can execute the necessary behaviors to achieve a goal.

Getting out of your comfort zone means a trial-and-error phase, during which at least some level of success is inevitable. Experiencing this success builds our sense of self-efficacy, along with the belief that

Sources of Self-Efficacy

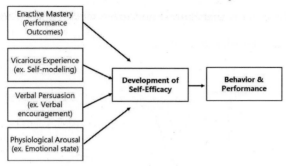

our abilities begin to grow.

Like any other benefit of stepping out of your comfort zone, this won't happen overnight. However, a cumulative upward spiral of achievement and confidence can be a powerful asset to anyone.

Let's review "Deliberate Practices" based on what we have learned so far. The table below consists of five principles.

The Five Principles of Deliberate Practice

① "Stretch" out of the comfort zone.

② Set specific goals that you want.

③ Focus on practice.

④ Receive appropriate feedback.

⑤ Develop a mental model of expertise.

3. Mindset that drives people

1) Fixed mindset and Growth mindset

Perhaps we are using only part of our potential. The problem isn't a lack of ability and potential, it's people's mindset. Our "mindset" is the way we perceive things.

The empirical exploration of the mindset seems to have begun in the early 1900s (Gollwitzer 1990, 2012). The mindset is our individual worldview and philosophy of life.

Carol Dweck(1999. 2006), a former Stanford University professor, coined the concepts of a growth mindset and a fixed mindset. Here, "mindset" refers to the individual's beliefs about the constancy or variability of abilities or intelligence.

Depending on whether they believe in the immutability or variability of their abilities, people are divided into a fixed mindset and a growth mindset, respectively.

The two mindsets are defined as opposite concepts on a continuum.

Carol Dweck studied California university students. The results are summarized as follows.

Students with a "fixed mindset" lose confidence when they face problems, while those with a "growth mindset" accept it as another experience and use it as a stepping stone for growth.

The bottom line is that people with a "fixed mindset" are significantly less likely to succeed than people with a "growth mindset." Carol Dweck argues that this simple and obvious result reveals a huge gap over time.

Here's a comparison between a growth mindset and a fixed mindset: A growth mindset focuses on everything you can yet learn, whereas a fixed mindset focuses on everything you have already achieved. See some examples below.

FIXED MINDSET	GROWTH MINDSET
- Success comes from talent.	- Success comes from effort.
- I'm either smart or dubm.	- I can grow my intelligence.
- I don't like challenges.	- I embrace challenges as a chance to grow.
- Failure means I can't do it.	- Failure means I'm learning.
- Feedback is a personal attack.	- Feedback helps me grow.
- If you succeed, I feel threatened.	- If you succeed, I'm inspired.
- If something's too hard I give up.	- I keep trying even when I'm frustrated.

2) From limits of Growth mindset to Vactor mindset

(1) "Effort" is not everything

A common misconception about the growth mind-set is to equate it directly with "effort." In the world we live in, sports and business heroes say that what we need to succeed in everything is hard work and dedication. So people put motivational quotes on the walls of their rooms.

But this is not true.

While hard work is certainly a prerequisite for success in school, work and life, it is not sufficient. As we have seen, another study that has been misinterpreted in this context is Anders Ericsson's 10,000 hour rule popularized by Malcolm Gladwell in <Outliers>.

(2) From dichotomy to the world of "yin and yang"

Interestingly, people often mistake the "growth vs fixed mindset" as two isolated mindsets.

This misunderstanding is fundamentally derived from the Western view of the world, which perceives objects as antagonistic relationships. In particular, the conflicting picture of the two mindsets presented to the general public seems to have greatly aroused this misunderstanding.

An important concept involved is contradiction and contrariety(=opposition). However, many people cannot differentiate between these two concepts. To put it simply, contradiction has no middle, and opposition has a middle. Just as conservatives and progressives are not contradictory.

Life and death are contradictory. Because a being cannot be alive and dead at the same time. (Let's leave out the Copenhagen interpretation of Schrödinger's cat saying that "death and survival are superimposed.")

In the picture below, "white" and "non-white" are contradictory. However, white and black are opposite (not contradictory) because there is a gray middle.

There is a diverse spectrum between the "fixed mindset and the growth mindset". Therefore, the two are opposites, not contradictory.

Yin-Yang is the frame of Eastern philosophical thinking. It is marked as Yin (陰) and Yang (陽), respectively, and all things in the world are divided into Yin or Yang.

The oriental world view sees the world through the principle of yin and yang. Yin and Yang are complementary. Just as the moon gets smaller the next full moon, it turns yang when it is full of yin. And vice versa.

It is believed that the world is maintained through the coexistence and harmony of yin and yang.

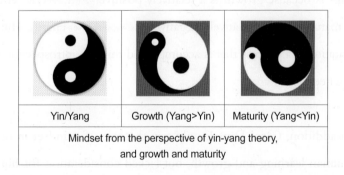

Yin/Yang	Growth (Yang>Yin)	Maturity (Yang<Yin)
Mindset from the perspective of yin-yang theory, and growth and maturity		

Carol Dweck recognizes that the two circles (fixed/growth mindset) are separate and isolated. This is a typical dichotomy.

However, from a yin-yang theory perspective, fixed and growth mindsets change. Yin and Yang are not isolated, but connected to each other. It can move from negative to positive, and it can also move from positive to negative.

(3) Mindset of growth and maturity

Carol Dweck saw the role of the mindset in terms of human learning and growth. This is an all-around growth mindset. She lacks consideration for what comes after human growth.

I express the "growth and maturity" of human beings as shown in the picture above. The second circle above represents growth, and the third circle represents maturity.

This is because growth is a relatively positive(=active, energetic) energy and maturation is a relatively negative(=passive, reflective) energy. Human maturation is a process that is accomplished through introspection and self-reflection.

In addition, Carol Dweck only saw the role of mindset in terms of human learning and growth, but lacked consideration for human excellence and human prosperity. However, it is necessary to consider human "excellence and prosperity", not simply growth through learning.

As we have seen from the case of Vincent van Gogh until now, humans reveal their existence through value creation. Man demonstrates his excellence and enjoys prosperity through his value creation. Vactor is such a human figure.

People with a scarcity mindset believe that resources are limited. They believe in the zero-sum game, one person's gain is someone else's loss. However, Vactor sees a world of abundance, not deficiency, and pursues plus-sum, not zero-sum. (See Chapter 9 for this.)

Vactor believes in a world of abundance and in the growth of human capabilities. So, people with a Vactor mindset believe that there are enough resources for everyone and that they can develop and grow their capabilities through their own efforts.

The Vactor mindset is the growth mindset and the abundance mindset. And it is a mindset that moves toward human excellence and prosperity. Therefore, the Vactor mindset guides human thinking and behavior and plays an important role in life experience, the journey of development, and excellence and human prosperity.

4. What are the beliefs that give us strength?

Our actions change us and change the world. And "mindset" drives our actions. So, what makes someone have a fixed/growth mindset in the first place? And if he had a new mindset, what would have driven such a change?

This is a very important question.

That is our "Beliefs." As you can see in the picture, there is a mindset behind our behaviors(actions). And behind the mindset are Beliefs. Our "Beliefs" is the driving force that moves all of this.

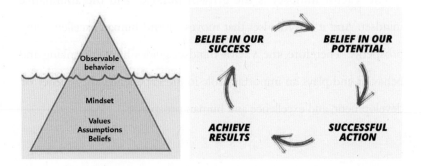

"Belief in our potential" leads to "successful action." We achieve "results." And "belief in success" creates a virtuous circle that leads to "belief in our potential." In the end, belief is the key. So how can we have this kind of belief?

1) Message from Steve Jobs

Do you remember Steve Jobs' commencement address at Stanford University in 2005? Jobs tells three stories of his life. The first is about turning points in life. He said he couldn't connect the dots to the future. What does this mean? I will quote part of his speech.

(skip) Of course it was impossible to connect the dots looking forward when I was in college. But it was very, very clear looking backwards ten years later. Again, you can't connect the dots looking forward; you can only connect them looking backwards. So you have to trust that the dots will somehow connect in your future. You have to trust in something - your gut, destiny, life, karma, whatever. This approach has never let me down, and it has made all the difference in my life.

(skip) Sometimes life hits you in the head with a brick. Don't lose faith. I'm convinced that the only thing that kept me going was that I loved what I did. You've got to find what you love. And that is as true for your work as it is for your lovers. (skip)

Your time is limited, so don't waste it living someone else's life. Don't be trapped by dogma - which is living with the results of other people's thinking. Don't let the noise of other's opinions drown out your own inner voice. And most import!!ant, have the courage to follow your heart and intuition. They somehow already know what you truly want to become. Everything else is secondary. (skip)

A ten-year plan should consist of one-year plans, one-year plans into monthly plans, and monthly plans into smaller dots. Considering that it is difficult for humans to know tomorrow, it would have been difficult for Steve Jobs to connect the dots to the future 10 years later.

Moreover, it would have been difficult for a person like Jobs who grew up in a single mother's family and dropped out of college to have a bright future.

The future is a world of uncertainty. Only an omnipotent god can know the future, and the future is an unknown world for all humans. Self-improvement books always say, "Be ambitious, have courage, dream bigger dreams," but this is not as easy as it sounds.

Carol Dweck talks about the "growth mindset." However, no matter how attractive it looks, not everyone can believe it and move on. In that respect, it can be heartless and irresponsible for teachers and parents to tell students and their children to have a growth mindset.

But everyone has a past and we can remember our past. The past of each of us is dotted with the joys and sorrows of life. The important thing is that we can connect the dots between our past events.

We can connect the dots from 10 years ago to the present. This is possible unlike connecting the dots from the present to the future. Because our past is not a world of uncertainty.

Only then are we ready to connect the dots from the present to the future. This is what Jobs said "the dots will somehow connect in your future."

Steve Jobs said:

"You have to trust in something-your gut, destiny, karma, whatever."

But what is karma? This is a term that refers to a relationship that is constantly connected from the past through the present to the future, and from the future to another world.

If we believe that we have come to this point today because we are connected to something, then we will be able to connect the dots from the past, through the present, and into the future.

So what makes it possible?

It is through our beliefs that we believe so. It is difficult for us to extend our beliefs from the present into a vague future. However, if we start with the belief that everything in the universe is connected, we can continue our belief into the future. We become beings who can do something.

Even if we discuss the distinction between a fixed mindset and a growth mindset, it does not give anyone the confidence and courage that they did not have. But Jobs' short speech gives us a chance to think about "What is faith?"

2) The Grounds and Amazing Power of Beliefs: The Hidden Link to the Growth Mindset (or Vactor Mindset)

And if someone has that belief, he or she will become what Dweck calls a growth mindset. What is important?

It is the source (or reason) for us to believe that I can do it too. Because when we believe in something (even if it's not because we're very skeptical) we need something to believe in.

For me, the story I heard as a child from my mother is the basis of my faith in life.

"Don't brag about how many children you have, raise this one well. This kid will be the person everyone will look up to."

This is what a blind fortune teller told my mother when I was less than 100 days old. Isn't it absurd?

But I've always believed this. I am already in my 60s. It doesn't matter who I become in the future. The really important thing is that I believe in that absurd word and try my best every day. And this is a very "realistic belief" that gives me strength.

I hope you, too, will build a foundation of these beliefs. This belief will always hold you firmly even when you are struggling, lonely and sad. This will enable you to step forward every day with strength.

Let us recall the "temple of success." Your rationally set vision and goals will look really good. Unfortunately, however, they are likely to be blown away by hurricanes. Rather, the "belief" that you irrationally cherish will be holding its place as a solid floor stone.

It doesn't matter if your faith is empty and people around you ridicule you. Gangsters trust their fists, and children trust their parents. It doesn't matter what it is.

When such a basis for belief (even if it is absurd) arises, amazing power arises. When you have a "ground of belief," it is easy for you to add confidence, enthusiasm, and hard work to your talents. When you believe "I can't do it," you tend to downplay your talents and lack a strong desire to try.

However, when you believe that "I can do it too," you try to find out why you came to this world and leave something valuable. A truly amazing change is about to happen.

Studies report that genetic and environmental factors (nurturing conditions, etc.) have a great influence on the initial determination of the above growth mindset and fixed mindset. So, the transition from a fixed mindset to a growth mindset is not easy.

What is the link that can lead to a paradigm shift from a fixed mindset to a growth mindset?

In summary, Jobs told us to have trust in something. I totally agree with what he said. We must have something to believe in. Only then can we sustain our lives.

And the Bible writes: "Now faith is being sure of what we hope for and certain of what we do not see." I like this phrase. The essence of faith is to believe in the invisible. Let's take a look at a few examples of the absurd beliefs that sports players play in.

What do Tiger Woods, Michael Jordan and Serena Williams have in common? Of course, these are all world famous sports stars. However, there is one more thing in common, and that is that they are willing to do superstitious things to win the game.

Golf tournaments usually have a final on a Sunday. Tiger Woods took out a red top and wore it every time in the tournament. While Woods' superstitious behavior was easily observable by others, Jordan and Williams' superstitious behavior was not readily apparent.

Michael Jordan says he always went to games wearing the blue shorts he wore for the University of North Carolina basketball team under his NBA uniform. Williams says she once played in the same socks throughout a tennis tournament.

So, are these superstitious behaviors just real superstitions? Or does it actually help with performance as well?

A study by Damisch et al, published in <Psychological Science> in 2010, showed that superstitious "beliefs" may actually improve "performance."

Researchers had participants perform a golf putting task. Participants were given 10 putting opportunities to put the ball into the hole 1m ahead.

Even though they actually used the same ball to putt, those who thought it was a "lucky ball" had a higher success rate than those who thought it was a "normal ball."

So how can superstitious thinking actually improve work performance?

One possibility is that someone's "belief" that they have a "lucky ball" can help promote "self-efficacy." Self-efficacy is the belief that you have the skills you need to succeed.

It is said that the stronger the belief that good luck will follow oneself, the more optimistic and hopeful people are about future outcomes. It also strengthens "confidence" in one's own capabilities. As a result, self-efficacy increases.

It is said that success is 1% inspiration and 99% hard work. So what makes 99% of the effort?

Damish et al.'s study shows that our confidence in success drives our efforts. And this certainty of success can be strengthened by the actually unscientific belief that "luck is with me." Maybe success is completed with 1% belief in luck.

Further reading: An episode of Dr. Youngwoo Kang

The year 2023 is a meaningful year for the 120th anniversary of Korean immigrants to America. On January 13, 1903, the steamship GAELIC, carrying 102 Koreans, entered Honolulu for the first time. By 1905, about 74,000 early Korean immigrants arrived in the Americas, opening the beginning of the history of Korean immigration to the Americas.

Related events to commemorate the 120th anniversary were held in Korea as well as in the United States. The National Assembly of the Republic of Korea held a forum commemorating the 120th anniversary of Korean immigration to the Americas on June 1, 2023. The purpose of this forum was to establish the identity of overseas Korean descendants.

At the event, presentations and discussions were held on <Make a Path on the Road>, which contains writings about 16 representative Korean Americans, including Dr. Syngman Rhee, the first president of the Republic of Korea. Presentations and discussions on 4 of the 16 figures continued. Among them, I introduce a discussion paper about Dr. Kang Young-woo. I think it will enhance your understanding of "belief", an important topic of this chapter.

The late Dr. Kang Young-woo was in an unfortunate environment. He had no parents and he became blind after being hit by a ball in middle school. He started studying five years later than others. everything was against him.

However, he became the first Korean doctor among blind people. He became Vice-Chairman of the United Nations World Commission on Disability, followed by Deputy Secretary of the White House National Commission on Disability. He has become a successful global leader and is regarded as a paragon of overcoming obstacles.

A person's life is bound to lie in connection and interaction with the people around him and the environment. So, even if it is just one human life, the content of that life is bound to be very complex. Therefore, I would like to examine the life of the late Dr. Youngwoo Kang, focusing on three things. Let's look at them one by one.

First, it is an episode of Dr. Kang's "30 Years of Stone, Silver, and Jade." This is related to his wife.

Youngwoo Kang, who entered the Seoul School for the Blind in 1961 at the age of 17, started the first year of middle school. In May 1961, a special fundraising project was carried out for young Kang Young-woo nearby Gwanghwamun, Seoul. At that time, female college students helped with the project, and one of them was Seok Kyung-suk, who later became Dr. Kang's wife.

On weekends, Kyungsook went to school to meet the boy. She read books to Youngwoo, helped him study English and math, and gave him various guidance. Seok Kyung-sook, who taught and helped Young-woo every weekend for a year, made Kang Young-woo her brother. About two years later, she looked at Kang's date of birth on his report card and found out that he was just a year and a half younger than her, but at the time it didn't matter.

The blind boy studied hard for Seok Gyeong-suk, who became his older sister. The university Kang Young-woo aimed for was Yonsei University, which was founded by missionary Underwood in the Christian spirit. After many difficulties, Kang Young-woo entered Yonsei University in 1968 and graduated second in class in 1972. He excelled, but missed the top because of poor athletic scores.

Meanwhile, Seok Kyung-sook, who graduated from Sookmyung Women's University, returned to Korea in 1968 after receiving teacher training for the blind in Pennsylvania, USA. She was a 26-year-old woman of marriageable age at the time, and was an elite who had gone to study in the United States. Kang Young-woo asked Seok Kyung-sook to write for her exam and entered the exam hall together. After the exam, he left the classroom and walked along Baekyang-ro together, proposing to Seok Kyung-sook and announcing his 30-year vision.

He said: "From today, I will call you Seok Eun-ok(石銀玉). 石 is an unchanging stone, 銀 is a precious silver, and 玉 means shining jade, so I will call you that." Then she liked it too. Here, the 30-year vision refers to 10 years of the era of "stone", 10 years of the era of "silver" and 10 years of the era of "jade." (Author's note: Each Chinese character has a meaning.)

The 10 years of "Stone" were 10 years like a rocky field from the time he first met Gyeongsuk Seok at Seoul Blind School to the time he graduated from Yonsei University. The 10 years of "silver" is 10 years when they get married, study abroad in the United States, receive a Ph.D., and raise children. And the following 10 years were the era of "jade" of a blessed and prestigious family that gave glory to God like a beautifully shining jade.

Seok Kyung-sook, who had only considered Kang Young-woo as her younger brother for 10 years, could not hide her emotion and surprise. She didn't know he had such a great idea. Finally, she prayed to the Lord that she would become a helper for Young-Woo Kang, helping him to grow strong, and then she made up her mind to become his wife. After getting married, the two went to study abroad.

While reading this episode, I was curious. How was Youngwoo Kang in his 20s able to present a "30-year" vision to Kyungsook Seok?

I was able to find the secret in Steve Jobs' 2005 commencement speech at Stanford University. Steve Jobs said he "couldn't connect the dots into the future." Considering that it is difficult for humans to know tomorrow, it would have been difficult for Jobs to connect the dots to the future 10 years later. Furthermore, it is estimated that it would have been difficult for a person like Jobs, who grew up in a family of single mothers and dropped out of college, to have a bright future.

But everyone has a past and we can remember it. The past of each of us is dotted with the joys and sorrows of life. So we can connect the dots from the past to the present. This is possible unlike connecting the dots from the present to the future. Because our past is not an uncertain world.

Then we are ready to connect the dots from the present to the future. This is what Jobs said, "The dots will somehow connect in your future."

Of course, this is purely my interpretation. Nowhere in Dr. Kang's testimony or book is it revealed how he was able to connect the dots into the future. Although he could not explain what made it possible without using the word "God," he must have known the logic anyway.

Among the 30-year vision of "stone, silver, jade" presented by Kang Young-woo, 10 years of "stone" was already a thing of the past. He had clear "evidence" of how he'd grown over the past ten years.

He was no longer an orphan from a rehabilitation center for the blind, but a student at a university founded by Missionary Underwood. On the other hand, he had "faith" in God who walked through fear, hardship, and adversity. Seok Kyung-sook was the witness.

That is why Kang Young-woo and Seok Kyung-sook were able to connect the dots toward the future with a vision of a total of 30 years, including the next 20 years, on the solid rock of the past 10 years. Just as the Bible says, "Faith is the substance of things hoped for," this is what we need.

(the latter part omitted)

As you might have noticed, the above article is actually a summary of the article I presented at the National Assembly event commemorating the 120th anniversary of Korean immigrants to the United States. The article about Dr. Kang was written by Kim Hong-shin (the first Korean million-selling author), and I wrote and presented a discussion paper about Kim's article.

I thought of Steve Jobs while reading the episodes of Dr. Kang Young-woo and Mrs. Seok Eun-ok. I hope that each of the readers will have "beliefs" through past achievements, big or small, and connect from the past to the present and future based on that beliefs.

Chapter 9

Value creation based on the Plus-sum mindset

1. Competition and Zero-sum

We all wish success and happiness. But the number of things we want is somewhat limited. As a result, we live in a fiercely competitive society.

We are used to competitive situations. Therefore, we believe that competition is inevitable to achieve goals. In other words, we often misunderstand that we achieve our goals only through "competition."

But it is not.

We can achieve our goals "independently", or through "competition or collaboration" with others.

For example, if you want to become better at writing than you are now, you can pursue and achieve that goal without competing or collaborating with anyone.

As we saw in the 10,000-hour rule, Benjamin Franklin developed his "writing skills" independently without competing with anyone else. He didn't even get help from a mentor.

You don't have to compete or cooperate with anyone when you put a term deposit or installment savings into the bank to buy a bigger house. There are three main ways you can create value in your life and workplace and achieve your goals. It is a competitive, cooperative and independent method.

The three are explained as follows.

① The competitive method is to achieve a goal by competing with others and winning. Examples include bowling, archery, boxing, lifting weights, beauty contests, college entrance exams, regime struggles, and war.

② The cooperative method is to achieve a goal together with others. For example, the relationship between the 400-meter relay team and the team members.

③ The independent method is to achieve a goal independently of others. For example, savings or self-study.

Nonetheless, we strive to stand above our opponents.

This is because people think that the sum is fixed in the world and that when someone gains, someone else loses. This kind of thinking is called "zero-sum thinking."

The Stone Age was a "zero-sum world" when people made a living through hunting and gathering. There was little investment or technology development. There was no possibility of getting rich by inventing a new stone axe. The food provided by nature was fixed.

Going through this era, it is understood that mankind has naturally inherited "zero-sum thinking" in its genes. This is because there was, and still is, a "zero-sum game" in the real world of people's lives.

On the other hand, "zero-sum bias" is a cognitive bias toward "zero-sum thinking." This is the tendency of people to intuitively judge that the real situation is "zero-sum" even though it is not. This bias promotes the "zero-sum fallacy", the false belief that a situation is zero-sum. These errors can lead to other poor judgments and bad decisions.

A "zero-sum fallacy" is an error because it is a "false belief." Unfortunately, it is a belief that can be self-fulfilling. If you believe there is no alternative but to split the fixed pie, you may fail to find where to create value. That's a real mistake.

In the world, there is both "zero-sum" and "non-zero-sum."

However, it is clear that someone can live a excellent and prosperous life by providing more value to others.

For example, each of the people who founded Internet companies, such as Google, Amazon, and Facebook, became rich. However, they did not take anything away from us. Rather, they enriched our lives by contributing to society beyond the money they earned.

Let's remember Karl Marx and Joseph Schumpeter again. They had different "mental models" of how they viewed the world.

Both Karl Marx and Joseph Schumpeter paid attention to the dynamism of capitalism and saw the subject of such dynamic destruction as capitalists and entrepreneurs.

However, Marx viewed the capitalist as an object to be overthrown, and Schumpeter highly evaluated it as a subject of innovation.

2. Plus-sum and Plus-sum mindset

In game theory, game situations are divided into negative sum, zero sum, and positive sum. In negative sum, "we all lose!" In zero sum, "I win. You lose." And in Positive-sum, "Either both win or all win."

Here I coined the concept of "Plus-sum" rather than positive sum. My point of view is that adding useful value to something so that it becomes new is "plus-sum."

It presupposes that someone can add value "alone" as well as "together" from a value creation point of view. For instance, a water molecule is made up of two hydrogen atoms "plus" one of oxygen atom. It has the formula H_2O. The "plus" here is not a simple addition. It created an entirely new substance called "water".

In Positive-sum, "Either both win or all win." It has the other person, namely "both or all" in mind. But in Plus-sum, comparison with anyone(or anything else) is meaningless.

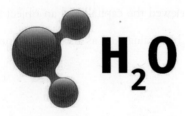

So I love the word "plus" rather than the term "positive" in game theory as opposed to negative. A good way to understand a new concept more easily is to learn an example. Let's look at some examples of value creation through plus-sum.

Asahiyama Zoo, which opened in 1967, faced a crisis of closure in the mid-1990s. The facility is old and there are no rare animals, so people are no longer looking for it. However, they found a new method of animals display.

It was to show the audience the way animals move according to their instincts and habits. The "zoo" was reborn as a "theme park." The penguins appear to be flying in the sky, and visitors can see them swimming in the wild through the glass tunnel below.

The number of visitors increased from 260,000 in 1996 to 3.04 million in 2006. Asahiyama Zoo did not compete with other zoos. This zoo has created a unique value "on its own."

"Positive-sum" presupposes competition with opponents. On the other hand, the "Plus-sum" includes both independent value creation and value creation in a competitive situation with an opponent.

Japan's Asaiyama Zoo did not compete with other zoos. Grameen Bank in Bangladesh and KIVA in the US did not compete with anyone. They conceived and implemented their own independent business model.

So Plus-sum promotes creative thinking. "Plus-sum thinking" actively utilizes a shift in ideas and reverse thinking.

For example, the front desk of a hotel is usually located on the first floor. The funeral hall is in the basement of the hospital. This is common sense. However, someone broke the stereotype of the general public and opened a hotel front desk and funeral hall in the Sky Lounge.

<Fountain, 1917>

The urinal on the left is a work called <Fountain> by Marcel Duchamp, a surrealist artist. He exhibited a ready-made toilet (urinal, A) as his art work. This is the moment when the urinal is transformed into a work of art.

The urinal (A') placed in the bathroom is just an ordinary urinal (A), but the moment it becomes Duchamp's work (B), the urinal becomes a work of art.

Previously, it was only worth the price of market goods (A, A′), but after Duchamp's work, it becomes the price of the work of art (B).

Duchamp's <Fountain> has become an icon of 20th century contemporary art. Now, bananas on the wall are recognized as contemporary art in recognition of the artist's intention, but their work owes a debt to Duchamp. Like Columbus' eggs, the first attempt at anything is more likely to draw criticism than praise. When he tried to exhibit <Fountain>, the president of the New York Artists Association even declared, "It is not a work of art."

Duchamp said:

"As an artist, I chose the object. After purchasing a common object and giving it a new title and perspective, I placed it in a place where it lost its original functional meaning. This itself is an artistic act that creates a new concept."

History sided with Duchamp. Since his transformation of ideas, numerous artists have followed his footsteps, and we can see many everyday items in art museums.

Before Duchamp's <Fountain>, there is a work that inspired him first. Although it is relatively hidden due to the unconventional image of <Fountain>, it is a work of great significance in that it is the work that enabled him to create <Fountain>. In 1913, he made a work in which a bicycle wheel was fixed upside down on a wooden chair (stool) used in the kitchen.

This is his first "ready made" work. Until then, there was only the perception that a work of art was "something that a painter or sculptor puts their efforts into", but Duchamp completely overturned this concept. He emphasized "art of intellect", in which the artist's thoughts and actions are more important than "art of the retina", which focuses on the appearance of the work.

Duchamp redefined existing "concept(or schemas)" to create new and additional "value."

In 1850, Rudolf Clausius generalized the image of "system" to include the concepts of "surroundings and boundaries."

In this way, our eyes distinguish each object in the world with "boundaries." This understanding is our learning process and the starting point of "common sense." So we need to learn how to understand "systems" using "mental models."

On the other hand, creativity, innovation, and new value creation begin by overturning these "common sense" and assumptions.

I call this transformation of A into A' and B, "redefinition of the existing concept(or schemas)". This is like making the boundary of a concept from a solid line to a dotted line, and eventually getting rid of even the dotted line.

Redefine the concept: A → A' (or B)

We can make the dough from wheat flour. And we can make many shapes with this dough. However, while we can make dough into any shape by hand, when we put the dough into a noodle machine or bread mold, it only comes out in the shape of noodles and bread.

Gently massage your brain so that you can make anything with your head, just as you can make anything out of dough with your hands.

Creativity dies when the head becomes a rigid frame like a noodle machine. Don't put the concept (or schemas) in a noodle machine, knead it by hand.

Practice changing object A in front of your eyes to A', A", B, C,... Redefine the "concept(or schemas)" of things as you please. For additional learning, refer to my book, <Da Vinci's Perspective: The Creative Thinking Skills of Leonardo da Vinci.>

Now let's go back to the concept of plus-sum and look at it in more detail. Take the game of chess as an example. In the Zero Sum Mind-set, the important thing is to win and lose the game.

On the other hand, the important thing in the plus-sum mindset is whether or not to 'level up'. In other words, it can be said whether there is improvement of skills or not.

A zero-sum mindset in education is concerned with how we rank compared to other students in our class. In this case you are only interested in your rank in the class.

On the other hand, the plus-sum mindset is concerned with whether or not you are growing compared to who you were in the past (e.g. yesterday, 1 month ago, 1 year ago, etc.). What matters in the plus-sum mentality is whether or not you level up. As shown in the figure below, Vactors level up and grow through value creation experiences.

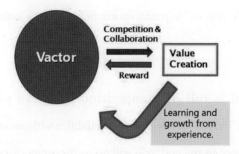

What matters in a zero-sum mindset in work meetings is the "order" of who added the most value. Or, whether your idea in its initial form has been accepted or not. If not, you consider that you did not add any value to the meeting.

In contrast, in a plus-sum mindset, it matters whether you are adding value to something, or whether you are adding more value over time on average.

The plus-sum mentality places more emphasis on self-improvement than on defeating opponents. Therefore, the setting of the competitor is not the other person, but the past you or the future you. So, winning this competition means growth.

"Apple Watch" continuously records the same running course, allowing you to compare your records a year ago, a month ago, yesterday's record and today's record.

The ad shows "today's me" patting "a year ago me" on the shoulder and getting ahead. This function is used not only for running, but also for "self-development" in many sports fields such as swimming, hiking, and cycling.

The world is full of competition. You can prepare in an "independent" way to develop your capabilities without competing with others. However, in the end, you will go to the arena of competition.

Therefore, it is very important to know that there is a field of "competition" and a field of "cooperation." This is because the "rules of the game" required by each place are different, so your response must be different.

Having a "plus-sum mindset" is key to being able to see "systems and events" that happen to you as "wins." Being able to see events as "wins" means you believe in yourself, enhance your abilities, and improve the world. It is a key that will help you.

It is natural and relatively easy for you to engage with a plus-sum mindset in the arena of "collaboration."

What you really need to master is learning how to play your game in the field of "competition" with a plus-sum mindset. And this is the key to growing yourself and others. Let's find out how to do that now.

3. How to create value?

We learned about "Mental models" and "Plus-sum mindsets." Now let's look at some examples of how to create value. In general, learners tend to regard these cases as irrelevant to them.

But keep in mind. Just as a bird flaps its wings to fly, we must create value to survive and prosper. And if you have the right Mental models and Mindset, you too can create value. In other words, you can build your own excellent and prosperous life.

We perceive external objects as "patterns." For example, we perceive "birds" as "animals" with wings, feathers and a beak.

We have a schema for birds. In our heads, we have a "common attributes" about birds. That's why we can distinguish numerous birds from other animals by calling them all "birds" despite their different appearances. On the other hand, we can distinguish each bird with different attributes.

We also learned what a "system" is. There are many different systems in the world. We learned about the economic system, political system, and business system and so on.

I have explained the "common properties(=attributes)" of these systems to make it easier for you to understand them. This is because we can understand the mechanism of all things in the world more easily without considering many things in the world as different from each other like grains of sand on the beach.

There are several descriptions of "business systems" in my book. There are several mental models for looking at business systems. One of them is the "business model canvas." Just as Vincent Van Gogh had a canvas, Jeff Bezos has a canvas like the one below.

The Business Model Canvas

Key Partners	Key Activities	Value Propositions	Customer Relationship	Customer Segments
	Key Resources		Channels	
Cost Structure			Revenue Streams	

The "business model canvas(BMC)" is a kind of "mental models" that entrepreneurs will refer to for value creation. BMC is a graphic template designed to show at a glance the 9 major business elements that should be included in the business.

Osterwalder's canvas has nine boxes: customer segments, value propositions, channels, customer relationships, revenue streams, key resources, key activities, key partners, and cost structure.

In conclusion, a business model is how a business makes money. BMC helps companies understand how to generate profits through the organic connection of each block.

However, "idea generation" is missing here. Surprisingly, this is not a problem unique to the business model canvas, but the fact that business curricula as a whole rarely deal with "idea generation."

This is because the realm of creativity requires consilience among very diverse disciplines, and management scholars in detailed majors such as finance and marketing do not know well about areas other than their own majors.

We'll look at how we turn external "information" into "ideas" for value creation using "mental models" in our heads.

The elements you need to create value for your customers(or for you or the world) are:

① "Information" from outside

    Cf. sometimes "idea" devised by yourself from inside

② Mental models for value creation

③ Relevant knowledge and skills

④ Activities and resources for implementation

⑤ Partners, Customer relationships and Channels

Here we will learn about ①, ② and ③. Because this is something that is not covered anywhere else, let alone in a traditional MBA.

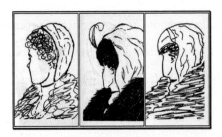

What do you see in this picture?

Known as "My Wife and My Mother-in-Law", this drawing was published in an American humor magazine in 1915 by British cartoonist William Eli Hill. Some see a young woman, others an old woman.

It became famous in 1930 when American psychologist Edwin Boring introduced this picture in a paper published. This kind of painting is also called a multi-objective figure because a single painting can be perceived as two or more objects and can be interpreted in various ways.

The same stimulus looks different depending on what you expect, and what you are interested in becomes the foreground and what you are not interested in becomes the background and is buried.

Even if people see the same opportunity and information in their domain, their lives are totally different depending on how the Brain works. Some people create value, some don't. In order for someone to create value, this brain must be formed and operated in a suitable form.

Do you remember how you learned calculation (arithmetic)?

First, we learn numbers and operators (+, -, ×, ÷). And we learn the counting rules. Next, memorize the multiplication table and practice arithmetic. And we grow to a level where we can even do "mental calculation."

The same goes for chess. We learn the chessboard and the pieces and learn the rules of the game. We learn the chess notes of masters and grow to a level where we can play chess in our heads.

In the process of learning and practicing computation and chess, "schemas" and "mental models" are formed in the brain that enable computation and chess play.

If your brain doesn't have the English alphabet and sentence patterns, you can't understand English. Without numbers, operators, and calculation formulas in your brain, you cannot calculate.

Your brain must have "schemas" for English and arithmetic. Likewise, if someone doesn't have concepts, theories, examples, and stories to create value in the brain, he can't create proper value. The brain must have schemas and "mental models" for value creation.

So you need to learn concepts, theories, etc. from school and books, while learning cases, stories, etc. from the world. It is desirable to learn these things in a balanced way. That is the "latticework of mental models."

That way, it's easier for you to use your brain to create value to improve your life. Concepts, theories, examples and stories. These are the seeds to be sown in the field of your brain. Just as you have to sow seeds in your soil to harvest crops, you have to make soil and sow seeds to create value.

Right in your brain!

When good seeds are well sown in good fields, good crops can be reaped. And these fields and seeds, as seen in the example of the "compound effect", bring better harvests the earlier they are cultivated.

If expressed graphically, it looks like the next.

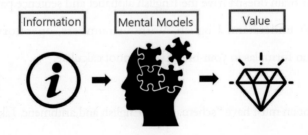

Charlie Munger emphasized the use of practical wisdom through understanding "mental models."

He said:

If you memorize fragmentary facts and try to bring them back up, you really don't know anything.

When you see or hear any external "information", if your "mental models" are well organized in your brain, you can interpret and assign meaning to the information through your mental models to create useful "value."

Facts cannot be in usable form unless they are hung together over the latticework of mental models. I call a brain with well-formed mental models "Vactor Brain" to be able to "create value."

The Vactor Brain is equipped with a "plus-sum mindset" as well as knowledge and skills for value creation. As such, Vactors can create value that is useful to themselves and to the world, even if they see the same things as everyone else.

We studied the mechanisms of capitalist systems in Part I. At its core, capitalism is a successful problem-solving and value-creating system. Therefore, those who have a good mental model of how this system works are inevitably more likely to create better value than others.

4. How to create value? : Case Study

McDonald's is synonymous with "fast food." At the same time, McDonald's is also synonymous with "franchises" operating all over the world. Let's take a look at the formation process of the "Mental Model" through the story by which McDonald's could become the current McDonald's.

The McDonald brothers, who founded McDonald's, focused on speed when they started their business. At the time, most drive-in restaurants in the United States had a system in which a customer ordered and the staff brought the food directly to the customer's car. The bowl was heavy and it took quite a while to get it to the customer's car.

So the McDonald brothers develop what is called "Speed Service System". First, the number of foods was reduced. And the types of food to order have been standardized. They numbered the menu to make ordering simple. And the kitchen was designed so that the chefs could move in the fastest and most efficient way.

Like Henry Ford's conveyor belt system, they streamlined the hamburger production line. This is what made the McDonald's myth that food comes out 30 seconds after ordering today.

(Source : Movie, The Founder)

There may be people who have a well-formed mental model of "Labor of Division" and people who do not. The McDonald brothers used this principle to make hamburgers quickly. This was their competitive advantage over other competitors.

There are three types of people in this picture.

① People in line at McDonald's : just customers

② McDonald's Brothers : Owners of Small Stores

③ Ray Croc : The future global McDonald's entrepreneur

Adam Smith wrote that "division of labor" in the pin mill produced 240 times higher productivity. The McDonald brothers applied "division of labor" to their restaurant business. The division of labor gave wings to their business as a kind of "mental model" we saw earlier.

Division of Labor → McDonald Bros. → Fast Food

The McDonald brothers created value by connecting 'hamburger' with 'division of labor'. The McDonald brothers were not the first to create a food called 'hamburger' that did not exist in the world, nor were they the first to create a labor system in the form of 'division of labor'. What they did is to 'connect' the food called 'hamburger' and the labor method called 'division of labor'.

People share and exchange their knowledge through the "division of labor." The higher one's knowledge and skill level, the greater value can be created. This isn't taking someone's share, it's creating value.

A man named Ray Kroc saw a long line of people in front of a McDonald's. He sees hamburgers being made at a high speed by the principle of "division of labor" in McDonald's.

And he tried to connect the speed system to the operating principles of restaurants he knew while supplying to various restaurant industries, especially franchises.

Although McDonald's restaurant had many customers in line, Ray Kroc was the only one who saw the restaurant's "speed system" differently. Eventually, he acquired McDonald's, founded by the McDonald brothers, and grew it into the world's largest fast-food chain brand.

Let's look at the following example. This is an example of creating value by introducing McDonald's Speed system into a hospital.

12 million people, or 80% of the world's visually impaired, are Indians. The unfortunate thing is that they are in a situation where they can see if they receive the right treatment at the right time.

A representative disease is cataract. In India, people who can live a normal life after undergoing an hour-long operation become disabled due to the high cost of surgery.

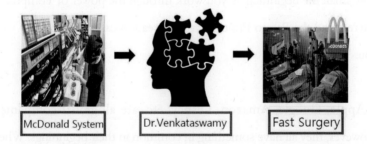

Indian ophthalmologist Venkataswami founded Aravind Eye Clinic, which offers cataract surgery for $18, compared to $1,800 in the United States. He has helped countless Indians to avoid losing their light. How did they manage to keep the price so low?

It lies in "standardization and specialization", as McDonald's did. They standardized and specialized the "surgical system." In general, there is one bed in the operating room and one patient is lying on it. However, at Aravind Eye Hospital, several beds are placed side by side, and patients are lying on each bed.

In this way, even if people see the same thing, each person has a different judgment according to their intellectual level and experience.

Do you feel that the preceding examples of value creation are irrelevant to you? We learned earlier about compound interest and the Pareto Principle.

Remember the power of "compound interest" and the "Pareto principle." Just as Archimedes lifted the earth with a lever, no matter how small the beginning, if you work through the power of compound interest and the Pareto Principle, value creation cases can connect with you.

Apple, Google, Amazon, Disney, etc. are all global companies. However, they all have something in common in their beginnings. When Jeff Bezos started Amazon, when Ray Kroc discovered McDonald's, when Google developed the search engine, they were all so-called "Garage startups." It's not much different from you now.

"Even though the beginning was weak (garage), the end will be prosperous (successful)."

Of course, this process is not as easy as it sounds. This requires "belief" as well as a mental model. The cases we have seen so far are by no means irrelevant to you. If you create value with "mental models", you can succeed like them.

Further reading: <One red paperclip>-from Plus-sum

The next story is the story of <One red paperclip> based on the true story of Canadian young man Kyle McDonald. He started with "one red clip" and had his own three-bedroom house within a year.

Kyle McDonald used to play "Bigger and Better" with his childhood friends. It is a game of changing from a small thing to a bigger thing through Barter. However, he never had much success in the game as a child.

After he became an adult, he was looking for a job. However, the job did not come easily to him. He stopped sending resumes for a while, and he decided to play "Bigger and Better" again.

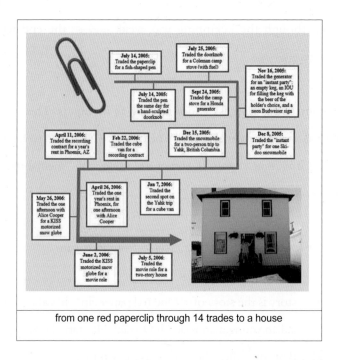

July 14, 2005:
Traded the paperclip for a fish-shaped pen

July 25, 2005:
Traded the doorknob for a Coleman camp stove (with fuel)

Nov 16, 2005:
Traded the generator for an "instant party": an empty keg, an IOU for filling the keg with the beer of the holder's choice, and a neon Budweiser sign

July 14, 2005:
Traded the pen the same day for a hand-sculpted doorknob

Sept 24, 2005:
Traded the camp stove for a Honda generator

April 11, 2006:
Traded the recording contract for a year's rent in Phoenix, AZ

Feb 22, 2006:
Traded the cube van for a recording contract

Dec 15, 2005:
Traded the snowmobile for a two-person trip to Yahk, British Columbia

Dec 8, 2005:
Traded the "instant party" for one Ski-doo snowmobile

April 26, 2006:
Traded the one year's rent in Phoenix, for one afternoon with Alice Cooper

Jan 7, 2006:
Traded the second spot on the Yahk trip for a cube van

May 26, 2006:
Traded the one afternoon with Alice Cooper for a KISS motorized snow globe

June 2, 2006:
Traded the KISS motorized snow globe for a movie role

July 5, 2006:
Traded the movie role for a two-story house

from one red paperclip through 14 trades to a house

The beginning was small. On July 12, 2005, the red clip became a fished-shaped pen, and the pen was replaced with a sculpted doorknob. Then it got bigger and bigger, and Macdonald finally got his own three-bedroom house on July 12, 2006, a year after he started his exchange. It was the fruit of the 14th transaction. He currently runs "oneredpaperclip.com."

If you made 14 deals in a year, could you own a house like Kyle MacDonald? Of Kyle's 14 trades, which trade made the value of the trade significantly greater than the previous trade? Let's take a closer look at each of his deals. For reference, individual product prices were calculated through an internet search.

370

number of trades / items	1/red paperclip	2/fish-shaped pen	3/sculpted doorknob
value (dollar)	0.02	0.31	1.92
4/Coleman camping stove	5/Honda generator	6/instant party things	7/snowmobile
11.54	38.48	138.51	1,154.29
8/trip to Yahk, B.C.	9/cube van	10/Recording contract	11/One year's rent in Phoenix
3,847.63	7,695.27	15,390.53	19,238.17
12/Afternoon with rocker Alice Cooper	13/KISS snow-globe	14/A Movie role contract	15/A House in Kipling
23,085.80	7,695.27	34,628.70	42,323.97

The table above is a table summarizing the value of the items Kyle bartered. Kyle first began his barter with "a red paperclip," as the title of his book suggests. This clip was the Paperclip that he had been putting on his resume when he was about to submit it. New ones are worth around $3 for a box of 100. Kyle's clip is a used clip, so it's worth about $0.02.

What he exchanged for a clip was a fish-shaped pen. Fish-shaped pens can be easily found in foreign countries, but these are also second-hand items and cost about $0.31. The next thing I exchanged was an unusually shaped vintage doorknob. It's a broken doorknob, but it's a decorative item worth about $1.92.

The next thing Kyle traded was a camping stove. This product was valued at around $11.54. The next exchange was a portable generator that could also be used while camping. It is a generator that can charge 100w capacity and is valued at $38.48 on a used basis. As a result of the bartering, though for products under $40, Kyle has bartered very effectively. From the first $0.02, the value rose about 2,000 times in 4 transactions.

Exchanges after the portable generator proceeded smoothly as if they were on track. The generator was exchanged for a set of Budweiser beer party supplies, which were traded for Michelle's snowmobile preparing for the beer party.

What followed was the first transaction that was not "barter". It was a travel ticket package for Canada's YAHK region, and the contents of the package were ① round-trip air tickets for 2 people ② ski resort tickets for 2 people ③ meal tickets for 2 people (3 meals). Kyle wanted to trade it right away, as it was worth a lot more than a used snowmobile, but there were pitfalls to this deal.

That was the condition that Kyle could only do business in the YAHK area. In other words, Kyle would have to go directly to YAHK, in which case the meaning of this exchange would be cut in half. It was a kind of unfair transaction, as the other party thought that the transaction would not work considering the cost of Kyle's trip to YAHK. However, Kyle came up with an idea and asked a citizen living in YAHK to make a deal for him, and the deal was successful.

Through this transaction, Kyle's red paper clip will rise in value tremendously. The next transaction was a box truck (lorry) called Cube Van. This cube van was an item with a price of about $ 7,695 on a used car basis. After that, Kyle again proceeds with a transaction with an intangible product. That was the contract for Kyle to record. The record company was in need of a truck, and the deal was made on the condition that they provide their own recording studio.

The record contract was a very unconventional condition. The conditions are as follows. ① 30 hours of recording time ② 50 hours of mixing and post time ③ Invitation from anywhere in the world to Toronto ④ Temporary residence in Toronto ⑤ Recording using Sony-BGM and XM radio, etc. It was a contract with tremendous value to musicians. On the one hand, it may be a contract that does not mean much to ordinary people who do not play music.

Kyle is well aware of this, so he wanted to exchange a recording contract with someone who really wanted to make music. Just then, singer-songwriter Jodie contacted him, and he wanted to exchange a contract for a "lease right" to live in a house in Phoenix (name) for one year. The lease was valued at approximately $19,238. Since the last thing Kyle wanted was a house, the lease was the closest thing to the goal of the deal so far. However, Kyle continued his trade.

In the next transaction, the person who happened to want to use the one-year lease on the Phoenix home was an employee at a store run by rock star Alice Cooper. With this deal, Kyle gradually increased his value exponentially through transactions with intangible values, such as the right to spend an afternoon with rock star Alice Cooper and the right to appear in a movie starring actor Corbin Bernson. went.

A record contract worth $15,390 was exchanged for movie rights worth well over twice that amount. And finally, in the last transaction, he was able to exchange his "movie rights" for a two-story house with three rooms.

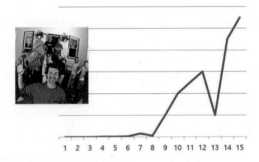

A graph of Kyle McDonald's 14 trades in a year and the value of those trades is as follows: The X-axis is time (t), which is divided into 14 times in one year. The Y-axis is Value. The graph shows how the value increases with each transaction. As can be seen from the graph shown in the present example, the value of McDonald's' transaction is increasing exponentially as it gets closer to the 14th transaction (getting a house).

A simple comparison of the value of the first clip he had ($0.02) and the value of the final three-room house ($42,323.97) shows an incomparably greater difference. However, after repeating the exchange using the relativity of the transaction, Kyle made the impossible a reality.

The magic of turning his clip (real object) into a house (real object) is not limited to "exchange". Both the clip and the house are tangible things, but looking at the list of things he bartered, it is not necessarily just the exchange of things.

In the eighth transaction, he exchanged the snowmobile for an invisible "intangible value" called "a ticket to a YAHK (area)". Kyle had exchanged goods for goods in the previous transaction. Then he exchanged goods with intangible values for the first time.

And the YAHK travel ticket is exchanged for a cube van vehicle. If Kyle had intended to turn the snowmobile straight into a 'cube van', the deal wouldn't have been easy. However, the Yak travel ticket was worth as much as a cube van to the person going on the trip, so they were able to get the deal done. As if Kyle realized about "intangible value" in the 8th transaction, he starts bartering with intangible value in earnest in subsequent transactions and finally succeeds in getting the house he wants.

In the barter exchange between tangible objects (tangible assets), the value of the object is determined. For example, the price spectrum is not as wide as the prices of goods in department stores that are implementing the price-fixing system. This is because it is difficult to make a big difference in the utility that can be obtained from a certain object.

However, intangible assets have different values. It is like products displayed without a price tag in a traditional market. Even with the same record contract, the value that a singer thinks and the value felt by the general public are bound to be completely different. This is the magic of "exchange", and in general, intangible values tend to vary more widely than tangible objects.

Also, rock star Alice Cooper is a very famous singer in America, but to a Korean who doesn't know him well, spending an afternoon with him may be painful rather than enjoyable. As such, the utility obtained from intangible assets varies greatly, which is also a characteristic of intangible assets.

Therefore, in order to maximize the relativity of these transactions, a greater increase in value can be expected by trading mainly intangible assets rather than tangible assets.

However, if you look at the graph, the value of the item he exchanged gradually increases, then suddenly decreases in value in the 13th transaction. Why? This is because Kyle made a deal that could be called "One step back for two steps forward." When we looked at the transaction alone, Kyle clearly had a transaction of diminished value.

In the thirteenth deal, Kyle traded the right to spend an afternoon with rock star "Alice Cooper" for a "snowglobe," a limited-edition but seemingly insignificant souvenir of the rock group KISS. However, through a seemingly losing deal, Kyle finally got the two-story house he really wanted. How could that be?

There is a principle that Kyle kept while playing 'Bigger and Better' starting with PaperClip. That is, he makes an exchange only when the other party sincerely wants an exchange. This seems natural, since the act of exchanging requires the consent of both parties. However, for Kyle, this was a very important factor in determining whether or not he actually made an exchange in the ongoing exchange transaction.

In trade 13, the snow-globe-holder was a huge fan who had dreamed of spending an afternoon with Alice Cooper for the rest of his life. Spending an afternoon with Alice Cooper was a meaningful time for his fans worth about $23,058.80.

But none of his possessions, tangible or intangible, were worth more than $23,058.80. So he presented Kyle with the least valuable snow globe he had. Kyle shared this deal with people around him, and most people told Kyle the exchange. He could not understand the choice to go back after he had worked hard to raise his value.

But after seeing how much he really wanted an afternoon with Alice

Cooper, Kyle decided to trade it out. Kyle's exchange, which proceeded despite the disapproval of the people around him, became famous. And thanks to that, the KISS snowglobe that Kyle exchanged became famous. A snow globe collector and film producer who recognized the value of snow globes offered to exchange them for film appearance rights, and the value of the exchange voucher reached a whopping $34,628.70.

In addition, these deals became famous, and the "City of Kipling", which had a two-story house, offered Kyle a deal as a publicity measure. In the end, the 13th transaction became the decisive opportunity to connect him to the two-story house he really wanted.

In this way, Kyle Macdonald gradually increased the value from a single red paper clip by connecting over and over again. But how could he find someone who would appreciate what he had?

For example, when looking for a room, in the past, we visited the real estate agent and took our time and effort to find out, but now we can get the necessary information about vacant rooms through Internet sites. Like this, Kyle posted the items he had on Craigslist.

It was because of the "platform" called Craigslist that a Canadian young man, Kyle MacDonald, had a 3-bedroom house he wanted within a year after trading 14 times with a single red paper clip. This platform drastically lowered the "transaction cost" that Ronald Coase said.

For most people, paperclips are just for organizing papers. After 14 trades with paperclips, Kyle Macdonald had his own house within a year.

Could you trade a red paperclip for a house?

No, you can't.

Could you trade a red paper clip for a pen? Could you trade a pen for a diary? Those trades definitely seem possible.

You can't trade a red paperclip for a house. You can trade a red paperclip for a diary. Here, you need to understand the concept of "adjacent possible."

The concept emerged from the work of complexity scientist Stuart Kauffman on biological evolution. In general, good ideas are not created out of nowhere, but are created from existing parts and their possibilities are expanded.

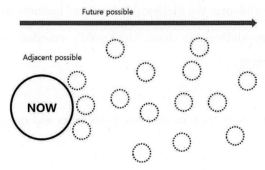

In the past, Korea was a country with a weak technological foundation. There were few indigenous products and most of the good quality products were imported.

At the time, the presidents of companies importing foreign products (e.g. rice cookers, blenders, etc.) were mostly engineers. Even if they did not graduate from engineering colleges, most of them graduated from technical high schools.

They imported excellent foreign products, sold them to consumers, and did A/S. In this process, they saw inconveniences and room for improvement in existing products, invented their own products to solve them, and became rich with them.

Korea was not the country where automobile inventors were born. Chung Ju-yung, an automobile repairman, founded Hyundai Motor Company. He learned how cars work by repairing them. That's what helped his business.

While working as a traveling salesman in the food service industry, Ray Kroc took over the McDonald's brothers' business and created the present-day McDonald's chain. McDonald's recorded sales of $23.18 billion in 2022.

Like this, every trade creates new possibilities and moves things into the "adjacent possible", that weren't possible before. Each trade you make creates new options that did not exist before. So, when you're frustrated you can't make the changes you want, think about the red paperclip.

We looked at high-value areas in Chapter 6. You should see a huge wave outside. But on the other hand, you have to look at the edges of your circle of competence. The edge of your Circle of competence(CoC) shows you the maximum of your competence. And close to it, you get good ideas and connections that help you in your life. Everything starts close to you. So, you have to observe and study nearby places.

Now I'm going to try to sort out the red clip cases. What next steps can help you make possible change?

If you want to do the impossible (or seem impossible), start with the possible. You can then ultimately trade the red clip for the house.

Part IV.

Social Networks

★★★★★ Chapter 10. ★★★★★

The Impact of Social Networks on Success and Prosperity

1. How did Einstein become a celebrity?

Asked to think of genius, almost everyone would imagine a wild-haired Jewish refugee with a soft smile who came to America from Nazi Germany. His mass-energy equivalent $E = m c 2$ from the theory of relativity has been called "the world's most famous equation."

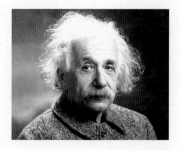

Albert Einstein's intellectual achievements and ingenuity made the word "Einstein" synonymous with "genius."

But among the many geniuses of mankind, how did Albert Einstein occupy such a unique place on the human mental maps?

Before Einstein was adored as a messy gray-haired genius, most Americans viewed him as an arrogant elitist. It was not until 1919 that he began to gain public attention. It was 14 years after his first paper on the theory of relativity had been published.

On November 6, 1919, British scientists presented experimental evidence that light does not travel in a straight line but curves around the sun.

On the left is a photo of an eclipse taken by Arthur Eddington. This was a testament to Einstein's theory. The British press was excited about the discovery. Joseph Thompson, president of The Royal Society, described the discovery as one of the momentous, if not most important, declarations in the history of human thought.

But Americans reacted differently. The New York Times review was a mixture of awe, doubt and resentment. Einstein was an intellectual from Germany who caused a disaster in World War I, and he was also Jewish.

At that time, a deep antipathy towards Jews and xenophobic sentiment prevailed in the United States. These points complicated the evaluation of Einstein.

After a brief burst of interest in 1919, public and media interest in relativity waned. Had it not been for a single fateful reversal a few years later, Einstein's fame would likely have disappeared like a comet. Perhaps he would remain a known figure only in academia.

Then, when and how did Einstein become a symbol of genius?

According to a literature review by scholars, there was an exact date when Einstein became famous. As the philosopher Marshall Missner wrote in a paper in 1985, everything goes back to Einstein's arrival in New York on April 2, 1921.

On this day, the New York Times and the Washington Post sent reporters to Battery Park on the south side of Manhattan to interview the controversial physicist. But reporters weren't the only ones who gathered on the East River to greet Einstein's steamboat. Reporters were bewildered.

A crowd of nearly 20,000 had gathered and were cheering with their throats exploding. Nearly 20,000 people gathered and cheered until their throats burst. Einstein disembarked from the boat and rode in a convertible with his party for a car parade through the streets of

Manhattan.

A scientist's visit to the United States was a story worthy of filling the back of a major newspaper with one of many short stories.

It was beyond reporters' expectations that a large crowd welcomed Einstein as ardently as they welcomed the return of a hero. The press saw Einstein's visit to the United States as big news. Given the enthusiastic reception of the public, Einstein was an important figure.

Reporters were taken by surprise again while interviewing Einstein. When Einstein arrived in the United States, some reporters were prepared to meet a scary or callous professor. However, the Einstein they discovered was a humble and informal person who provided a great news story by pouring out unconventional quotes.

The next day, Einstein appeared on the front page of The Washington Post. The New York Times also ran a front-page article titled "Professor Einstein in America Explains the Theory of Relativity," with the following subheadline: Thousands of people warmly welcomed the visit of the physics theorist and his party to the United States.

The tone of the newspaper article suddenly changed favorably. He was no longer the snobbish, arrogant scientist.

He was a childlike artist, an intuitive physicist, and a witty and playful conversationalist. He was a likable person. Besides, he was popular. From that moment on, Einstein was treated as a famous movie star wherever he went.

Before arriving in New York, Einstein was a physicist. Any news about him was about the theory of relativity and his achievements as a scientist. But the very next day, Albert Einstein made front-page headlines as large crowds welcomed the steamboat he boarded.

But why the hell did 20,000 ordinary New Yorkers make a fuss close to a riot at the visit of an obscure physicist? Why did they take vacations from work to welcome a controversial scientist?

Einstein's monumental reputation was born of a great misunderstanding. Missner argues that Einstein came as part of a delegation to the International Zionist Organization (IZO), and the majority of the Jewish crowd would have been primarily enthusiastic about the cause.

Einstein did not come as a scientist. He had only come to New York from Rotterdam as part of a delegation that accompanied IZO President Chaim Weizmann.

Wiseman and his entourage traveled to the United States to publicize the idea of creating a new Jewish state in what was then Palestine. This was an issue that touched the hearts of Jews living in New York.

And, in fact, Einstein was not in favor of the creation of a Jewish state promoted by Wiseman and IZO. Einstein feared that establishing a Jewish state in Palestine would lead to new conflicts.

Einstein boarded a steamboat to help raise money for the founding of the Hebrew University. Einstein was a scientist. He did not come to New York to build a Jewish state.

The major newspapers had little interest in Zionism as a Jewish state-building. The press focused on Einstein because they were interested in the idea of relativity.

That's why the headline of the Washington Post added the expression "A triumphal procession in honor of him" with the subtitle "Thousands gathered at the docks to greet Einstein."

So who were the 20,000 people who welcomed the arrival of the steamer? They were ardent supporters of Zionism. Jewish community leaders encouraged Jews to come out to welcome the delegation.

Jews came out to greet Wiseman, the hero of Zionism. Even to them, as Jews, Einstein was a brilliant scientist, but they were not interested in the theory of relativity.

Thanks to the Jewish newspapers, this fact has been documented. The headline of <Forward>, which carried the welcome news of the steamship, was as follows. "The Massive Street Procession of the Zionist Delegation Visiting New York"

This article describes the same street procession covered in headline articles by The New York Times and The Washington Post.

The only difference is that only the Jewish press, including <Forward>, knew exactly why the crowd had gathered. Not only does Einstein not appear in the headlines, but he is mentioned in passing in the article as an entourage of Wiseman.

Mainstream non-Jewish newspapers, such as the New York Times, blundered about Einstein in their headlines, giving Einstein a huge boost to his reputation. And this bizarre incident created a decisive opportunity to put Einstein in the ranks of celebrities.

Jewish journalists soon caught on to widespread recognition of Einstein in the United States and began to acclaim him as a hero. After that day, Einstein became a celebrity, and crowds flocked to him like clouds wherever he went.

Einstein's unprecedented fame as a scientist was due to an accident completely unrelated to his scientific achievements. He just happened to be in the right place at the right time.

Einstein, who came to the United States in April 1921 as a curious figure at best, left two months later as a respected man, especially in the Jewish community. When he left America, his status as an icon of genius was firmly established.

He published an essay called <My First Impression of the U.S.A.> in July 1921. He tried to outline some characteristics of the American people, much like Alexis de Tocqueville presented his impressions in <Democracy in America (1835)>. He wrote that Americans are kind, confident, optimistic and not envious.

Einstein and his wife, Elsa, left on October 8, 1922, on the Kitano Maru cruise from France to Japan. He traveled to Asia and Palestine as part of a six-month excursion and speaking tour. And it was on his way to Japan that he heard the news that he had been selected for the 1921 Nobel Prize in Physics.

He was touring Kyoto on December 10th when the awards ceremony was held in Stockholm, Sweden. Naturally, he was unable to attend the awards ceremony. Instead, the dinner speech was delivered by a German diplomat who praised Einstein as an international pacifist and activist as well as a scientist.

Compared with other Nobel Prizes, the nomination and selection process for the prize in physics is long and rigorous. Below is a brief description of the process involved in selecting the Nobel Prize laureates in physics.

September – Nomination forms are sent out. The Nobel Committee sends out confidential forms to around 3,000 people – selected professors at universities around the world, Nobel Prize laureates in physics and chemistry, and members of the Royal Swedish Academy of Sciences, among others.

February – Deadline for submission. The completed nomination forms must reach the Nobel Committee no later than 31 January of the following year. The Committee screens the nominations and selects the preliminary candidates. About 250–350 names are nominated as several nominators often submit the same name.

March-May – Consultation with experts. The Nobel Committee sends the names of the preliminary candidates to specially appointed experts for their assessment of the candidates' work.

June-August – Writing of the report. The Nobel Committee puts together the report with recommendations to be submitted to the

Academy. The report is signed by all members of the Committee.

September – Committee submits recommendations. The Nobel Committee submits its report with recommendations on the final candidates to the members of the Academy. The report is discussed at two meetings of the Physics Class of the Academy.

October – Nobel Prize laureates are chosen. In early October, the Academy selects the Nobel Prize laureates in physics through a majority vote. The decision is final and without appeal. The names of the Nobel Laureates are then announced.

December – Nobel Prize laureates receive their prize. The Nobel Prize award ceremony takes place on 10 December in Stockholm, where the Nobel Prize laureates receive their Nobel Prize, which consists of a Nobel Prize medal and diploma, and a document confirming the prize amount.

Although only $750,000 was raised, rather than the $4 million hoped for, the project to which Einstein was most attached, the Hebrew University, came to fruition and opened in April 1925.

Einstein left Germany in December 1932 and he never returned.

Hitler came to power a month later. And Einstein settled permanently in the United States in October 1933.

The State of Israel was founded in 1948 and Weizmann served as its first President. Einstein, who spent his final years at Princeton, lived another seven years. He said this at the end of his life. "My relationship with the Jews has become my strongest human bond."

2. Mixed fortunes of SAMO partners.

In May 1978, "SAMO©" spray text graffiti appeared all over the streets of Manhattan, New York.

The East Village and the immediate surrounding area of the School of Visual Arts were the main targets of graffiti. SAMO was primarily written on buildings, but was also used in elevators, public toilets, and D trains on the New York City Subway.

The scribbles were poetic puns with the copyright symbol © attached to SAMO.

SAMO© SAVES IDIOTS AND GONZOIDS.
SAMO© AS AN ALTERNATIVE TO GOD.

Diaz graduated from City As School, one of America's oldest alternative public schools, in 1978. Although he was only 20 at the time, his graffiti career was quite old.

Diaz's work was already featured in <The Faith of Graffiti> by Norman Mailer three years ago. His collaborator, on the other hand, was born in 1960, dropped out of school, and spent time homeless with mischievous friends in Manhattan.

Diaz worked alone or collaborated with his friend to publish works under one person's name. The two who smoked cannabis called it "Same Old Shit," and the phrase became "SAMO."

Concealed, the two took paint cans and took to the streets, scrawling graffiti as they roamed the city.

On December 11, 1978, <The Village Voice> published an article about SAMO graffiti. According to the article, those who did these bizarre graffiti were identified as Al Diaz, who was born and raised in New York in 1958 as a Puerto Rican, and one of his collaborators.

And in 1979, it was declared that "SAMO is dead". It wasn't that SAMO was really dead.

This is how SAMO came to an end when the two artistic collaborations fell apart and went their separate ways. Then what happened after that?

As of 2023, Al Diaz is still an artist in New York. However, his name is not very well known to the public. His greatest fame so far is still the SAMO project. However, this project has already died after his collaborator took to the streets alone.

And Diaz's collaborator died of a drug overdose in 1988 at the age of 28. However, his works are still alive and breathing.

Two years after "SAMO IS DEAD" was scrawled on a wall in New York City's SoHo neighborhood, Diaz's collaborator painted a skull with spray paint and oil sticks. The untitled painting recently broke records when it sold for $110.5 million. His name is Jean-Michel Basquiat.

In terms of success, Diaz and Basquiat are classic examples of how people who start out the same can end up with very different outcomes.

Both started their careers at the same time and place. Their works were so similar that at first it was hard to tell them apart. However, Diaz's artistic activities have not been well known since SAMO. On the other hand, Basquiat created a lot of buzz as an artist even during his lifetime and achieved tremendous success even after his death.

So, how did Diaz and Basquiat come to very different results from similar beginnings?

The two were essentially different in one way. While Diaz was a loner, Basquiat had a shameless network of people. Even in the SAMO era when the two were very young, the difference was evident.

Diaz insisted on hiding their shared identities, but Basquiat revealed their partnership to the media in exchange for $100 from a reporter. In 1978, Basquiat was the background for an article about SAMO to be published in the <Village Voice>. Basquiat told reporters that he and Diaz were both SAMOs.

These differences persist. Basquiat was a completely different person from the less fortunate artists (such as Vincent van Gogh) who silently created masterpieces during his lifetime and were praised as masters posthumously.

He wanted to gain fame as soon as possible. Basquiat has always dreamed of being a star since he was 17 years old. Basquiat always had idols like Charlie Parker and Jimi Hendrix in mind. And he was curious and romantic about the way people became famous. He crowned his idols in his works.

The two, who continued their SAMO activities, eventually drifted apart due to differences in their views on fame. Since then, Basquiat has built up personal connections in the art world, just as he meticulously prepared for a gallery exhibition.

In 1982, Basquiat met Andy Warhol through the introduction of Bruno Bischofberger, who became one of the most important pop art dealers of the day and his own dealer.

It was Andy Warhol who gave Basquiat wings. Warhol recognized Basquiat's talent. Warhol used his resourcefulness to help the young artist succeed. In his early twenties, Basquiat was as popular as a rock star, earning both money and the crown of an artist genius. He became famous enough to be rumored to be dating Madonna, the star of stars at the time. Basquiat, who continued his artistic sympathy with Andy Warhol, also presented a collaborative exhibition in 1983.

Perhaps the most important of Basquiat's connections is the East Village artist and super connector Diego Cortez. He included as many as 20 of Basquiat's works in a group exhibition.

Basquiat's works were exhibited side by side with the works of the greatest artists and celebrities of the time, such as Keith Haring and Andy Warhol.

Intense primary colors, enigmatic symbols, brushwork far from restrained expression. Like most graffiti, Basquiat's work is rough. Starting with strong forms such as totems of primitive tribes, Basquiat drew free forms of Batman, baseball players, cars, musicians, and skeletons.

The times were on the side of Basquiat. In the 1980s, a new wave was rising throughout the American cultural scene. The times were on the side of Basquiat. In 1981, the MTV channel appeared with the pop song "Video Killed the Radio Star." MTV played music videos armed with a unique format and editing never seen before.

Fascinated by avant-garde music videos, the "MTV generation" wanted a new star and culture that overturned the grammar of the older generation. Superstars such as Michael Jackson and Madonna were born. Black painters, graffiti, street art, unconventional forms. Basquiat was the person New York wanted in the 1980s, when the craving for new things surged.

Basquiat's works look like a child's drawing, or scribbles. It is concise, but emits intense energy with unique colors and expressions. He left over 3,000 drawings, paintings, and sculptures in a short period of eight years. The total value of the works alone is estimated to be over 900 million dollars.

But in 1987, Andy Warhol, who was like his father to Basquiat, died. Shocked by this, Basquiat gave up his will to live and ended his life in 1988. He was only 28 years old.

With his death, the existence of Basquiat, a black artist from the street who turned the academic white-dominated art world upside down, became even more remembered.

Today, Basquiat's works are not confined to the lofty art realm. Uniqlo sold T-shirts with Basquiat's pictures all over the world. Korean conglomerate CJ also launched a golf apparel brand under the name "Jean-Michel Basquiat."

Warhol, who said "making money is an art", used commercial means to promote Basquiat. Even today, Basquiat enjoys more commercial success and fame than when he was alive, shaping the history of auction houses. Basquiat's success is regarded as the most successful collaboration between capitalism and art.

3. Lessons from Einstein and Basquiat

Einstein was a scientist who showed outstanding competence and achievements. However, the reason he boarded the steamship was Einstein's human network, his connections with key hubs outside the scientific world, and his cause (raising funds to build a university).

That network rarely comes up when we often talk about Einstein's success story. How about the case of Basquiat? What was the difference between Basquiat and his colleague Diaz? In fact, their talents do not seem to differ much. Maybe Diaz's talent was better. But while we don't remember Diaz, Basquiat remained in people's memories.

What lessons do Einstein and Basquiat teach us?

You have to take the opportunity to be recognized for your achievements. All the discussions we have seen so far are valid. But if you have a stereotype that someone has to climb from the bottom to get to the top, now you need to drop that prejudice.

Use the bridge that connects you to opportunity (not the corporate ladder). No one works alone. They just think they did it alone. If you want to be successful in your group and society, you must think about how your achievements affect others.

If you want to get to the top, keep in mind that it is not enough for you to work hard. You must reach out to them by finding the hubs that will quickly put you on high orbit. Just as Basquiat reached out to Andy Warhol through someone's help.

In sports, performance is accurately measured. The athlete who crosses the finish line fastest in the 100m race is in first place. And the ranking is determined in the order of the following records.

In soccer or basketball, the team with the most points wins. These principles apply regardless of the type of sport. Of course, in boxing (especially amateur boxing), when judges decide the match, there are cases where the judgment is considered inaccurate.

However, in the case of the arts, it is virtually impossible to measure performance. At Art Basel in Miami, USA in 2019, Maurizio Cattelan simply attached a banana to the wall with duct tape.

The title of the work is "Comedian." Galerie Perrotin revealed that two of the three works in this series were sold to a Frenchman for about $106,000 each. Since bananas are a material that rots and disappears, what the buyer takes is a "certificate of authenticity."

At Sotheby's auction house in London in 2018, British faceless artist Banksy's <Balloon and Girl> was sold for £1.04 million to a bidder who participated by phone. The moment the presenter hit the bid stick, the canvas of the painting came down under the frame. Then the picture was cut vertically.

It was the painter Banksy who orchestrated this. The next day, Banksy released a video showing the process of installing a shredder on a picture frame. He said he secretly installed a shredder in the frame several years ago in preparation for the painting to be sold at auction. He quoted Picasso as saying, "The urge to destroy is the urge to create."

Banksy has once ridiculed the scene of an auction where works of art are sold at exorbitant prices. "I really didn't know an idiot like you could actually buy this crap," he wrote on his piece.

However, the painting that Banksy shredded was again submitted to London Sotheby's auction in 2021. The painting became more famous for the unprecedented event in which an artist vandalized his work after winning it at an auction. Also, a new title was added, <Love is in the Trash Can>.

It was predicted that the work would sell for between £4 million and £6 million. However, the actual winning bid exceeded expectations. It was sold for £18.7 million. That's a 20-fold increase in 3 years. This is the highest price ever for a Banksy work sold at auction. The purchaser of the work is said to be a private collector in Asia.

What is very interesting is that sports and the arts are placed at the extremes of the game of "success" that most people hope for. Despite many similarities in arts and sports, they have a very big difference in the success equation.

Usain Bolt from Jamaica emerged like a comet at the 2008 Beijing Olympics, breaking world records in the 100m and 200m, winning numerous gold medals. His 100m best is 9.58 seconds. He has won a total of 21 gold medals (8 at the Olympics, 11 at the World Championships, etc.). His fortune is estimated at $90 million as of 2022. However, all his assets during his lifetime are only 10% of the value of Basquiat's works.

As of 2022, the fortunes of world-class soccer players are as follows: Cristiano Ronaldo at $460 million and Lionel Messi at $400 million. In addition to transfer fees and annual salaries, soccer players increase their wealth through lucrative advertising contracts. Of course, their salaries are determined by performance.

However, in the field of art, as seen in the case of Basquiat, the value of an artist and his work is determined not by competence and performance, but by the network. This is because it is very difficult for us to evaluate the value of a work of art.

In fact, no one can assign a value to a masterpiece. No one can estimate the value of a work of art just by looking at it. That's why we have to look at the invisible network of curators, art historians, gallery owners, dealers, agents, auction houses, and collectors.

This is because they decide which works will be displayed in which museums and set prices for the works. These connections not only determine which works are displayed on the walls of museums, but also the paintings that ordinary people like us line up to see.

At the time Joseph Duveen was active as an art trader, art trade was not activated due to forgery issues between Europe and the United States. Even today, when science and technology have developed, forgery disputes often become an issue, but in the early 1900s, it was more difficult to determine whether a painting was genuine or fake.

As a result, there were not many people who wanted to buy it with a lot of money, and it was difficult to make a transaction. Duveen got this right. He solved this problem by collaborating with Bernard Berenson, an art appraiser who distinguishes between genuine and fake goods.

Berenson majored in humanities and art history at Boston University and Harvard University, and was particularly an authority on the history of Renaissance art. So, getting an appraisal from Berenson was tantamount to receiving a security with the highest face value.

In this context, it can be said that the collaboration between art dealer Joseph Duveen and art connoisseur Bernard Berenson was truly a fantastic combination. The title of a book published about their collaboration in the 1980s was <Artful Partners>.

However, it was revealed through Colin Simpson's book that behind Duveen and Berenson's collaboration, there was a secret agreement in which Berenson shared 25% of the sale price. The two were a partnership that was thoroughly connected by money.

Duveen sold works to business magnates including J.P. Morgan, Rockefeller, Henry Clay Frick, and Andrew Mellon. He, of course, used Berenson's authentic judgment as a way to guide their buying decision.

Duveen was a skillful player who thoroughly utilized his networks and the authority of experts. However, this applies not only to art but also to other fields. It is especially evident in areas where it is difficult to evaluate the value.

As the examples of Einstein and Basquiat show, success is a collective phenomenon, measured by the response of communities (or groups, companies, and societies) to individual performance. That is why it is impossible for us to understand the phenomenon of success without looking inside the networks in which it occurs.

The performance of value creation, including invention and innovation, is realized through a social atmosphere. It is the market and society that decide whether an idea is new and valuable. Warhol and Basquiat were people who knew this all too well, but unfortunately Vincent van Gogh did not seem to realize this.

Let's take an example of an invention. In the 1800s, America's core business was agriculture, but productivity was very low. The most important resources for harvesting wheat were people and horses. No matter how well wheat was grown, it was of no use if no one could harvest it.

Cyrus McCormick, through trial and error, received a patent in 1834 and created a new harvester. This harvester showed groundbreaking performance.

At the time, it took six men a day to harvest two acres of wheat. However, with the automatic harvester, only two people could easily harvest 10 acres of wheat five times larger than that. This was 15 times higher performance.

However, although this harvester was an innovative product, this new invention did not sell at all. He sold one in 1840 and none in 1841.There were two reasons for the sluggish sales. The problem was the overflow of similar products and lack of awareness.

McCormick fought a public performance battle and a lawsuit. Whenever an imitation came out, he caused a lawsuit and put his rivals down. Among the lawyers who stood on the other side of the patent dispute lawsuit was Abraham Lincoln.

He overcame the problem of lack of awareness with an on-site demonstration. When a farmer showed interest, he immediately ran to it and gathered people and showed an open demonstration.

After demonstrating the machine on the farm, McCormick actively promoted the fact that when farmers use this product, productivity increases dramatically, which greatly increases the profits of the farmer.

McCormick entered the world's first exhibition held in London in 1851 and won a gold medal. He also introduced installment sales. Then, sales increased exponentially. He used his marketing skills to sell his products.

He won the hearts of farmers with the promise of money back if they failed to harvest 15 acres a day. As word of mouth spread about the product, sales increased. McCormick sold 23,000 harvesters by 1865.

And by 1884, when McCormick died, annual sales of reapers had risen to 55,000.

Mihai Tsiksentmihai says of this:

> "Any idea, invention or work must go through a period of social evaluation to determine whether it is new andvaluable. We don't know if it's new, innovative, or valuable unless it's actually evaluated by people."

McCormick's harvester was a product of outstanding performance. However, in order for this product to succeed in sales, it had to go through rigorous evaluation by farmers. This principle also applies to individual performance and success. Performance is the driving force of success.

But there are areas where people find it difficult to measure the performance of something (or someone). Works of art fall into this category. Strange as it may sound, many exam interviews fall into this category.

Many areas where qualitative rather than quantitative assessments are conducted also fall into this category. In this case, social connections determine someone's success.

4. Social Networks

1) Weak ties

Mark Granovetter, professor of sociology at Stanford University, published a paper titled "The Strength of Weak Ties" in 1973. In this paper, Granovetter argued that people receive practical help more often from people they are not close to than from close people such as family and friends.

In fact, Granovetter conducted an empirical study on how people who changed jobs found a new job. According to the study, 27.8% got a job through a weak tie, 16.7% through a strong tie, and 55.6% through a medium tie.

Here, strong ties refer to family, friends, and colleagues, and weak ties refer to strangers and acquaintances. In his research, the criteria for distinguishing these relationships are the time spent forming the relationship, the strength of the relationship, and the level of intimacy.

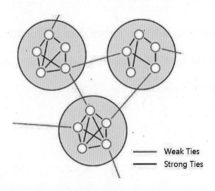

Weak Ties
Strong Ties

This effect is based on a social network, a connection between people. Components of the network include "strong ties", "weak ties" and "hub". A "hub" is a node that is connected to many other nodes in a network.

Strong ties are family members, best friends, etc. Weak ties are people who do not fit into the same circle. What do these two distinctions mean for our lives and our success?

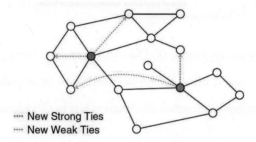

···· New Strong Ties
···· New Weak Ties

According to research results, poor people are obsessed with "strong-ties" and cannot escape poverty. Therefore, if someone's environment is poor, it is important for him to create "weak-ties" that are closely related to new work and employment.

In 1993, Robin Dunbar, a cultural anthropologist at Oxford University in the UK, based on studies of primates such as monkeys and apes, published a thesis that the average limit for the number of friends was 150. Since then, 150 people, which means the maximum number of personal connections, have been called "Dunbar's number."

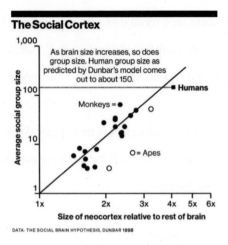

The Social Cortex

As brain size increases, so does group size. Human group size as predicted by Dunbar's model comes out to about 150.

Humans

Monkeys = ●

O = Apes

Average social group size

Size of neocortex relative to rest of brain

DATA: THE SOCIAL BRAIN HYPOTHESIS, DUNBAR 1998

Since the announcement of Dunbar's Number, 1400 papers (based on Google Scholar search) using it as a keyword have been published, and Dunbar's Number has reached 26.5 million hits in Google searches.

Meanwhile, researchers at Stockholm University, Sweden, published in the international journal <Biology Letters> in 2021, titled: "The number of Dunbar disintegrated," said that the size of the cerebral cortex does not limit the size of relationships, and that if people make an effort, much more He said he could have friends.

Critics also say that today's social networks allow us to maintain a much wider range of relationships than "Dunbar's Number". Social networks aimed at career management, especially LinkedIn, say that the person at the end of the chain also counts.

However, Professor Dunbar argues that "Dunbar's number" is still valid in today's hyper-connected world because the strength of social networks is often weak. Dunbar says that the Dunbar number means closer relationships than just face-to-face acquaintances.

According to Dunbar, human relationships are composed of several layers according to emotional intimacy. Depending on the level of intimacy, the average number of friends is 5, 15, 50, 150, etc., and the size of the network triples each time the level goes up. "More than 60% of social time is spent with 5 best friends," Dunbar said.

Can the dispute between the two sides over Dunbar's number come to an end? It is impossible to predict the outcome of an academic debate. However, the monologue-like words of professor Lindenfors leave a lasting impression.

Dunbar's number is easy to understand. So it is widespread even among scientists. Therefore, our claim that the size of a group cannot be calculated by a specific number will not be very amusing.

Now let's go back to the weak ties. According to the results of the study, poor people (region, district) are obsessed with too strong ties and cannot escape poverty.

Therefore, if someone sees his/her environment as poor, it is important for him/her to create weak ties that are closely related to new work and employment.

We can enter a new hub, a new network. We can form great connections with people of different values and lifestyles, people who grew up in different places. By doing so, we can acquire life-changing skills on a fundamental level and increase our chances of change.

The task of choosing whom to collaborate with is more important than your personal determination and effort. Luck comes in through weak ties. Therefore, making as many weak ties as possible will help you reach success.

People who have a better understanding of how networks and systems work are more likely to create greater value than those who do not. For various reasons, these people are usually on weak ties.

We can enter a new network by networking. We can form great connections with people of different values and lifestyles, people who grew up in different places. By doing so, we can acquire life-changing skills on a fundamental level and increase our chances of change.

The task of choosing the "people to cooperate with" is more important than personal determination and effort. "Luck" comes through weak ties. Making as many weak ties as possible is advantageous for reaching "success."

People with a better understanding of how networks and systems work are more likely to create greater value.

2) Success formula : "3 Elements of Success, PIE"

But there are more important factors than this. According to Harvey Coleman's research, "success" can be broken down into three components:

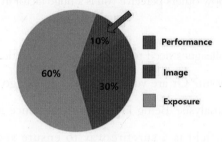

① Performance accounts for 10% of success.

② Image accounts for 30% of success.

③ Exposure accounts for the other 60% of success.

These three factors, easily memorized using the acronym PIE, suggest a completely different theory from what we are taught in school and throughout our careers. The other two non-performance factors account for a much larger amount of what makes a successful person.

① Performance

10% may not seem like a big deal, but it remains a determining factor in success. You won't get far if you don't work hard and persevere for your dreams. Ask yourself: Am I maximally productive?

② Image

What would you say if asked to describe who you are and what role you play in your professional team or business? Having a firm idea of what your role is and how others perceive you is a huge factor in your success.

When your colleagues need to brainstorm creative ideas, are you the first reference point? Or are you the person people go to when they need numbers analysis? Being known for excellence in a particular department/or field is a surefire way to ensure success in your professional life.

③ Exposure

Research has shown that success is largely based on exposure. To be successful is to be remembered—talked about one's work, achievements, and personal strengths.

Hard work is important but never enough to be successful. Especially in a competitive world. You need to find a way to stand out from the crowd, and exposing yourself and your business as much as possible is the way to do that.

The "cognitive revolution" was literally a revolution. This is very good news for us. Because the cognitive revolution is saying that each of us can enjoy a better life for ourselves if we use our brains well. Each of us can make better decisions through better thinking. And better decisions lead to better performance.

Nevertheless, uncertainty still lies ahead of us. We know that better performance does not necessarily guarantee success. And, as we just saw, some studies show that performance contributes only 10% of success. This news depresses us. But see the next picture.

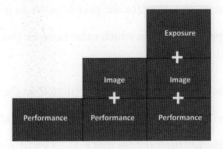

As you can see in the picture, performance is the starting point for your success in life and work, and it is a solid foundation for your success.

Your current performance lays the foundation for your growth and success before you. Performance is an entry ticket to the halls of growth and success and is a reputation builder.

3) Value network

A value network is a set of "connections" between organizations or individuals that interact with each other to benefit the entire group. Like businesses, people become part of a larger network of relationships.

And in order for someone to create value and succeed in a specific area, he or she needs not only to accumulate specific knowledge and experience, but also to communicate and cooperate with various stakeholders.

As a result, they together form a value network. And that value network becomes the source of power for the people active in it to create value. Your success depends largely on which value network you belong to.

Harley-Davidson has a fandom culture centered on the riders who ride Harley-Davidson (HOG: Harley Owners Group). Harley-Davidson is a group of people who like big motorcycles that make a lot of noise. It is a place where such staff and riders gather.

This corporate culture encourages ideas based on these cool motorcycles. The voluntary passion of employees and customers is the source of value creation.

In this respect, Harley-Davidson has a value network that creates value together centering on its employees and customers. A value network is a system. It is defined as "a value creating system in which all relevant stakeholders jointly create value."

In human history, there are countless people who lived on this earth before us. They have created ideas, sponsors, partners, and supporters to improve their lives in the field of their lives. Michelangelo in the Renaissance, Rubens in Belgium, Monet in France, and Beethoven in Germany all created their own value networks.

They drew the encouragement and support of strong patrons (even popes and kings) before there was a market for buying and selling paintings and music. And after the market was created, they also utilized transactions through a system called the market.

Meanwhile, Jean-Claude Monet, who lived at the same time as Vincent van Gogh, made a living by writing sad letters to friends and borrowing money until the Impressionist painter's work was recognized and sold.

Although Monet had a natural talent and creativity, his paintings were not sold at all because of the atmosphere of the times that did not recognize Impressionist paintings. Around the birth of his first son, Jean, in 1867, he fell into extreme financial difficulties and his father was reluctant to help the Monet couple.

Monet attempted suicide in the Seine River in 1868, and to make matters worse, he failed consecutively at the Salon exhibitions in 1869 and 1870. Monet, with his wife and small child, had to rely on the support of those around him due to financial difficulties.

Luck came to the poor painter Monet. A businessman named Oshede, who runs a department store, liked Monet's work enough to fill his house with Monet's paintings and became his sponsor.

Although Jean-Claude Monet suffered in his youth, he lived an 86-year-old life and enjoyed wealth and honor while he was alive. He was a successful painter. What would his value network look like?

His work right below tells the secret. As a painter of light, he mainly worked outdoors, not in the atelier. Most of his paintings were painted outdoors.

< Japanese Bridge in Monet's Garden, 1899 >

He arranged a flower and water garden near Paris. And he made the flowers and garden beautiful every day there. And there he invited his friends, patrons, customers, journalists and critics.

People who visited the beautiful garden and talked while appreciating Monet's work became Monet's customers and fans. He has demonstrated his business skills. In contrast, Vincent Van Gogh tried to form a community of painters based on socialist equality in the "Yellow House" but failed.

Andy Warhol is synonymous with the commercial painter. One day reporters asked him, "What's your favorite thing?" Then he replied, "I love money. I want to make a lot of money." He made a work called <Dollar Sign (1981)> using the dollar as a motif.

He often said that making money is art, and art is business. To him, life was art and business at the same time. He was born into a family of Czechoslovak immigrants and grew up in a poor family. For this reason, it is said that he had a strong desire for wealth and an obsession with success, and he liked the American dollar.

He said: "Everyone works for someone else. The shoemaker makes shoes for you, and you entertain him. It's always give and take." He seems to have known all too well that the capitalist system has division of labor, specialization and exchange at its core.

He learned early on how to connect himself to a value network that would grow him. He not only made connections with Leo Castelli, New York's most competent art dealer and exhibition planner in the 1960s, but also made celebrities his patrons.

Warhol entered the ranks of popular artists after being selected as an exclusive artist of the Leo Castelli Gallery, and was later called the "King of Pop Art."

In the Hollywood film industry, led by Walt Disney, many people are creating value through cooperation. Disney's <Frozen> and <The Avengers>, 20th Century Fox's <Avatar>, etc.

By the way, is it possible to produce, promote, and sell these films with the power of one person?

The film crew refers to people who have professional skills and participate in the production of film works at the request of the director.

In a broad sense, it also refers to staffs in areas beyond the director's authority, such as publicity and distribution. They are organizing "camps or divisions."

The number 1 box office movie worldwide is <Avengers: Endgame>.

Many people participated in the success of this film. After filming the movie, the cast and staff took a commemorative photo together.

However, the number of people who participated in this film was so large that it was not included in one picture, so a total of four cameras were used to complete the commemorative photo shoot. All of them worked together to create the greatest box office hit ever.

Almond flowers survive the long winter and bloom the earliest in early spring. <Almond Blossoms (1890)> is the first gift Vincent van Gogh gave to his nephew and the last flower painting he painted in the last spring of his 37-year life.

In February 1890, Vincent van Gogh, while in the Saint-Rémy Asylum, received a letter from his brother Theo containing the happy news of a new son.

"As I said before, the child is named after you. And I also wished that this child would be determined and courageous like you."

Gogh was both sorry and grateful that his nephew inherited his name

(Vincent), which he had no health, happiness, or success. So Vincent van Gogh painted a pretty flower tree as a gift for his nephew.

It was a picture of a blossoming almond tree in pink and white colors against a blue sky. Theo, who received the painting, said it was very beautiful and hung it over the baby's crib.

Almond flowers that bloom in early spring symbolize new life and hope. Also, the almond tree is known as a symbol of resurrection. Paradoxically, Vincent Van Gogh painted the most hopeful and brightest picture in the darkest and most difficult time. Five months later he died, and his lifelong brother, Theo, followed six months later.

So what happened to baby Vincent? He cherished the flower paintings his uncle gave him for the rest of his life, and later donated them along with all his uncle's posthumous works to the Van Gogh Museum.

Would the painter Vincent Van Gogh have imagined the image of his nephew who created an art museum with the name and gift he received from his uncle?

Among the fruits of the plant, there are exceptionally many red ones. Why?

Plants bear fruit in order to spread offspring through seeds. However,

young plants do not grow well near the mother. Young plants born near their mother do not grow well because they cannot compete with their mother for nutrients and sunlight.

Therefore, plant seeds must be moved to a faraway place and sprouted there so that they can grow well without competition and spread over a wide area.

Birds have wings and can travel quite far. Then the plant can spread its seeds as far as possible. That is why plants attract birds with their fruits. Birds do not have teeth, so they cannot bite the seeds in the fruit and swallow them whole. The flowers therefore encase the seeds in the "red" flesh that birds love.

Plants make their fruits look "attractive" in order to spread their seeds. Even plants have evolved to adjust the size of their fruit to match the snout size of birds that love their fruit.

Plants have been "co-evolution" to survive in the natural "ecosystem."

Vincent seems to have failed to package his works to look "attractive or valuable" like the fruit of a plant. Vincent should have adjusted the subject, composition, and color of the painting to suit the tastes and needs of the customers and art dealers, just as trees adjusted the size of fruit to match the size of a bird's snout.

Humans are small systems. The world is a system larger than humans. We need to know how the "system" works. And we need to know how to adapt and use the system, while also improving it (just as birds evolve with their ecosystems).

The better we understand the system (including the market), the easier it is for us to make better decisions and create better value. To do this, we must form a good "latticework of mental models" in our brain.

Albert Einstein said:

"Try not to become a man of success, but rather try to become a man of value. He is considered successful in our day who gets more out of life than he puts in. But a man of value will give more than he receives."

How can we become "a man of value"?

I interpret Einstein's words as follows. A man of success is someone who has grown from good to better. A man of value is a man of excellence. He is a person who has matured from better to best self.

As such, success and excellence are both growing and maturing into a higher self. And in the process, prosperity is when you feel the meaning of life. Simply put, a prosperous life is when you feel happy in your everyday life. It is here that we excel as human beings and enjoy a prosperous life. And this is the way to become "a man of value".

You are the main character of your life and the subject of history, the Vactor. Vactor does not stay in a specific state (v), but grows by accumulating experiences of $v \rightarrow v^1 \rightarrow v^2 \rightarrow v^3$ according to the time flow of t, t1, t2, and t3.

$$V \rightarrow V^1 \rightarrow V^2 \rightarrow V^3 \rightarrow$$

To elaborate a little more, growth and maturity are concepts of process, not completion. Growth can be measured and compared quantitatively. Physical height, academic performance, and sales performance can all be expressed in numbers. Growth means bigger numbers in quantity.

But maturity is qualitatively better. That is why excellence defies measurement and comparison. If each one uses his talents in his own life and lives to the best of his own and his neighbor's, then he excels in that.

It would be difficult for a normal person to feel the meaning of life while being pointed at by others. If we have virtues in this respect, it is easier for us to reach prosperity.

And if prosperity is the ultimate good of man, surely it would be good for as many people as possible to enjoy it. That is why Einstein encouraged us to become a man of value, not a man of success.

We are social beings who live together with others. Therefore, we must have the virtues of caring for others and cooperating with them.

Adam Smith first spoke of empathy and consideration for others in <The Theory of Moral Sentiments(1759)> before writing <The Wealth of Nations(1776)>. We must seek true prosperity that comes from excellence.

Prosperity should come from a plus-sum mindset where people live well together, not a zero-sum mindset where only one person can eat well and live well.

And as we have seen, the wonderful secret of excellence and abundance is that our performance and success depend on the evaluation of others and society (not our competence).

I am about to close this book while appreciating Austrian composer Johann Strauss II's <Voices of spring (Fruhlingsstimmen in German)>. Opus No. 410.

This piece represents Strauss II, and is a song that is always played at spring concerts. Although it was composed in 1882, when Strauss II was about to turn 60, it is full of youthful energy like a spring day.

Although it is a waltz style, it was originally composed for soprano solo, not for dancing. It is a concert aria, not an accompaniment for a ball.

Bertha Schwartz (alias Bianca Bianchi), a famous coloratura soprano at the time, premiered it at a charity concert held in Vienna on March 1, 1883, and achieved great success. This waltz was hotly loved in Russia, where the winter is exceptionally long.

Coloratura means "with color" and refers to a soprano with high notes and splendid technique, enough to sing Mozart's Queen of the Night Aria.
<Voices of Spring> became famous after being arranged as a piano piece, but now it is played not only in vocal version but also in orchestral music.

The lyrics, written by Austrian playwright Richard Genée, begin as follows:

The lark into blue heights escapes, the thawing wind blows so gently; its delightful mild breath revives and kisses the field, the meadow.

Spring awakes in beautiful splendour, ah, all anguish may have come to an end, all suffering has fled far away! Pain becomes milder, happy pictures, Belief in luck returns; Sunshine, ah, please come in, ah, everything laughs, ah, ah, awake!

There also flows the fountain of songs, That for too long already seemed to be silent; tinkling sounds pure and bright again sweet voices from the branches!

Ah, quietly let the nightingale soon sound the first notes,
so as not to disturb the queen, be quiet, all you singers!
Her sweet tone soon sounds fuller. Oh yes soon, ah, ah yes soon! Ah, ah, ah, ah! (omitted)